MURDER!

The 25 Most Intriguing Private Eyes in Books, Movies and TV:
Their Lives, Cases, Dives, Digs, Drives & Drinks

By Lan Sluder

MURDER!
The 25 Most Intriguing Private Eyes in Books, Movies and TV: Their Lives, Cases, Dives, Digs, Drives & Drinks

By Lan Sluder

Published by Equator.
Printed in the United States.

ISBN 13: 978-0-9994348-0-2
ISBN 10: 0-9994348-0-2

Library of Congress Control Number: 2017914418
Equator, Asheville (Candler), NC

Cover photograph is from an MGM production/publicity still of *The Thin Man* (1934) featuring William Powell and Myrna Loy, in the public domain. Illustration on back cover is courtesy Shutterstock.com.

Table of Contents

INTRODUCTION

The origin of the mystery story is, well, mysterious.

One can suppose that it dates back to a clan of primitive humans around a fire speculating on how and why one of their tribe has disappeared. Was he killed by a sabretooth tiger or by a warring group? Did she fall into the glacier river while gathering water? Did he just go on a walkabout?

The Bible story of Cain and Abel, in which Cain kills Abel, has been viewed by some as the first mystery story, with the Hebrew God as the first detective.

Many of the classic texts of antiquity have elements of mystery. Homer's *Odyssey* is a mythic tale of adventure, yes, but it has its mysterious side. How can Odysseus and his men possibly escape from the giant Cyclops? Why does he not want to stay with beautiful Calypso? And where indeed is Odysseus' home, "sunny Ithaca"? The Homeric "Eleusinian Mysteries" involve Demeter's search for her lost daughter, Persephone.

Oedipus Rex by Sophocles (c. 430 BC) draws on some elements of mystery story, with a murder, a small group of suspects and a gradual process of uncovering the truth.

The Chinese Ming Dynasty (1368–1644) is another source of early crime fiction. The hero of these novels is usually a highly educated Mandarin magistrate. The stories are based on likely real men including Bao Qingtian and Di Renjie.

In more recent centuries, the author Henry Fielding (1707-1754) was also a magistrate in London who developed the Bow Street Runners, an early attempt at creating a police force. The work of the Bow Street Runners was the subject of several books of the time.

A mainstream classic that is also in some ways a detective story is *Emma* by Jane Austen, published in 1815. Charles Dickens provides a murder mystery in *Bleak House* (1853) and later, in 1873, his friend Anthony Trollope does as well in *Phineas Redux.*

Here, however, we are dealing with modern mystery and detective story genre. As in all things literary, critics and readers disagree, but it is generally accepted that the first modern fictional detective was C. Auguste Dupin, a Parisian aristocrat and amateur solver of crimes by "ratiocination."

Dupin was created by Edgar Allan Poe. Monsieur Dupin first appeared in the short story, "The Murders in the Rue Morgue" in 1841. *Das Fraülein von Scuderi* (1819) by E. T. A. Hoffmann is often cited as an early German mystery story that likely influenced Poe's "Rue Morgue."

It is also generally agreed that the first modern mystery novel, at least in English, was *The Moonstone* by William Wilkie Collins, published in 1868. The novel was serialized in a magazine, *All the Year Round,* run by Charles Dickens, Collins' close friend. The plot involves the theft of a valuable diamond called The Moonstone from a young Englishwoman, Rachael Verinder. Suspicion falls on a number of different people. Over the course of a year, Rachael's onetime romantic interest but with whom she has a falling out, Franklin Blake, sets out to solve the mystery. He finally does so, and Franklin and Rachael marry. Modern mystery and detective stories have their own customs and rituals. While these tales have changed and evolved over time, most have common elements that appear in most, and it is this familiar pattern that has helped make the genre a favorite of hundreds of millions of readers.

Distinctions are often made between mystery fiction and detective fiction, and indeed many libraries shelve the two in different places. Clearly, Poe's "The Murders in the Rue Morgue" is a detective story, while Collins' *The Moonstone* is more of a mystery, although a character in it acts as an amateur detective in solving the mystery of the stolen diamond. The two categories tend to blur, except to the extent that detective fiction has a prominently featured detective of some kind, whether that detective is a cop, an amateur who solves a murder or other crime, or some other character who "detects," whereas some mysteries may be solved not by a purposeful individual action but by the unfolding of circumstance or the passage of time.

There are sub-genres and related genres, such as police procedurals, puzzle mysteries (e.g., locked room mysteries), cozies (Agatha Christie's Miss Marple popularized this category), hard-boiled private eyes, suspense, true crime and thrillers that further blur the distinctions between detective and mystery fiction.

Whenever we think of mystery/detective writing, our minds naturally go to Britain and the United States, which are the two great mother lodes of this kind of fiction.

France, to a smaller degree, also is known for its detective and mystery fiction. Some posit that the father of detective fiction was a Frenchman, ´Emile Gaboriau, who wrote four detective novels in the 1860s. While a Belgian by birth, not French, Georges Simenon lived in France for much of his life and is viewed as the father of contemporary European mystery and detective literature. He wrote more than 500 novels, and his Paris Inspector Maigret appeared in 75 of them.

As the late G. J. Demko, a professor of geography at Dartmouth College has pointed out, the detective/mystery story has diffused throughout the world:

"Normally the genre first infiltrates each country via translations of the immensely popular British or American works such as those of Poe, Doyle and others. These imports are usually followed by indigenous imitators and finally by native authors who adapt and alter the formula of the genre to meet the conditions and culture of the country."

Dr. Demko pointed to mystery/detective authors around the world, including Leonardo Sciascia, Umberto Eco and Carlo Emilio Gadda in Italy. In Spain Pedro Antonio de Alarcon was an early mystery author, publishing *The Nail and Other Tales of Mystery and Crime* in 1853, and today Arturo Perez-Reverte's mystery novels are some of the most widely read in the world. In Japan, mystery publishing dates to the 1880s but began flourishing in 1923 with the writings of Edogawa Rampo, whose name is a punning transliteration of Edgar Allan Poe.

In Argentina, crime fiction went mainstream as leading authors such as Jose Luis Borges and Rodolfo Walsh used genre, focusing on why crimes are committed rather than whodunit. Israel, the Czech Republic, Mexico, South Africa and many other countries are vital mystery publishing centers.

In Russia, mystery fiction also began very early, and one could argue that Dostoyevsky's *Crime and Punishment* (1866) and *The Brothers Karamazov* (1880) are forms of psychological mysteries. During the Soviet era, *"Pinkertonista"* stories were popular, based on the first American detective agency, Pinkerton, but these usually depict the KGB or Russian heroes defeating capitalist spies.

It is notable that authoritarian regimes, such as Mussolini's Fascists in Italy, Franco in Spain, Stalin in the Soviet Union and Mao in China banned, at least for a time, some or all detective/mystery stories. The Nazis under Hitler had a policy of banning many translated books, and during the war about one-third of all banned translated books were in the mystery/detective genres.

Each regime probably had different reasons for banning detective and mystery novels, but one common theme for the banning is that many of these works had heroes that exposed government corruption or that glorified the individual over the state.

Nonetheless, regardless of the genre or subgenre or where written or set, most critics and readers tend to agree that certain elements should be present in both mysteries and detective fiction:

• A serious crime occurs, or a series of crimes, usually murder but occasionally another serious crime, such as a theft or attempted murder. The crime is significant in that it cannot be reversed, so it is worth the reader's time to engage with it.

• The person or persons attempting to solve the crime must be interesting or different in some way – eccentric, very smart, observant, unusual in age, place of residence, occupation or in another way. Again, this is so the detective or other protagonist is sufficiently interesting to engage the reader.

• All the suspects, including the perpetrator, must be presented, typically fairly early in the story, although in some stories the guilt individual may appear fairly late.

• The author must "play fair" in that all the clues that the detective or other protagonist uses to solve the crime has to be available to the reader as well, even though the clues may be disguised or the reader's attention misdirected through the use of a "red herring" or other device.

• The solution to the story must make sense and be logical enough that it is believable to the reader. In short, the reader will say, "yes, if I had the same information I would probably have come to the same conclusion."

Of course, some successful mystery and detective works break one or more of these rules, and that is probably truer now than in the past.

In this book, we are dealing with detective fiction, and specifically with a particular type of detective – one who is not officially employed by the police, even though some, such as Dupin, Hercule Poirot or Adrian Monk, may consult with or work with the police from time to time. Others, such as Charlie Chan, may have some official connection to the police, but in the stories we examine they are acting mostly on their own. Some, such as Jim Rockford, Sharon McCone and Kinsey Millhone, are licensed private detectives – AKA private eyes, private dicks, PIs – while others, such as Travis McGee, Spenser, Hercule Poirot and the "Hallmark Blondes" are unlicensed and work on an unofficial basis.

This book is by no means a representative history of detective fiction. How could it be? In the United States alone, about 15,000 mystery novels are published each year, and that does not include ebooks. Since the mid-19th century, hundreds of thousands and possibly millions of detective/mystery titles have been published, by tens of thousands of authors. This does not include the thousands of film and television, and now internet, detectives who have flickered across our vision.

Of all those, I have selected 25 private detectives. In fact, there are more than 25 individuals.

Among the 25 profiles are a couple, Nick and Nora Charles, two teams – Perry Mason and Paul Drake, and Nero Wolfe and Archie Goodwin – and four different "Hallmark Blondes."

I could attempt to make an argument for why each of these 25 detectives is featured. Some are without doubt important to the development of the genre. As noted, Poe's C. Auguste Dupin appears in what most agree is the first detective story. Sherlock Holmes's DNA is in nearly every detective story or film created since he first appeared in 1887 in "A Study in Scarlet."

Agatha Christie, the undisputed grand dame of mystery writers, made her Miss Marple novels and stories the most widely read detective tales in the world. The hard-boiled school of detection, from the typewriters of Dashiell Hammett, Raymond Chandler, Ross Macdonald and Mickey Spillane, and later, John D. McDonald and Robert B. Parker, sold millions, nay billions, of books.

Instead, I will just say that these 25 are my favorites, for all kinds of different reasons. In some cases, as with Dashiell Hammett, Raymond Chandler, Ross Macdonald and Robert B. Parker, it's because I admire the writing. In other cases, such as Sue Grafton's Kinsey Millhone and Aurora Teagarden (played on TV by Candace Cameron Bure), it's because I'm a little in love with the detectives. Yet in other cases I'm interested in the settings of the stories or films, in Sam Spade's San Francisco, in Judge Deborah Knott's fictional Colleton County, North Carolina, or Jessica Fletcher's Cabot Cove, Maine.

Several I've included just because. Just because they've given me so many hundreds of hours of pleasure reading about them or watching their antics. Jim Rockford and Trav McGee fall into this category. Most will be well known, if only by name, to most crime fiction buffs, although one or two, such as P. D. James' Cordelia Grey and Poe's Dupin, appeared only a few times.

At least one, Mickey Spillane's Mike Hammer, I actually don't care for. Hammer is a bigot, a sexist and very possibly a sociopath. I included Hammer because, while immensely popular in his day – at one time seven of the 10 books on the best-seller lists were Hammer novels – today he is not appreciated for how much he changed the reading habits of Americans. Many of his readers, and the children of his readers, may be the hardcore Trump supporters of today.

For each detective, I've sketched his or her unique style, looked at some of their best-known cases and provided a brief biography of the detective's creator or creators.

In most cases, I've also included personal details about all the detectives: where they lived and worked, what they liked to drink, (with a recipe or two for their favorite cocktails or other drinks) and what vehicle if any they drove. (Travis McGee's vintage 1936 Rolls-Royce pickup takes the prize.) Also I've included lists of their major appearances in print or broadcast.

I've divided my picks into four fairly arbitrary categories of detection: Talented Amateurs, The Professionals, Tough Guys and New Women. Talented Amateurs are individuals who solve murders and other crimes essentially for the fun of it. The Professionals have made detection their business, whether or not they are licensed.

Tough Guys include the founders of the hard-boiled private eye genre and those that followed them. New Women are resourceful, independent women who, with their creators, came to prominence about the time, starting in the early 1970s, that feminism became an important movement. In a number of cases, detectives could fit in more than one category. For example, Jessica Fletcher is both a Talented Amateur and an accomplished member of the New Women. In those cases, I have had to make a judgment call. Within each category, chapters are in alphabetical order by the last name of the detective. My lists include not only detective novels and short stories, but also film and television detectives.

In the end, this is my highly personal list of the most fascinating, intriguing and interesting detectives. If you already know them, I hope that you will learn something new about them, and if some are new to you, I hope you enjoy getting to know them.

My look at these detectives required my reading of hundreds of books, both about the detectives and the biographies of their creators. I confess to stealing the ideas of many wonderfully talented and hardworking detectives and writers.

Over the course of many years, I've followed the murder most fowl of several thousand (mostly) innocent men and women. With so much murder in mind, I'm sure I've made mistakes, and for that I apologize in advance.

Lan Sluder
Asheville, North Carolina

TALENTED AMATEURS

There are two kinds of detectives in this world: amateurs and professionals.

Professionals may be trained in criminology, forensic medicine and other investigative and enforcement subjects in colleges and universities, or they may be trained in police academies and work for local, state or federal law enforcement agencies. Amateurs also come in several varieties, from little old ladies who simply are wise about human nature and very good at observing people. Agatha Christie's **Miss Marple** of course is the archetype, working from her home in a little English village. Or they may be self-taught in criminology or have had previous experience in police work but are no longer employed in the field. **Sherlock Holmes** and **Hercule Poirot** respectively are two prime examples.

In this book, we focus on *private* detectives, whether amateurs who solve cases on the side or professionals such as licensed private eyes. In this section, we look at the true amateurs, those who try to discover whodunit for the intellectual and psychological rewards, not for money.

Besides the three famous amateurs already noted, we look at Edgar Allan Poe's Parisian aristocrat **C. Auguste Dupin,** who is widely considered the main character in the first true detective stories ever written.

We also take a tour with that delightful couple, **Nick and Nora Charles**, created by Dashiell Hammett, who would in just five novels change the course of crime fiction. The hard-drinking, wisecracking couple came to life in a series of six *The Thin Man* movies in the 1930s and 1940s.

Dorothy L. Sayers, one of the most intelligent and talented of all detective fiction writers, created the eccentric and sometimes irritating honorary peer, **Lord Peter Wimsey,** whom we join in his luxurious flat in Piccadilly, London. Lord Peter, like the other amateurs in this section, is still read with pleasure by millions of detective fans many decades after he first appeared on the page.

Finally, we present two created-for-television amateurs, the inimitable Jessica, or J. B., Fletcher of *Murder, She Wrote.* In her years on TV, she popularized the little town of Cabot Cove in Maine as the murder capital of New England.

We also have a little fun with what we're calling the **"Hallmark Blondes,"** engaging amateur murder magnets who bake cookies, run an antique shop, renovate old houses or work in a library.

These, all staples of the family-friendly Hallmark Movies & Mysteries Channel, are not ditzy blondes, and in fact not all are real blondes; they are engaging female sleuths, American-Canadian throwbacks to the British "cozies" of Christie and Sayers.

Remember, the detectives are presented in each section alphabetically by their last names.

Nick and Nora Charles

From The Thin Man novel by Dashiell Hammett (1894-1961) and The Thin Man movie (1934) and its sequels

"The important thing is the rhythm. Always have rhythm in your shaking. Now a Manhattan you shake to fox-trot time, a Bronx to two-step time, a dry martini you always shake to waltz time."

William Powell as Nick Charles in *The Thin Man*

A publicity still from the 1934 MGM film The Thin Man *from the novel by Dashiell Hammett featuring (L-R) Myrna Loy as Nora Charles, William Powell as Nick Charles and Maureen O'Sullivan as Dorothy Wynant*

Nick and Nora Charles doubtless are the most famous married couple in the history of detecting. To be precise, Nick was the detective, nominally retired from the business after marrying Nora and her money ("[Nora's] father died and left her a lumber mill and a narrow-gauge railroad and some other things"), and it was he who mostly solved the cases.

However, Nora was always there to help and cheer on Nick, and usually to share a few jokes and many drinks with him.

The Thin Man was the fifth and last novel of Dashiell Hammett, published in early 1934. With those five novels, published over a short period from 1929 to 1934, Hammett transformed the detective novel. *The Thin Man* novel was the basis of the MGM movie of the same name, starring William Powell and Myrna Loy as Nick and Nora. It was shot in just two weeks by director W. S. "Woody" Van Dyke and came out in May 1934. The screenplay, which in many ways closely follows the Hammett novel, incorporating verbatim some of the witty banter between Nick and Nora, was by Albert Hackett and Frances Goodrich, also a married couple.

Following the success of the original movie, five other films in *The Thin Man* series were produced, all featuring Powell and Loy. Hammett worked on the synopsis, treatment and screenplay of the first two of them. *After the Thin Man* was released by MGM on Christmas Day, 1936, and *Another Thin Man* premiered in 1939. After this, three other Nick and Nora films were produced, without any involvement by Hammett except for an eight-page treatment he wrote for the first of the three, a treatment that was rejected by the MGM studio: *Shadow of the Thin Man* (1941), *The Thin Man Goes Home* (1944) and the last and weakest of them all, *Song of the Thin Man* (1947).

The Thin Man is set in New York City at the end of Prohibition. In Hammett's novel, Nick Charles is the son of Greek immigrants and has left "the Agency" after marrying Nora, who has inherited a great deal of money and several businesses. The cases involves the disappearance of Clyde Wynant, an eccentric, divorced inventor whose family, except the daughter, played by Maureen O'Sullivan, are a money-grubbing and unpleasant bunch. The skeletal Wynant, played by Edward Ellis, is actually the "thin man," but later movies capitalized on the nickname to refer to Nick Charles.

Early on Nick and Nora are childless (from the third movie, they are parents to Nick Junior), but they have a dog to which they are deeply attached. In the novel it is a female schnauzer named Asta, but in the movies it is a male wired-haired fox terrier.

In the first two *Thin Man* movies, Asta was played by a trained dog named Skippy, which also appeared in other 1930s movies including *The Awful Truth* starring Cary Grant and Irene Dunne and in *Bringing Up Baby* starring Katherine Hepburn. In later *Thin Man* movies other trained terriers were used to portray Asta.

Nick and Nora's Digs: Nick and Nora Charles spend most of their time in San Francisco and New York City. Since Nick no longer works regularly as a private detective, he does not need an office.

Both the novel and film versions of *The Thin Man* are set in Manhattan, mostly during the Christmas and New Year's holiday period. The Charleses are staying The Normandie, a residential hotel at Broadway and 38th Street. The movie was shot primarily at MGM's studios in Culver City, Calif.

The second *Thin Man* movie, *After the Thin Man,* is set in San Francisco, with the first scenes at New Year's Eve. Nick and Nora Charles' lavish home, actually Coit Tower atop Telegraph Hill. The base of the art deco Coit Tower is used in the movie as the set for their home. Other scenes take place at the Victorian home of Nora's aunt, cousin and other relatives and in San Francisco's China Town.

In the third film in the series, *Another Thin Man,* Nick and Nora are returning to New York from a long vacation, with luggage and Asta in tow. They are staying in what appears to be a residential hotel on the Upper East Side. Although shot at MGM's Culver City studios, the setting for much of the movie is supposed to be the Long Island estate of Col. McFay, who manages Nora's business affairs.

Shadow of the Thin Man reverts back to a San Francisco setting. Nick and Nora are living in a pleasant but not lavish apartment near a park. Some of the action takes place at a horse track (Golden Gate Fields in Berkeley). Most scenes were filmed at MGM's Culver City studios.

In *The Thin Man Goes Home,* the Charleses are back in New York City. But they are on their way to visit Nick's father, Dr. Bertram Charles, a physician, and mother in Sycamore Springs, N.Y., Nick's hometown. Much of the movie takes places in Nick's parents' rambling white frame home.

The last, and the worst, of *The Thin Man* movies, *Song of the Thin Man,* again takes place in New York City, at times on a docked gambling boat, the *U.S.S. Fortune.*

Nick and Nora's Drives: In *The Thin Man* movies, the Charleses show relatively little interest in cars. Since they live in large cities, New York and San Francisco, often they take taxis. In *After the Thin Man* and *The Thin Man Goes Home,* they get to their destinations by train, San Francisco and Sycamore Springs, N.Y. respectively. In *Another Thin Man,* they are picked up at their hotel in New York by a car and driver sent by Col. McFay (C. Aubrey Smith), who looks after Nora's business interests. They are taken to McFay's home on Long Island in a 1934 Lincoln.

However, in one film, *Shadow of the Thin Man,* Nick drives a beautiful convertible, a 1941 Lincoln Continental Cabriolet. He is stopped for speeding by a motorcycle cop on the then newly completed San Francisco-Oakland Bay Bridge.

In *After the Thin Man*, Nick and Nora are picked up from the train in what is probably their 1936 Packard Super Eight Drophead (convertible) and taken to their hilltop home in San Francisco.

Nick and Nora's Drinks: Both in the novel and film versions of *The Thin Man,* alcohol is consumed casually and in great quantities. In the film, when Nora meets Nick at a bar, she asks how many drinks he has had. He says he is on his sixth. She tells the bartender to set up six martinis. Drink or drinking is mentioned 61 times in the 259 pages of the novel. Cocktail is referred to 12 times, whisky eight times, Scotch five times, champagne three times and wine once.

Today, by almost any standard, Nick would be considered an alcoholic. Although he is rarely seen drunk, he frequently seems unsteady on his feet and seems to speak carefully to avoid slurring his words.

Nick's drink of choice in the original novel and movie and in the movie sequels generally is Scotch and soda, but he often drinks martinis, champagne and various other wines. Nora seems to prefer martinis but likes Scotch and sodas as well and will gladly accept other cocktails or wine. Only in one of *The Thin Man* movies is Nick always sober. In *The Thin Man Goes Home,* Nick switches to apple cider to please his father, a physician in Sycamore Springs, N.Y., who disapproves of drinking.

Nick's Scotch and Soda

2 oz. or more of Scotch

Soda water

In an old-fashioned glass (ice cubes optional), pour 2 oz. or more of Scotch. Add a splash of soda water, preferably from a siphon bottle.

Nora's Dry Martini

2 oz. gin

Small splash of dry vermouth

Combine ingredients in a shaker with ice. Shake well (to waltz time). Strain and serve straight up in a small chilled martini glass. Garnish with olives. Repeat 32 times.

The Charles' Bronx

1½ oz. gin

½ oz. dry vermouth and ½ oz. sweet vermouth

1 oz. orange juice

Combine all ingredients in a shaker with ice. Shake well (to two-step time). Strain and serve straight up in a chilled martini glass, garnished with orange peel.

About Author Dashiell Hammett:

(For additional information on Hammett, see The Maltese Falcon *chapter of this book.)*

Dashiell Hammett is widely considered the founder of the hard-boiled detective genre.

Born in St. Mary's County, Md., in 1894, Samuel Dashiell Hammett grew up in Baltimore. Leaving high school to help support his family, he worked at various blue-collar jobs. He never finished high school nor attended college. During World War I, he served in the U.S. Army near Baltimore, where it was thought he contracted tuberculosis.

It was at a TB sanatorium where Hammett met a nurse from Montana, Josephine (Jose) Annis Dolan. After Jose became pregnant in 1921, the two married. They had two daughters, Mary and Josephine.

Hammett would again enlist in the Army during World War II, serving as editor of an Army newspaper in the Aleutian Islands. He was briefly stationed in Alaska, near Anchorage.

After the First World War, at age 21 Hammett answered an intriguing classified newspaper ad and took a job with Pinkerton's National Detective Agency in Baltimore. He worked for Pinkerton's for the next seven years. Hammett spent part of the time in the company's office in San Francisco, the city with which the writer is most closely associated.

Although Hammett used a glamorized version of his detective experiences with Pinkerton's in many of his early detective stories and novels, Hammett likely worked on occasion for the agency as a strikebreaker. At that time, Pinkerton's biggest source of revenue came from breaking union strikes at big companies. Indeed, at one point Pinkerton's was the country's number one buyer of Thompson machine guns, to arm its force of violent union busters.

Hammett arrived in San Francisco in 1921, assigned to the Pinkerton's office there, and it was in that city that he wrote most of the fiction for which he is known and where most of his most famous works are set. He wrote the ground breaking hard-boiled detective novels *Red Harvest, The Dain Curse* and *The Maltese Falcon* in San Francisco and also wrote almost all of his approximately 100 short stories there. Two of his best known characters, private eye Sam Spade in his trench coat and snap-brim hat, and the Continental Op, an unnamed, short, fat operative for the Continental detective agency, lived in San Francisco. Nick and Nora Charles also were residents of the city by the bay, splitting their time between there and New York City.

In his late 20s, seriously ill with tuberculosis and unable any longer to hold an outside job, Hammett decided to become a writer. He enrolled in a journalism program at a vocational school in San Francisco, mainly to learn how to type. Hammett soon began selling detective stories and novellas, first under a pseudonym and then under his own name, to the pulp detective magazines popular at the time, mainly *Black Mask*. Hammett first sold a story to the magazine in 1922. Under editor Joseph T. Shaw, *Black Mask* became the premier outlet for the new, hard-edged, tough-guy style of detective fiction, the mystery equivalent of Ernest Hemingway's terse style in his more literary fiction, and Dash Hammett was the star writer at *Black Mask*.

Knopf published Hammett's first hardcover novel, Red Harvest, in 1929. Originally titled *Poisonville*, the Continental Op tale was based in part on the bloody Industrial Workers of the World strike in Montana, finally broken by hired thugs working for Pinkerton's.

By a stroke of luck, Hammett sent *Red Harvest* over the transom to Knopf, where it found its way to Blanche Knopf, wife of Alfred Knopf and co-founder of the publishing firm. Blanche Knopf was then and remained until her death in 1966 the most important woman in publishing. She had the great talent of spotting and nurturing talented writers: Over the course of her career, 27 of her writers won Pulitzers for literature and 16 won Nobel Prizes. Among the American authors with whom she worked, besides Hammett, were Willa Cather, H. L. Mencken, John Updike and Langston Hughes. She traveled frequently to Europe and worked with Sigmund Freud, Thomas Mann, Albert Camus, André Gide, Jean-Paul Sartre, Simone de Beauvoir and Mikhail Sholokhov, often striking deals to publish translations of their works in the United States.

Red Harvest was followed soon thereafter by another Continental Op novel, *The Dain Curse.* The Continental Op stories and novels, told in the first person, were set against a background of political and social corruption. This was the period of Prohibition (1920-1933), when organized mobs ran the illegal alcohol business and sleazy bureaucrats in the Warren Harding and Calvin Coolidge administrations made bribery a highly profitable part of government service.

Hammett's famous 1930 novel, *The Maltese Falcon,* was first run as a five-part serial in *Black Mask.* (*Also see the chapter on Sam Spade.*)

The Glass Key was recast as a novel from a group of *Black Mask* stories. This 1931 work features Ned Beaumont as a gambler, friend of a mobster and amateur detective who finds the dead body of a politician's son. Hammett considered *The Glass Key* his favorite of all his books, although today it is not as widely read as his other works.

In the early 1930s, several of Hammett's works were made into films. But he was drinking a lot and spending money faster than he made it, and by 1932 Hammett was nearly broke. Although Hammett was unfaithful on a number of occasions to his wife Jose, and they divorced in 1937, Hammett remained emotionally close to Jose throughout his life. At one point in the 1950s he bought her a house.

Hammett had met playwright and leftwing intellectual Lillian Hellman in 1930, and they began an on-and-off relationship that would last until his death in 1961. Hammett's relationship with Hellman was portrayed in the 1977 film *Julia.* Jason Robards won a Supporting Actor Oscar for his depiction of Hammett, and Jane Fonda was nominated for her portrayal of Hellman.

Staying with Hellman at the Sutton Club Hotel in New York in late 1932, in a short but intense three-week burst of creativity, aided by Hammett temporarily going on the wagon, Hammett wrote much of what would be his final and most successful book, *The Thin Man.* Nathanael West was then acting as manager of the Sutton while he finished his classic novel, *Miss Lonelyhearts*, and he allowed Hammett and Hellman, along with several other writers, to stay free.

The Thin Man, featuring the witty, hard-drinking duo of Nick and Nora Charles – patterned partly on Dashiell and Lillian – was published about a year later, first in December 1933 in condensed and somewhat expurgated form in *Redbook* magazine and then as a hardcover novel by Knopf in January 1934. The book was dedicated to "Lily."

Hammett sold the rights to the novel to MGM for $21,000 (about $350,000 in today's dollars). The movie, starring William Powell and Myrna Loy, shot in just 14 days, debuted to great success later in 1934.

As noted, *The Thin Man* plot centers on an inventor, Clyde Wynant, who mysteriously disappears.

Wynant is in fact the eponymous very thin man of the novel (a photograph of a rail-thin but dapper Hammett appeared on the front dustcover of the novel) and of the movie. MGM, realizing that the public thought of Nick Charles as "the thin man," went along with that charade in all the movie sequels.

The novel opens with San Franciscans Nick and Nora Christmas shopping in New York. Nick, a former private eye, has married money and no longer takes cases.

However, Wynant's daughter, Dorothy (Maureen O'Sullivan) introduces herself to Nick at a 52nd Street speakeasy and tells Nick about her missing father, for whom Nick had formerly worked. Nick suggests calling Clyde Wynant's lawyer, Herbert Macaulay (played by Porter Hall).

The plots of the novel and the film differ in a number of respects, and the novel, with its references to sexual sadism, cannibalism and lesbianism, is much darker, and racier, than the movie. The Canadian government banned the book.

In part because of its notoriety, the novel was a success. It sold 20,000 copies in hardback in the first three weeks and 30,000 copies in the first year. The novel also received good critical reviews.

Most importantly for Hammett, who long had struggled to make ends meet on a Veterans Administration pension and freelance writing, *The Thin Man* ended most of Hammett's financial worries, at least for a while (when he died in 1961, he was effectively bankrupt, with assets of less than $10,000 and liens against his estate of $220,000 including nearly $180,000 in federal and state tax judgments). From 1933 to 1950, it has been estimated that Hammett's total earnings from the novel, its spin-offs and movies came to about $1 million (well over $10 million in today's dollars.) Hammett and Hellman spent the winter of 1933-34 in Homestead and Key Largo, Fla., fishing and drinking. Here, Hellman wrote her best-known play, *The Children's Hour,* based on a plot Hammett had found for her about a Scottish girls' boarding school. Hammett acted as Hellman's editor, forcing her to do rewrite after rewrite. Hellman dedicated the play to "D. Hammett With Thanks."

The year 1934, when Hammett was 40 years old, essentially marked the end of Hammett's productive creative life. He still hired out to Hollywood, working on the screenplays for the first two of the five sequels to *The Thin Man* film, briefly wrote a comic strip, *Secret Agent X-9,* and worked on other projects.

In the late 1930s, he sold all the rights, except radio rights, to *The Thin Man* series and its characters to MGM for $40,000 (nearly $700,000 today).

Although Hammett did little writing in the 1940s, his name was constantly before the public as the originator of the characters in the later *Thin Man* movies, in various radio series, and, most notably, as the creator of Sam Spade, played by Humphrey Bogart in *The Maltese Falcon* in 1941, directed by John Houston, who also did the screenplay.

From the 1930s on, Hammett increasingly became involved with left-wing political causes, especially the Civil Rights Congress, of which be became president. The Civil Rights Congress had Communist affiliations. Hammett himself joined the Communist Party USA in 1937.

In 1951, Hammett declined to testify, citing the Fifth Amendment, in U.S. District Court about the whereabouts of several Civil Rights Congress members who had jumped bond and fled as fugitives. As a result, Hammett was jailed and then transferred to federal prison, spending about six months behind bars. He later was a target of Joe McCarthy's House Un-American Activities Committee.

Hammett's lover, Lillian Hellman, speculated that his espousal of Marxist ideals was a reaction to his guilt at being a strikebreaker while working for Pinkerton's. Hellman claims that Hammett told her that in 1917 he was assigned to help break the IWW strike against Anaconda Copper in Montana and had been offered $5,000 (around $70,000 today) to assassinate the Wobblies' strike leader. Hammett's first novel, *Red Harvest,* was set in a town like Butte, Montana.

Blacklisted, hounded by the Internal Revenue Service for unpaid taxes, ill and drinking heavily, in 1957 he moved in with Lillian Hellman in her apartment on East 82nd Street in New York City. During his last years, he was a near invalid and a hermit, spending most of his time watching television. In 1961, Hammett died of lung cancer and complications of TB and alcoholism in a New York hospital.

Novels by Dashiell Hammett

The first four of Hammett's five novels were serialized in several parts in pulp magazines, mostly *Black Mask*. *The Thin Man* appeared first in *Redbook* magazine, in a condensed and expurgated version.

Red Harvest (1929)
The Dain Curse (1929)
The Maltese Falcon (1930)
The Glass Key (1931)
The Thin Man (1934)

The Thin Man Movies

The Thin Man (1934)
After the Thin Man (1936)
Another Thin Man (1939)
Shadow of the Thin Man (1941)
The Thin Man Goes Home (1945)
Song of the Thin Man (1947)

Notable Works about Dashiell Hammett and The Thin Man

Cline, Sally. *Dashiell Hammett, Man of Mystery* (2014). This biography, the first Hammett biography since the early 1980s, is short but covers the ground well.

Layman, Richard, *Shadow Man, The Life of Dashiell Hammett* (1981). Many consider this the best general biography of Hammett.

Tranberg, Charles, *The Thin Man: Murder Over Cocktails* (2015). Profiles of the characters and actors in the film series.

C. Auguste Dupin

From the short stories by Edgar Allan Poe (1809-1849)

"EXTRAORDINARY MURDERS. — This morning, about three o'clock, the inhabitants of the Quartier St. Roch were aroused from sleep by a succession of terrific shrieks, issuing, apparently, from the fourth story of a house in the Rue Morgue, known to be in the sole occupancy of one Madame L'Espanaye, and her daughter Mademoiselle Camille L'Espanaye."

Edgar Allan Poe, "The Murders in the Rue Morgue"

Edgar Allan Poe, from a daguerreotype, circa 1847

In the views of many, C. Auguste Dupin is the template for all the thousands of detectives in fiction. Edgar Allan Poe, the troubled genius of 19th century American literature, brought him to life in three short stories: "The Murders in the Rue Morgue" (1841), "The Mystery of Marie Rogêt" (1842) and "The Purloined Letter" (1844).

Some consider Poe's "The Gold Bug" (1843) also a detective story, because its solution involves a cipher, but it does not feature Auguste Dupin, and it is not included here.

When Poe penned his stories, the word "detective" did not even exist in the sense that it is used today. Now, the Mystery Writers of America present annual awards, the Edgars, named in honor of the inventor of the detective story.

"The Murders in the Rue Morgue," the first and best of Poe's three famous detective stories, was published in April 1841 in *Graham's Magazine,* owned by a Philadelphia lawyer, George Graham. Poe was then working as the editor of the literary magazine, which had a circulation of only around 5,000, but due to Poe's reputation as a biting literary critic and the author of some of the most famous poems and short stories of the first half of the 19th century the magazine's impact on the literary world was much greater than its circulation numbers would suggest.

Auguste Dupin is a Parisian, an aristocrat who comes from a wealthy family but who through untoward circumstances has been reduced to near-poverty. He lives with the unnamed narrator in a flat in an old mansion. The two have little money to spare, with their only luxuries being old books. That common interest is how the two met, when both were searching for a rare volume in an obscure library in Montmartre.

Dupin is introduced as a man of analytical mind, "fond of enigmas, of conundrums, hieroglyphics."

As Sherlock Holmes would do later with Watson, Dupin is able to deduce what his friend the narrator is thinking by putting together a series of clues.

The character of Auguste Dupin is thought to have been based on Eugène François Vidocq (1775-1857), a French criminal who reformed and became the founder and first head of the *Sûreté Nationale,* the state security police. Later, Vidocq established the world's first private detective agency, *Le bureau des renseignements* (Office of Information). Vidocq is considered by many to be the father of modern criminology. Poe likely saw a series of articles on Vidocq published in *Burton's Gentleman's Magazine,* another Philadelphia literary magazine that Poe briefly edited.

In "The Murders in the Rue Morgue," the narrator and Dupin discuss newspaper accounts of the brutal murders of a mother and daughter. The body of the mother, Madame L'Espanaye, had been found in the yard behind their apartment building in Quartier St. Roch, with multiple bones broken and her throat cut so deeply that when police try to move the body her head falls off.

A tuft of reddish hair is clutched in her cold hand. Her daughter has been strangled and her body stuffed upside down in a chimney in the flat.

The door and windows of the fourth-floor room on Rue Morgue where the murders took place were closed and locked. This street did not actually exist in Paris at the time, but a place where dead bodies are kept was the perfect title for the story.

Four thousand French francs in gold (around $8,000 in today's money) had been delivered from a bank three days before the murders, but the gold had not been taken, so robbery was ruled out as a motive. Neighbors and passersby, including a Spaniard, an Englishman, a Dutchman, an Italian and a Frenchman, were interviewed. They had not seen anyone enter or leave the apartment. They all heard a man speaking French, but they could not agree on what language was spoken by the presumed murderer. Despite a lack of evidence, a bank clerk, Adolphe Le Bon, who had arranged the delivery of the gold francs, was arrested for the murders. Le Bon had once done a good deed for Dupin, so the French aristocrat decides to solve the crime and get the bank clerk set free.

Mostly from information from newspaper accounts, with consultation with the Prefect of police, "G—" and with a visit to the scene of the murders, Dupin is able to determine that the bank clerk had nothing to do with the murders. He concludes that murderer (now so well known that there is no need to avoid giving away the ending) in fact is an "Ourang-Outang" or orangutan kept by a sailor.

Dupin places an advertisement in a newspaper asking the owner to claim the animal. It turns out that the primate escaped from its locked room, ran away from its owner carrying a straight razor that it had seen the sailor use for shaving, committed the murders and escaped through a fourth-story window, with the spring-loaded sash closing on its own.

Under French law of the time, neither the orangutan nor its owner could be held responsible. The wrongly arrested bank clerk is released. The sailor sells the ape and goes his way. Dupin, despite his poverty, refuses to accept an offer of a reward from the sailor.

"The Murders in the Rue Morgue" likely derives from Poe's recollection of the display of an orangutan at the Masonic Hall in Philadelphia in July 1839.

The story ends with a quote from Rousseau in French (Poe was fluent in French) about the incompetent Prefect of Police G. whom Dupin believes to be "too cunning to be profound:" *"de nier ce qui est, et d'expliquer ce qui n'est pas"* ("to deny that which is, and explore that which is not").

The other two of Poe's stories featuring Auguste Dupin, while popular at the time, are inferior to "Rue Morgue" in several ways.

"The Mystery of Marie Rogêt," published in two parts in the December 1842 and January 1843 issues of *Snowden's Ladies' Companion,* was based on a real murder, that of Mary Cecilia Rogers. Known as the "Beautiful Cigar Girl," her dead body was found floating in the Hudson River in Hoboken, N.J. Later, her fiancé committed suicide, leaving a note confessing the murder.

In the Dupin story, the young woman's body is found floating in the Seine in Paris. Dupin uses his skills in ratiocination to determine that the murderer dragged Rogêt by the cloth belt around her waist, then switched to a cloth around her neck and dumped her body off a boat into the river.

The third Dupin story, "The Purloined Letter," was published in December 1844 in the literary annual *The Gift for 1845* and was soon reprinted in several newspapers and magazines. The still unnamed narrator and Dupin are discussing some of Dupin's cases when the Prefect of police G calls on them and seeks Dupin's help in the matter of a compromising letter stolen from the bedroom of a woman by an unscrupulous government minister, who is blackmailing the woman.

The Prefect says that he and his officers have searched the minister's rooms and have not found the letter. Eventually, the police offer a reward of 50,000 French francs (perhaps $100,000 U.S. dollars today).

By thinking like the criminal minister, Dupin is able to find the stolen letter, which has been hidden in plain sight, and replace it with another. This time, Dupin accepts the 50,000 franc reward.

Readers today may find the Dupin stories a little slow to start. "The Murders at the Rue Morgue" begins with a kind of dissertation on chess and checkers. In the way of 19th century literary works, they are a little wordy, with long sections of narration and not a great deal of dialogue. Yet, if you stick with them, you can clearly spot many of the conventions that have made up the detective story to this day – the clues, the red herrings, the locked-room puzzle and others. The end of "Rue Morgue," while well known now, was original and even shocking for its time.

Auguste Dupin's Digs: Dupin lives with his unnamed Boswell in a fourth floor flat in a decaying "time-worn and grotesque" mansion at 33 Rue Dunôt in Faubourg St. Germain in the third *arrondissement* of Paris.

The eccentric Dupin rarely goes out except at night, and during the day the windows are covered to shut out the light.

Dupin and the narrator of the stories accept few visitors.

As the narrator tells his readers, "Indeed the locality of our retirement had been carefully kept a secret from my own former associates; and it had been many years since Dupin had ceased to know or be known in Paris. We existed within ourselves alone."

Dupin's Drives: Dupin, though born to a wealthy family, now lives on a small income, so he does not own a horse and carriage. When he and the narrator go out at night, they walk arm-in-arm, wandering on foot around the city and often returning late at night.

Dupin's Drinks: In the three short stories devoted to Dupin, Poe does not have his character take anything to drink. The reclusive, eccentric Dupin does not seem to have an interest even in wine. Poe, however, began drinking at an early age. Trouble with alcohol plagued Poe all his life, costing him many jobs and contributing to his early death at the age of 40. Poe was the type of alcoholic who would go for weeks or months without drinking. But, then, if he took just a glass of beer or wine, he could not stop drinking. His alcoholic binges sometimes lasted for weeks. Poe would, and did, drink almost anything. He did not savor his drinks but craved them, drinking one after another until he passed out. However, especially in his time at the University of Virginia and as a cadet at West Point, apple brandy or cognac seemed to be his favorites.

At West Point, Poe excelled at mathematics (as would Dupin) but left before graduating as an army officer. He was said to spend as much time as he could at a tavern near the cliffs of Highland falls about 1½ miles from the student barracks. The tavern was called Benny Havens, after the name of its proprietor.

For about 70 years, from the 1930s to 2009, on Poe's birthday, January 19, a mysterious masked man, or perhaps a series of men, would leave a bottle of cognac and three roses on Poe's tombstone in Westminster Hall and Burying Ground in Baltimore. Often the masked man would also leave a short note addressed to Poe, often along the lines of "We haven't forgotten you." The media tagged the man the "Poe Toaster." Here is a recipe for a fictional Poe Toaster Cocktail, based on the classic Sidecar:

Poe Toaster Cocktail

2 oz. VSOP Cognac

1 oz. Grand Marnier (substitute Cointreau if you prefer)

1 oz. freshly squeezed lemon juice

Orange peel for garnish

Add all the ingredients to an ice-filled cocktail shaker. Shake and strain straight up into a cocktail glass. Garnish with a slice of orange peel.

About Author Edgar Allan Poe:

Edgar Allan Poe is the author of some of the best known works in American literature: classic, macabre short stories such as "The Tell-Tale Heart," "The Fall of the House of Usher" and "The Masque of the Red Death" and also memorable poems such as "The Raven" and "Annabel Lee."

Some consider Poe the first true professional writer, in the sense that he tried, if often without much success, to make his living from writing. Besides inventing the detective story as a literary genre, Poe also was an important pioneer in science fiction, with his novel *The Narrative of Arthur Gordon Pym of Nantucket* and other works. Today, he is best known for his dark, Gothic tales of madness and death and for unforgettable Romantic poetry. "The Raven," published in 1845, a lament for the beautiful Lenore by her lover, was a sensation and made Poe famous, not only in America but also in Europe, especially France. Despite making him a household name on two continents, "The Raven" earned its author only $9.

During his lifetime, Poe was known as a literary critic and later as a public lecturer. He edited five different magazines and contributed hundreds of book reviews and literary critiques to them and to other magazines and newspapers.

Unfortunately for Poe, many of his caustic reviews made enemies of some of the leading authors of the day including Longfellow.

Poe's life was to a great degree a series of failures, losses and disappointments, dropping out of the University of Virginia and West Point, gaining and soon losing jobs as the editor of literary magazines, spending years in poverty, constantly trying to borrow money from friends, losing his mother and wife to illnesses. He habitually alienated his friends and employers, especially those who tried to help him. Bouts of depression and alcoholic binges plagued him, and he died from the effects of his last drinking binge.

Born January 19, 1809, in Boston to parents who were traveling actors, Poe's father abandoned the family the following year, and then his beautiful mother died of tuberculosis. Taken in by a wealthy merchant of Scottish heritage in Richmond, John Allan, Poe grew up expecting to be the heir to a considerable fortune. That was not to be, however, as the young Poe and John Allan had an increasingly angry relationship. Poe matriculated at the University of Virginia, where he spent much of his time drinking and gambling, much to his foster father's dismay. He left Virginia after only a year. After finding he couldn't support himself, he joined the army as a private and within two years had risen to the highest enlisted rank, sergeant major.

Poe left the army early, and, after staying briefly in Baltimore where he lived with his widowed aunt, her daughter Virginia (Poe's first cousin, whom he would later marry) and his brother, he managed to get an appointment to West Point. At first he excelled, especially at mathematics and French, but then he began drinking heavily, neglecting his duties. Eventually he was court martialed and expelled.

By this time, Poe had published three slight volumes of poetry, none of which received much notice. From this point on, Poe attempted to make a living as a writer and editor. He was hired, and usually soon fired, as a writer and editor for five magazines, in Richmond, Philadelphia, Baltimore and New York. His goal was to start his own magazine, a goal he never achieved.

In 1835, Poe, then 26 years old, married his cousin Virginia Clemm, who was 13. By most accounts, the marriage was a loving one, despite Poe's battles with alcohol and depression. Virginia died in 1847 in a cottage in Fordham, N.Y. (now a part of the Bronx), of TB at age 24.

Poe's life went increasingly downhill after Virginia's death. He had relationships with several women, but all ended badly due to Poe's drinking and his inability to find stable work. He endlessly tried to borrow money from family, employers and friends. Returning to Richmond and then Baltimore, he continued his self-destructive drinking, suffering from hallucinations and delirium tremens.

On October 3, 1849, he was found delirious on a street in Baltimore, barefoot and wearing someone else's clothes. Poe was hospitalized in a small cell-like room with barred windows at Washington College Hospital. He died a little over three days later, at 5 am on October 7, 1849, at age 40. The cause of death has never been known sure, but it has been variously attributed to acute alcohol poisoning, cerebral bleeding, hypoglycemia, heart disease and rabies. Poe's last words were reported to be "Lord help my poor soul."

The Auguste Dupin Stories:
"The Murders in the Rue Morgue" (1841)
"The Mystery of Marie Rogêt" (1842)
"The Purloined Letter" (1844)

Notable Books on Poe:
Collins, Paul, *Edgar Allan Poe: A Fever for Living* (2014)
A short (144 pp.) but informative biography.
Meyers, Jeffrey, *Edgar Allen Poe, His Life & Legacy* (1992)
Perhaps the best full-length biography.

Jessica Fletcher

From the Murder, She Wrote television series (1984-1996) starring Angela Lansbury

A 1888 Victorian in Mendocino B&B, the exterior of which was used as Jessica Fletcher's home in Cabot Cover – from Blair House website

"'I've been here one year, this is my fifth murder. What is this, the death capital of Maine? On a per capita basis this place makes the South Bronx look like Sunny Brooke farms! ... I mean, is that why Tupper quit? He couldn't take it anymore? Somebody really should've warned me, Mrs. Fletcher. Now, perfect strangers are coming to Cabot Cove to die!"

Sheriff Mort Metzger, in *Murder, She Wrote,* "Mirror, Mirror on the Wall" Part 1 (1989)

Jessica Fletcher is a former high school teacher turned mystery writer and amateur detective. Although technically not a private detective, as the well-known author of many mystery novels she is frequently sought out by acquaintances and sometimes the police to help solve murders. She uses her powers of observation – her friend Dr. Seth Hazlitt remarks that Jessica "is the most observant person I've ever known" – and her deductive skills to gather clues and find the killer.

Murder, She Wrote is set in the small ocean side town of Cabot Cove, Maine, population around 3,600. Cabot Cove does not appear on Maine maps, although in various ways it resembles Penobscot Bay, Castine, Boothbay Harbor and a number of other small coastal towns in the state. *Murder, She Wrote* producers Richard Levinson and William Link did not film the show on location in Maine. The exteriors were shot in Mendocino, a popular artist's colony on California's North Coast about four hours north of San Francisco. Parts of some 60 movies have been filmed in Mendocino. The Pacific fills in for the rugged Atlantic coast.

Many of the early settlers of Mendocino were from the East, and some of the town's historic architecture is reminiscent of New England, so it was not too difficult to transform the picturesque California town into a Maine village. An inn in Mendocino, Hill House Inn (sometimes using its actual name and sometimes called Cabot Cove Inn in *Murder, She Wrote)* is featured prominently in the TV series. Ten episodes of *Murder, She Wrote* had scenes filmed on the Mendocino coast, and virtually every episode set in Cabot Cove showed views of the area. Exteriors of Blair House B&B was used to represent Jessica's home in Cabot Cove *(see below)*.

Additional New England backdrops were shot in Oregon and other parts of northern California. Most interior scenes and many street scenes in Cabot Cove and elsewhere were filmed at Universal Studios in Universal City, Calif., which also was a setting for at least one *Murder, She Wrote* episode featuring the Bates Mansion from *Psycho* ("Incident in Lot 7"). Some buildings in the series, such as hospitals and police stations, were shot in Los Angeles and elsewhere in California.

A retired English teacher living alone, her beloved husband Frank having died in the early 1980s, Jessica becomes a published writer by accident.

Her nephew, Grady, whom she helped raise, sees her mystery manuscript and, unknown to Jessica, sends it to a friend at a New York publishing house.

To Jessica's apparent perturbation, the manuscript is accepted and published. It soon zooms to the top of the best-seller lists, and Jessica is on her way to becoming a highly successful mystery writer and globetrotting amateur detective.

In early episodes, Jessica types her manuscripts on an old Royal typewriter. Later, she gets an IBM computer and a printer. During the course of the series, Jessica writes 28 books, the best known of which is *The Corpse Danced at Midnight.* All 28 novels appear to have been best sellers. It is thought she becomes quite wealthy from the royalties, movie rights and other income from her books. Jessica only rarely meets anyone who hasn't read at least one of her books, or at least who hasn't heard of her and her work.

As befits a successful writer, Jessica dresses well, albeit conservatively. In many episodes, she wears many different well-tailored and expensive outfits, sometimes changing several times a day.

Almost from the beginning of the series, Jessica is away from Cabot Cove a lot, on book signings and book promotion trips, visiting friends (she seems to have friends in almost every city and country) or family (Jessica has a huge number of nephews and, especially, nieces) on business or on vacation. Of the 263 episodes, only about three dozen were set primarily in Cabot Cove. The producers usually limited Cabot Cove as the setting to just five episodes per season.

This, it turns out, is a good thing for Cabot Cove, because otherwise, at the rate of one to three murders per episode, the little town of Cabot Cove would have been greatly depopulated. As it is, many jokes have been made about Cabot Cove having the highest murder rate per capita of any place in the world. No matter where Jessica travels, to New York, Nashville, Las Vegas, San Francisco, Los Angeles, or to Ireland, Australia, Jamaica, Moscow, Paris, London or wherever, she is sure to stumble up at least one homicide.

Fletcher's Digs: Jessica is supposed to live in an old white wood house 698 Candlewood Lane in Cabot Cove, Maine, zip code 03041. In fact, shots of Blair House, an 1888 white Victorian house in Mendocino, Calif. that is now operated as a B&B are used to represent Jessica's home in Cabot Cove.

If you want to see it for yourself, rates for Blair House start at an affordable $120 a night double. The V.I.P. suite, named the Angela Suite in honor of Angela Lansbury, is around $240.

In the eighth season of the series, Jessica rents an apartment in Penfield House Apartments at 941 West 61st Street in Manhattan.

Jessica uses the apartment when she is teaching courses in criminology and crime writing at Manhattan University, a fictitious institution on the West Side. She keeps her house in Cabot Cove.

Fletcher's Drives: Jessica never learns to drive, and she never owns a car. This is ironic, because Angela Lansbury is a car buff who often has often owned Cadillacs. Whenever she needs to go somewhere, Jessica bums a ride with her friend Dr. Seth Hazlitt, Sheriffs Tupper or Metzger (who has a Cadillac convertible) or someone else. Otherwise, she walks or rides her bicycle. When traveling, she uses taxis or a limo with driver, usually provided by her publisher. On long trips, she travels by air, usually in first class. (With the royalties she earns, she can afford it.) In one episode in the first season ("Hit, Run and Homicide") Jessica is forced to take the wheel of a runaway car, which crashes.

Fletcher's Drinks: Jessica isn't a prude about alcohol. She keeps a bar in her Cabot Cove home stocked with bourbon and other booze. She will drink dry sherry or champagne, and at a bar often will ask for white wine. On the other hand, she's not a writer who needs a drink to fuel her writing. On deadline, she'll sit down at her Royal, or later her IBM computer, and bang out the last chapters with at most a cup or two of tea to keep her going.

About the TV series: *Murder, She Wrote* is one of the most-successful and longest-running television series of all time. The series, starring Angela Lansbury, aired on CBS for 12 seasons from 1984 to 1996 with 263 episodes. At its peak, the show attracted some 23 million viewers to its Sunday night slot. After the series ended, there were four made-for-TV movies also starring Lansbury that aired from 1997 to 2003. A brief-lived spinoff series, *The Law & Harry McGraw,* ran for 16 episodes in the 1987-88 season.

Murder, She Wrote – the title is believed to come from the 1961 film adaptation of Agatha Christie's novel *4:50 to Paddington* called *Murder, She Said* owes its existence to producers Richard Levinson and William Link. Writer-producer Peter Fischer, who was later to go on to become the writer of a series of mystery novels collectively titled "The Hollywood Murder Mysteries" was also instrumental in creating it.

Levinson and Link had co-created the *Mannix* detective series starring Mike Connors that ran from 1967 to 1975. The duo then created the *Ellery Queen* show starring Jim Hutton. It lasted only one season, 1975-76. *(See the chapter on Ellery Queen.)*

The duo also co-created the highly successful *Columbo* series starring Peter Falk as a cigar-chomping, bedraggled LA homicide detective. Columbo was on television for about 35 years, airing a total of 69 movie-length episodes on NBC and ABC from 1968 to 2003. The first episode was based on a play that Link and Levinson had written.

Levinson and Link previously had worked with Peter Fischer as a writer on the *Ellery Queen* and *Columbo* shows. Fischer had co-written four *Ellery Queen* episodes and wrote or co-wrote seven *Columbo* episodes. During the first season of *Murder, She Wrote* Fischer was a writer on eight of the 22 episodes and wrote many of the shows in subsequent seasons. Link and Levinson also had a hand in writing some of the *Murder, She Wrote* episodes.

The producers-writers initially wanted Jean Stapleton for the starring role in *Murder, She Wrote,* but Stapleton was burned out from nine years of sitcom TV playing Archie Bunker's wife, Edith. Doris Day also turned them down. Levinson, Link and Fischer didn't think Lansbury, a leading stage actress and multiple Tony winner, having starred in the Broadway musicals *Mame* and *Gypsy* and in Stephen Sondheim's *Sweeny Todd,* and veteran film performer *(The Picture of Dorian Gray, The Manchurian Candidate, Bedknobs and Broomsticks, Death on the Nile, The Mirror Crack'd* and *The Lady Vanishes,* among many others) would consider the role, but they sent her a script and to their surprise she quickly accepted.

Born in London in 1925, to escape the blitz Lansbury, her mother and her siblings moved to New York in 1940, where she studied acting. She began her movie career with MGM, moving to stage and Broadway, where she enjoyed even greater success, and finally to television. *Murder, She Wrote* made Lansbury a household name in the U.S. and later worldwide, with millions of fans around the globe. Lansbury was part of the last group of film actors in the old studio system, on Broadway at the height of its celebrity and on television during the last period when the major American broadcast networks provided huge national audiences.

The show debuted September 30, 1984, with a two-part episode, "The Murder of Sherlock Holmes," written by Peter Fischer and directed by Corey Allen. Although it initially received only lukewarm reviews, *Murder, She Wrote* quickly became very popular, dominating its Sunday nighttime period during the years it aired then. It was especially popular with older viewers, in part because the show, even though it was about murder, eschewed graphic violence.

The televisions in the White House during the presidency of Ronald Reagan were always tuned to *Murder, She Wrote* on Sunday nights, according to Peter Fischer in his book, *Me and Murder, She Wrote.*

Through Corymore Productions, which she owned with husband Peter Shaw, Lansbury gained control of *Murder, She Wrote* in 1982, and Lansbury became executive producer of the show during its last four seasons.

Although ratings remained strong, with the show often in the top five network programs, its demographics were skewed to a 50+ audience, while most advertisers sought the 18-35 age group. Efforts were made to attract a younger audience – for example, in the eighth season some of the settings of the show were changed to Manhattan, where Jessica was supposed to be teaching crime writing at a university that resembles Columbia, and there were episodes that involved video games, rock stars and other subjects designed to reach younger viewers, but the efforts never worked very well.

When CBS moved the show from its Sunday slot to Thursday night up against *Friends* and *Seinfeld,* Lansbury objected strongly. Ratings for the show dropped precipitously, and the show's viewership remained weak in the key younger age groups. The last episode aired May 16, 1996. It was titled, likely not coincidentally, "Murder by Demographics."

Lansbury was nominated for 10 Golden Globe awards for *Murder, She Wrote,* winning twice, and 12 Emmys, but she never won an Emmy for this or any other show, although over the course of her long career she was nominated 18 times. She won five Tony awards, was inducted into the American Theatre Hall of Fame and was nominated for three Academy Awards. In 2013, Lansbury received an honorary Academy Award for lifetime achievement. In 2014, Lansbury became Dame Angela Lansbury when she was named Dame of the Order of the British Empire (DBE).

After the series ended, Lansbury remained busy working in movies and the theater and doing television commercials. The actress divides her time among homes in Manhattan, Calif., and County Cork, Ireland.

There have been many reports of her doing follow-up versions of *Murder, She Wrote,* but now, in her 90s, it is increasingly unlikely.

Murder, She Wrote is in syndication in the U.S. and nearly 50 other countries and is available on online services including Netflix.

Donald Bain, a prolific ghostwriter with around 120 ghosted books under his belt, including 27 novels in the Margaret Truman Capital Crimes series, was picked to write a series of *Murder, She Wrote* mysteries under the byline "Jessica Fletcher and Donald Bain."

The first appeared in 1989 and through 2016 more than 40 of these novels have been published. The books feature the characters in the television series but have new plots. Like the TV series, some are set in Cabot Cove and the rest in locales around the world. In 2013, Bain published a novel, *Lights Out!,* under his own name. The caper thriller received mediocre reviews and had modest sales.

Notable Works on Jessica Fletcher and Angela Lansbury

Bain, Donald, *Murder HE Wrote: A Successful Writer's Life* (2002). Bain, author of more than 40 *Murder, She Wrote* novels based on the television series, writes about his life as a novelist, ghostwriter and biographer.

Fisher, Peter, *Me and Murder, She Wrote* (2013). The story of the creation and production of the television series by one of the people responsible for it.

Gottfried, Martin, *Balancing Act: The Unauthorized Biography of Angela Lansbury* (1999). The best biography of Lansbury.

Hallmark Blondes

From the Hallmark Movies & Mysteries Channel

"When I die, I want to go peacefully like my grandfather, in his sleep. Not screaming like the passengers in his car."

Dr. Trammel in *Garage Sale Mysteries*

They're hokey. They're nice. They're pretty. They're perky. They live in small towns, where everybody knows nearly everybody. Most run their own businesses. On the side, they solve mysteries. And, they're blonde. The few who aren't really blonde look like they should be.

We're talking about the stars of the Hallmark Movies & Mysteries Channel made-for-TV mystery movies. Among them: Jennifer "Jenn" or sometimes "Jen" Shannon (played by Lori Loughlin) in *Garage Sale Mysteries;* Aurora Teagarden (Candace Cameron Bure) in *Aurora Teagarden Mysteries;* Shannon Hughes (Jewel Kilcher) in *Fixer-Upper Mysteries*; Hannah Swenson (Alison Sweeney) in *Murder, She Baked Mysteries.* Hallmark has other mystery series, including *Emma Fielding Mysteries,* about an archeologist turned amateur sleuth; *Hailey Dean Mysteries,* about a former assistant district attorney who has become a psychologist and an amateur detective; *Flower Shop Mysteries,* about a former lawyer played by Brooke Shields who opens a flower shop and, of course, solves murder mysteries on the side; *Mystery Woman,* about a book store owner with a mystery side; *Signed, Sealed and Delivered,* about the Postable family who, yes, solve mysteries; and others. *Darrow & Darrow,* which debuted on Hallmark Movies & Mysteries in October 2017, features a mother-daughter team of lawyers. However, here the focus is on the first four – *Teagarden, Garage Sale, Fixer-Upper* and *Baked.*

In many ways, these are the modern video equivalent of British "cozies," of which Agatha Christie's Miss Marple is the most famous archetype. Most of the Hallmark mystery series feature women in the starring roles, although *Signed, Sealed and Delivered* has an entire family and another, *The Gourmet Detective,* features a male former chef and a female police detective.

All are adamantly G or at most PG fare. Although they are movies about crime and murder most foul, they generally avoid on-screen gore and violence. The featured females are smart, practical and mostly enjoy a happy home life, either single but looking (Aurora Teagarden, Hannah Swensen and Shannon Hughes) or happily married (Jenn Shannon).

Despite their lack of hot sex and edgy realism, most of these mystery series are doing surprisingly well in the ratings. The Hallmark channels are bucking the trend of many in this cord-cutting era. Ratings are up, and both the Hallmark Channel and Hallmark Movies & Mysteries are among the top-rated networks on cable and satellite, offering real competition to Fox News, ESPN and CNN. The audience, while still predominantly female, is skewing younger, and an increasing number of men are watching.

Some media critics say the fans of these mysteries, with their family-oriented, middle-class and mostly white characters are reflections of the Donald Trump base. Many others, however, say it's a reaction to the divisive political period we're in. A segment of viewers, whether pro- or anti-Trump, just want an escape from the news headlines and angry talking heads. It's *Brady Bunch* déja vu all over again.

Garage Sale Mysteries

This series, now up to 11 movies from 2013 through 2017, is set in a small town in Washington State, near the coast. Most episodes are filmed in and around Vancouver, British Columbia, Canada, with some location scenes in the towns of Mission, Maple Ridge, Fort Langley and elsewhere. The production company is Front Street Pictures, with studios in Vancouver.

Jenn Shannon (Lori Loughlin) and her business partner Danielle "Dani" (Sarah Strange) run Rags to Riches, a vintage/antiques/consignment shop. Rags to Riches is patterned after Country Lane Antiques in Fort Langley, B.C., and that shop has been used for location filming. Jenn and her husband, Jason (Steve Bacic) have two children, Hannah (Eva Bourne), a live-at-home college student, and Logan (in earlier movies, played by Brendan Meyer; in later ones, by Connor Stanhope), a high school student and computer geek who often helps his mother to do research online.

Most of the murders in the *Garage Sale* series, naturally enough, are related to Jenn's business. In the *Murder Most Medieval* episode, Jenn buys a 100-year-old suit of armor, immediately sells it at a profit to a local collector and medieval fighting buff, and a local history professor is found dead in the suit of armor, which turns out in fact to be authentic medieval armor. In *The Beach Murder,* Jenn sells a collectible and valuable surfboard that she had found at a garage sale to a wealthy entrepreneur, who is then killed while surfing. A local police detective, Frank Lynwood (Kevin O'Grady) often is involved in investigating the cases Jenn stumbles on.

The town of Squamish, British Columbia, Canada, has been used for many exterior scenes of the Hallmark Movies & Mysteries show

The movie series was originally adapted from the three-part *Garage Sale* book series by author Suzi Weinert. The books are set not on the West Coast but in McLean, Va. The director on the movie series is Peter DeLuise.

Jenn's Digs, Drives and Drinks: Jenn's Rags to Riches store is in an unpretentious building in a commercial area of town. She and Dani are keeping the business going, but occasionally they have to forego their salaries. She drives a late-model dark blue Ford SUV and often shares a glass of wine with her husband Jason after work. At parties she drinks champagne. She and her husband live in a large upper-middle class home in a suburban area (Jason is a successful commercial and residential real estate builder.)

Aurora Teagarden Mysteries

Aurora Teagarden, a librarian in the fictional town of Lawrenceton, Wash., is a murder magnet. She is constantly stumbling on dead bodies, and in onc memorable scene the body of the local chief of police is dropped from a small airplane into her front yard.

Aurora also heads up the Real Murders Club, which meets regularly to discuss and try to solve past murders.

Among the club's members are Aurora's mother, Aida Teagarden (played by Marilu Henner), a real estate agent; Roe's best friend Sally Allison (Lexa Doig), a reporter at the local newspaper, the *Lawrenceton News*; John Queensland (Bruce Dawson) whom "Roe" hopes will marry her mother and Martin Bartell (Yannick Basson), a senior executive at manufacturing company PanAgra and a former CIA agent who served two tours of duty in Afghanistan. Roe is sweet on Martin, who is known for his good looks and long eyelashes.

The character of Aurora is based on a series of 10 novels, published from 1990 to 2017, by Charlaine Harris. (The books are set in the fictional town of Lawrenceton in Georgia.) Hallmark Movies & Mysteries Channel has so far done six of the *Teagarden Mysteries* starring Candace Cameron Bure as Roe.

Candace Cameron Bure is also executive producer of the *Teagarden Mysteries,* with her production company iCandy. Among her many roles was as D. J. Tanner in the long-running *Full House* series. She also is co-host on ABC's *The View.* Bure also has published three books and is an inspirational speaker. She and her husband also own a boutique vineyard in the Napa Valley.

Most of the location filming is done in Squamish, British Columbia, near Vancouver. The library where Aurora works is actually the Squamish Public Library at 37907 2 Avenue. The exterior of the Lawrenceton newspaper office where Sally is a reporter is at 37989 Cleveland Avenue in Squamish.

Aurora's Digs, Drives and Drinks: In the early episodes, Aurora lives in an apartment, with the rent paid by her mother, due to Roe's low salary as a librarian. However, in *The Julius House,* a former librarian and Real Murders Club member dies and bequeaths Aurora enough money to buy a large house about 5 miles outside of town. Of course, the house has a murky history and the previous occupants had disappeared without a trace, a mystery that Aurora is left to solve.

The ever-practical Aurora drives a silver Prius. When she drinks, which isn't often, she usually has a glass of wine. Is the wine from her own vineyard in the Napa Valley?

Murder, She Baked Mysteries

Based on the best-selling series of 21 bakery cozies (through 2017) by Joanne Fluke. *Murder, She Baked* is set in the fictional small town of Lake Eden, Minn. Fluke, who now lives in Southern California, grew up in a small rural town in Minnesota.

Altogether, Fluke has written more than 50 novels in the mystery and thriller genres, some under the pseudonym Jo Gibson.

Fluke also has done a Lake Eden cookbook, which combines recipes with stories. Fluke's *Murder, She Baked* novels also contain many recipes.

The Hallmark Movies & Mysteries series, which through 2017 is up to five episodes, features *Days of Our Lives* soap opera actress Alison Sweeney as Hannah Swensen, owner of The Cookie Jar bakery and coffee shop in Lake Eden. (Coincidentally or not, there are now more than a dozen bakeries in the U.S. named Cookie Jar, in Kentucky, Illinois, Indiana, Maine, Florida and other states as well as one in Lagos, Nigeria.)

Hannah's mother, the youthful-looking, and also blonde, Delores Swensen (Barbara Niven) is constantly hoping Hannah will get married. Hannah's blonde sister, Andrea Todd (Lisa Durupt), is married to a sheriff's deputy, Bill Todd (Toby Levins). Although Hannah dates an earnest dentist, she is more interested in Cameron Mathison (Mike Kingston), a detective in the Lake Eden sheriff's department. He stays busy investigating the homicides Hannah turns over.

In *Murder, She Baked: A Chocolate Chip Murder Mystery,* Hannah finds a delivery driver shot to death behind her bakery. In *Murder, She Baked: A Peach Cobbler Mystery,* Hannah finds her new bakery shop competitor dead in her new store, and Hannah is the prime suspect in the murder. In *Murder She Baked: Just Desserts,* Hannah is in a televised bake-off, and a judge on the show is murdered. And so it goes in Lake Eden, the murder capital of Minnesota.

Like most of the other Hallmark Movies & Mysteries programs, *Murder, She Baked* is filmed in British Columbia. Location scenes are shot in Langley, Maple Ridge, Squamish and other places in BC.

Hannah's Digs, Drives and Drinks: Much of the action in *Murder, She Bakes* takes place in her shop, The Cookie Jar. The Cookie Jar exterior used in the series is at 38055 Cleveland Avenue in downtown Squamish. In the real world, this is The Ledge Community Coffee House. At home, she pampers her cat, Moishe. (Moishe is yellow in early episodes, gray in later ones.) In some episodes, Hannah drives a silver Dodge Caravan with the license plate COOKEEZ. Especially at holiday parties, Hannah enjoys champagne with her cookies.

Fixer Upper Mysteries

Shannon Hughes (played by pop singer-songwriter Jewel Kilcher, who prefers to go just by Jewel) is a contractor in the small fictional coastal resort town of Lighthouse Cove, Ore.

Hughes owns Hughes Construction, a company that specializes in Victorian home renovations. She's savvy, competent, independent, knowledge about construction and, of course, attractive.

One of her jobs is the restoration of a large, historic home – part of the lighthouse for which the town is named for Macintyre "Mac" Sullivan (Colin Ferguson). Mac, a former investigative journalist turned best-selling crime novelist, is looking for a getaway to write his next novel. He comes to Lighthouse Cove, buys the old lighthouse mansion with his book royalties and hooks up with Shannon, both in the business and personal senses.

This Hallmark Movies & Mysteries series, new for Hallmark in 2017, is based on the *Fixer-Upper Mysteries* by Kate Carlisle, an LA-born law school dropout. To date, Carlisle had published five Fixer-Upper novels. (The novels use a hyphen; the Hallmark movies don't. Go figger.)

In the books, Lighthouse Cove is not in Oregon but on the northern coast of California near Mendocino, and Shannon's last name is Hammer.

Carlisle also has done the successful *Bibliophile Mysteries* series, featuring Brooklyn Wainwright, whose bookbinding skills invariably lead to a murder or two. So far, there are 11 novels and one e-novella in the Bibliophile series.

Shannon's Digs, Drives and Drinks: As with other Hallmark mysteries, the Fixer Upper movies are filmed in British Columbia, Canada. So far, the location filming has been in the resort town of Victoria. Shannon's home in the Hallmark series is the exterior of a B&B at 1121 Faithful Street in Victoria, BC, according to IMDB. She drives a beat-up old green and white pickup truck. Most contractors seem to drink beer. Shannon doesn't. Yet.

About Hallmark and Crown Media Holdings:

Crown Media Holdings, Inc., which owns the Hallmark Movies & Mysteries Channel, Hallmark Channel and Hallmark Drama Channel, along with a streaming service, is a media production company with corporate headquarters in Studio City, California. It is controlled by Hallmark, the large privately owned company headquartered in Kansas City, Mo., best known for its greeting cards.

Originally called Hall Brothers, the company was established by Joyce Clyde Hall (1891-1982). Starting around 1906, J. C. Hall had sold postcards and other cards from a store in Norfolk, Neb.

In 1910 Hall moved to Kansas City and in 1916 bought an engraving company to print postcards and greeting cards. Hall began selling his cards under the Hallmark name in 1928.

The company name was changed from Hall Brothers to Hallmark in 1954. Hallmark is still owned and mostly run by members of the Hall family. Donald J. Hall, born in 1929, is the chairman and by far the largest stockholder. Donald J. Hall Jr., a grandson of the Hallmark founder, is CEO, and Donald's brother, David E. Hall, is president.

Hallmark's Crown Media Holdings subsidiary traces its history to the launch of two religious cable channels, the American Christian Television System (ACTS) and the Vision Interfaith Satellite Network (VISN), which began broadcasting in1992. The network was renamed as the Faith and Values Channel in 1993. It soon began adding a few non-religious programs such as health and cooking shows and family-oriented movies. In 1995, cable conglomerate Tele-Communications Inc. acquired a 49% ownership stake in the Faith and Values Channel, and took over operational control. It reduced religious programming to about 10 hours a day. In 1996, the network was rebranded as the Odyssey Network. Henson sold its interest in the channel to Crown Media Holdings in 2000.

In 2001, the channel re-launched as the Hallmark Channel. It completely dropped religious programming and focused on family-oriented sitcoms, movies and drama series. The Hallmark Channel became known for its original production and airing of family-oriented movies. A sister network, Hallmark Movies, was launched in 2004. It later changed its name to Hallmark Movies & Mysteries, running original mystery and other movies and also reruns of programs such as *Murder, She Wrote, Matlock* and *Diagnosis Murder* programs. This channel now is available to around 57 million pay television households (more than 48% of households with television) in the U.S.

William (Bill) J. Abbott, who has been with the company since 2000, is president and CEO of Crown Media Holdings.

Hallmark is the largest manufacturing of greeting cards in the U.S. However, the company is involved in a number of other businesses. Its owns Crayola, maker of Crayola-brand crayons, Halls (an upscale department store in Kansas City) and DaySpring Greeting Cards, the world's largest Christian greeting card company.

Hallmark operates some 2,000 Hallmark Gold Crown shops, most independently owned. The company has about 27,000 employees worldwide, of which only about 5,500 are full-time.

About 2,700 employees work at Hallmark's Kansas City headquarters. Hallmark's creative staff currently consists of about 800 artists, designers, stylists, writers, editors, and photographers. Together, they create nearly 20,000 new and redesigned greeting cards and related products each year.

Although a private company that doesn't disclose its financials in detail, it reported gross revenues of about $4 billion in 2016.

Crown Media operates the Hallmark Channel and its spin-off Hallmark Movies & Mysteries. The channels are shown on cable and satellite. In 2017, Hallmark announced it was starting another channel, Hallmark Drama, and a streaming service. Both debuted in October 2017. In 2016, Hallmark Cards announced it bought the remaining 3 percent of Crown Media Holdings from Liberty Media, a public company, and had taken Crown Media private.

As Heather Long wrote about the main Hallmark Channels in *The Washington Post* in August 2017, "It's feel-good TV. There's no sex or gore. Hallmark movies and series like "When Calls the Heart" and "Chesapeake Shores" have happy endings. The main characters do the right thing. The problems get worked out. The guy and girl, whatever their age or grumpiness level at the start, always end up together." You could say the same thing about Hallmark's sister channel, Hallmark Movies & Mysteries.

Long continues: "...[M]ore and more Americans are turning to the Hallmark Channel for relief from the daily news cycle. Hallmark is the complete opposite of the divisiveness that so many families felt during the election and President Trump's penchant for courting controversy. Turn on the news and you see people who can't get along, even in the same party. Turn on Hallmark and everyone ends the show smiling."

The Hallmark mysteries have been criticized not only for their sappy happy approaches, but also for their lack of diversity. Most characters are white and very middle class. However, the parent company, Hallmark, privately owned by the same family since 2010, while it is considered a family-focused, politically conservative company, and traditionally a number of Hall family members have been large donors to the Republican Party, it has diversity as one of its corporate goals. In its vision statement, Hallmark states, "We also support and rely upon Employee Resource Groups (ERGs) that offer opportunities for African American, Hispanic, Asian American, Millennial, Military, and Gay, Lesbian, Bisexual and Transgender employees to share common interests and give perspective on product development." Crown Media is adding more nonwhite actors to its programming, although executives admit it has more work to do in that regard.

The Hall Family Foundation, one of the largest philanthropic organizations in the United States, each year gives away tens of millions of dollars to public and private education, social welfare causes, religious causes and civic beautification in Kansas City and the surrounding region.

The Foundation was instrumental in the restoration of the Quality Hill area of Kansas City, once the city's premier residential area, but which by the 1970s had fallen into a serious decline. Today the neighborhood is a showcase for well-executed urban renewal and historic preservation.

In any case, the Hallmark/Crown Media approach seems to be working. Ratings for the Hallmark channels are booming. The Hallmark Channel in 2017 had 88 million subscriber households, and the Movies & Mysteries Channel had 67 million. In the November and December Christmas season of 2016, Hallmark claimed 85 million people watched during the period. At times since 2015, Hallmark's main channel has run neck and neck with ESPN and Fox News for total viewers, and it often leads in women in prime time.

While many of its shows appeal to older women, its ratings are growing in the coveted 18-49 female age group, according to Nielsen, and it is gaining more male viewers as well. In one quarter of 2017, Hallmark Movies & Mysteries increased its viewership by a whopping 22% over the same quarter of the previous year.

Hallmark Movies & Mysteries' four *Garage Sale Mystery* premieres in August 2017 averaged a 1.9 households Nielsen rating, making it the top-rated network in the Sunday 9-11 pm time period that month. During the month, Hallmark Movies & Mysteries also was the third most-watched cable network in that Sunday time period.

Garage Sale Mysteries
Garage Sale Mystery (2013)
Garage Sale Mystery: All That Glitters (2014)
Garage Sale Mystery: The Deadly Room (2015)
Garage Sale Mystery: The Wedding Dress (2015)
Garage Sale Mystery: Guilty Until Proven Innocent (2016)
Garage Sale Mystery: The Novel Murders (2016)
Garage Sale Mystery: The Art of Murder (2017)
Garage Sale Mystery: The Beach Murder (2017)
Garage Sale Mystery: Murder by Text (2017)
Garage Sale Mystery: Murder Most Medieval (2017)
Garage Sale Mystery: A Case of Murder (2017)

Aurora Teagarden Mysteries
A Bone to Pick: An Aurora Teagarden Mystery (2015)
Real Murders: An Aurora Teagarden Mystery (2015)
Three Bedrooms, One Corpse: An Aurora Teagarden Mystery (2016)
The Julius House: An Aurora Teagarden Mystery (2016)
Dead Over Heels: An Aurora Teagarden Mystery (2017)

A Bundle of Trouble: An Aurora Teagarden Mystery (2017)

Murder, She Baked Mysteries
Murder, She Baked: A Chocolate Chip Murder Mystery (2015)
Murder, She Baked: A Plum Pudding Mystery (2015)
Murder, She Baked: A Peach Cobbler Mystery (2016)
Murder, She Baked: A Deadly Recipe (2016)
Murder, She Baked: Just Desserts (2017)

Fixer-Upper Mysteries
Framed for Murder: A Fixer-Upper Mystery (2017)
Concrete Evidence: A Fixer-Upper Mystery (2017)

Notable Works on Hallmark

Regan, Patrick, *Hallmark A Century of Caring* (2009). While this is a corporate history authorized and subsidized by Hallmark, published to celebrate the 100th anniversary of the Hall family business, it nonetheless is a fascinating look at how Hallmark grew from a small business to one of the largest privately owned companies in America.

Sherlock Holmes

From the Sherlock Holmes stories and novels by Arthur Conan Doyle (1859-1930)

"How often have I said to you that when you have eliminated the impossible, whatever remains, *however improbable*, must be the truth?"

Sherlock Holmes in *The Sign of the Four* by Arthur Conan Doyle

Watson and Holmes in an illustration in Strand Magazine *by Sidney Paget*

Sherlock Holmes is by far the world's best-known fictional detective. Although he appears in just four novels along with 56 short stories by Scottish writer Arthur Conan Doyle, Sherlock and his companion and biographer, Dr. John Watson, have starred in countless movies, plays, television productions, cartoons and other works patterned after Doyle's creation.

Guinness Book of World Records lists Sherlock Holmes as the most portrayed character in film history, with at least 70 actors playing him in more than 200 movies. The first Holmes movie, *Sherlock Holmes Baffled,* came out in 1900.

Basil Rathbone is the best known of the more than 70 actors who have played Sherlock Holmes in movies

In film, arguably the most iconic Holmes was Basil Rathbone, who starred in 14 movies from 1939 to 1946, two produced by 20th Century Fox and 12 by Universal. Nigel Bruce portrayed Watson. The two 20th Century Fox movies were set in Victorian England, while all the Universal movies were set contemporaneously.

Sherlockian experts put the detective's date of birth as January 6, 1854, in rural England. He is believed to be the son of a country squire. He has one elder brother, Mycroft, who becomes an English civil servant.

Holmes attended a prominent English university, whether Oxford or Cambridge is a matter of debate, but he showed scant interest in most classical subjects, including the arts, literature and philosophy, although he does know Latin. He becomes expert in chemistry and has a knowledge of some other sciences, including geology, anatomy and botany (especially as regards poisonous plants). Holmes has a practical understanding of British law. He tends to learn only those things that will help him solve his mysteries and ignores other kinds of knowledge. Sherlock plays the violin and is an expert boxer, fencer and cudgelist.

Both Holmes and Watson frequently carry pistols. Holmes seems to prefer a Webley Bulldog revolver, while Watson has a Mark III Adams revolver, a pistol used at the time by the British Army. Frequently, Sherlock uses a cane or walking stick as a weapon, and sometimes wields a riding crop.

The consulting detective uses both abductive and deductive logic to solve cases and was among the first to use forensic science in criminal investigations. Some of Holmes' investigative techniques, including fingerprinting and handwriting analysis, were in their infancy when Doyle wrote the stories.

One expert estimated Holmes' IQ at 190.

We owe Sherlock Holmes' great fame as a detective to his friendship with Dr. John Watson, whom Holmes first meets when, due to financial reasons, he needs to take in a boarder at his apartment at 221B Baker Street in London. Holmes and Watsons become flatmates beginning in 1887 before Watson's marriage and then again after the death of Watson's wife.

At home, the detective is something of a hoarder, keeping old letters and papers stacked around the flat. He is addicted to tobacco, smoking both cigars and a pipe. He dabbles in the use of morphine but is an intravenous user of cocaine (both morphine and cocaine were then legal in Britain), which he injects with a syringe in a 7% solution.

The detective never marries and purports to not like women, although he is kind in dealings with them. He has an infatuation with at least one woman, Irene Adler.

Holmes works as a detective for 23 years, 17 of those years with Watson. Watson not only is his Holmes' friend and assistant, he is also the chronicler of Sherlock's cases. Watson narrates all but four of the Holmes stories. Two of the stories are narrated by Holmes himself, and two are written in the third person, as are parts of two of the novels, *A Study in Scarlet* and *In the Valley of Fear.*

Having become financially well off due to his consulting detective work, Sherlock retires sometime before 1904 to a small farm in Sussex. There he takes up beekeeping, writing a handbook on the subject, *Practical Handbook of Bee Culture, with some Observations upon the Segregation of the Queen.*

Holmes' Rides: When he needs to go somewhere, Holmes either goes by foot or uses horse taxis and trains. He never owns a horse and buggy or a car.

Holmes' Digs: Famously, Holmes lives at 221B Baker Street in London, a flat owned by his landlady, Mrs. Hudson. Holmes meets prospective clients here as well. The flat is a suite of rooms up 17 steps from the entrance. Holmes' room is behind the main study, and Watson's room is on the floor above.

The Baker Street area, known in Holmes' time as Upper Baker Street, north of Marylebone Road near Regent's Park, was then an upper class residential section of London.

At the time the Holmes stories were written, the numbers on Baker Street did not go as high as 221, so the exact location of Holmes' residence is debated by Sherlockian experts.

Later, in the 1930s, the street and its numbers were extended. When street numbers were reassigned, a block of odd numbers from 215 to 229 was given to the Abbey House, constructed in Art Deco style in 1932 for the Abbey Road Building Society. The building society no longer exists. Today, the Sherlock Holmes Museum is in an 1815 townhouse between 237 and 241 Baker Street. In some ways the townhouse is similar to 221B Baker Street as described in the Holmes stories.

After retirement, Sherlock moves from Baker Street to a small farm in rural Sussex.

Holmes' Drinks: Sherlock Holmes, a connoisseur of French wines, is fond of good drink, but he only rarely indulges in it. He prefers other drugs, including cocaine, which he injects, and nicotine, which he takes in pipe tobacco and cigars.

Holmes' favorite wines are burgundies, especially Montrachet and Meursault. In *The Sign of Four,* he drinks red burgundy for lunch, and in "The Gloria Scott" he has port after dinner. In "The Adventure of the Dying Detective" Holmes has a glass of claret.

The great detective also enjoys an occasional whisky and soda. He has a gasogene in his sitting room at 221B Baker Street for making soda water. A gasogene was a 19th century device for producing carbonated water. It consists of two linked glass globes, the lower containing water and the upper a mixture of tartaric acid and sodium bicarbonate. The two chemicals react to produce carbon dioxide.

It is not clear which brands of whisky Holmes prefers, but Watson drinks Glenkinchie, a classic malt whisky from the Glenkinchie Distillery in the East Lothian Lowlands near Edinburgh. Although Holmes makes his own soda water, the Schweppes Company, founded by J.J. Schweppe in Geneva in 1783, has been in London since 1792. Thwaites of Dublin sold bottled soda water in Britain starting in 1799, but this company no longer is in business.

Sherlock also drinks brandy for medicinal purposes. Occasionally, he has a glass of beer at a pub or tavern. Holmes finds spending time in taverns is useful in helping him pick up information. He discovers important clues while nursing a beer at the Green Dragon, a tavern in Berkshire ("Shoscombe Old Place"), at the Alpha Inn, a pub in London ("The Blue Carbuncle") and the Black Swan, an inn in Winchester" ("Copper Beeches").

Holmes uses his expert knowledge of wines and other spirits and of the habits of imbibers to solve some of his most difficult cases. For example, in "The Adventure of the Noble Bachelor," he retrieves an errant heiress and foils the plans of a unsuitable suitor by being knowledgeable about the price of fine wines at expensive London hotels.

Watson's Whisky and Soda

2 oz. Glenkinchie Scotch whisky

Schweppes soda water

Pour two fingers (about 2 oz.) of Glenkinchie Scotch in a glass and add a large splash of Schweppes soda. Do not add ice.

About Arthur Conan Doyle:

Arthur Ignatius Conan Doyle was born in Edinburgh, Scotland, in 1859. After attending Jesuit schools, he went to the University of Edinburgh for medical school, becoming a doctor in 1881. Later he did postgraduate study in Vienna and became an ophthalmologist, setting up a practice in London.

Doyle began writing while in medical school. His first Sherlock Holmes and Dr. Watson story, "A Study in Scarlet," was published in 1887. He said that the character of Holmes was partly modeled on one of his medical school professors, Joseph Bell. It may also have been partly modeled on two different police officers of the time.

Doyle wrote a total of four Sherlock novels (*A Study in Scarlet, The Sign of the Four, The Hound of the Baskervilles* and *The Valley of Fear*) and 56 short stories. His classic detective has appeared in countless other stories and novels, along with scores of movies, television shows and plays.

The author always had an ambivalent relationship towards his most successful creation. A prolific writer of historic novels, stories, poetry and non-fiction, he would have preferred not being tied to a single character. However, the Holmes stories were in such high demand Doyle was able to raise his price for the stories to such a point that Doyle was one of the highest paid writers in Britain.

In 1893, in "The Final Problem," Doyle had Sherlock and his great enemy, Moriarity, plunge to their deaths. Popular demand, however, required him to bring his famous character back to life in 1901 in the novel *The Hound of the Baskervilles.*

Twice married, with five children, in later life Doyle became greatly interested in mysticism. He was a member of The Ghost Club and was a friend of magician and escape artist Harry Houdini. Doyle also was a keen sportsman, playing soccer, cricket and golf.

Doyle died at home age 71 of a heart attack.

Sherlock Holmes Novels by Arthur Conan Doyle

A Study in Scarlet (1887 in *Beeton's Christmas Annual*)
The Sign of the Four (1890 in *Lippincott's Monthly Magazine*)
The Hound of the Baskervilles (serialized 1901–1902 in *The Strand*)
The Valley of Fear (serialized 1914–1915 in *The Strand*)

Sherlock Holmes Short Story Collections

Originally published in magazines, the stories were later collected in five anthologies:

The Adventures of Sherlock Holmes (stories published 1891–1892 in *The Strand)*

The Memoirs of Sherlock Holmes (stories published 1892–1893 in *The Strand)*

The Return of Sherlock Holmes (stories published 1903–1904 in *The Strand)*

His Last Bow: Some Later Reminiscences of Sherlock Holmes (stories published 1908–1917)

The Case-Book of Sherlock Holmes (stories published 1921–1927)

Notable Works on Sherlock Holmes and Arthur Conan Doyle

No other detective has been has there been so much written about as Sherlock Holmes. There are more than a half dozen "biographies" of Holmes. Hundreds of books, dissertations, essays and internet articles have been done on so-called Holmesian studies. *The Baker Street Journal* (www.bakerstreetjournal.com) describes itself as the "premier publication of scholarship on Sherlock Holmes." It is associated with The Baker Street Irregulars, established in 1934, and The Baker Street Irregulars Trust.

"Biographies" of Sherlock Holmes

Baring-Gould, William, *Sherlock Holmes: A Biography of the World's First Consulting Detective* ((1962).

Blakeney, Thomas S., *Sherlock Holmes: Fact or Fiction?* (1993).

Blegin, Theodore Christian & McDiarmid, Errett Weir McDiarmid, *Sherlock Holmes: Master Detective* (1952).

Keating, H. R. F., *Sherlock Holmes: The Man and His World* (2006).

Rennison, Nick, *Sherlock Holmes: The Unauthorized Biography* (2006).

Biographies of Arthur Conan Doyle

Costello, Peter, *Conan Doyle Detective - The Crimes Investigated by the Creator of Sherlock Holmes* (1991).

Lycett, Andrew, *The Man Who Created Sherlock Holmes: The Life and Times of Sir Arthur Conan Doyle* (2007)

Sims Michael, *Arthur and Sherlock: Conan Doyle and the Creation of Holmes* (2017).

Miss Jane Marple

From the Miss Marple novels and short stories by Agatha Christie (1890-1976) and from Miss Marple movies and television programs

"I'm afraid that, observing human nature for as long as I have done, one gets not to expect very much from it."

Jane Marple, in *Murder at the Vicarage* by Agatha Christie

Jane Marple is the English spinster and shrewd amateur detective featured in 12 novels and 20 short stories by Agatha Christie, along with numerous adaptations for radio, the screen and television. The Miss Marple books and stories are considered the epitome of the "British Cozy" style of murder mysteries.

Miss Marple first appeared in a short story in *The Royal Magazine* in 1927, and she first showed up in a novel in *The Murder at the Vicarage* in 1930. When we first meet Miss Marple, she is already in her mid- to late 60s. By the time of the last Marple novel, *Nemesis,* published almost four decades later, she would have been well over 100 years old, but in Christie's fiction she ages much more slowly than does the real world. She is around 80 in some of the later stories. Some Marple experts put her birth year as 1869, but that date doesn't fit with other known biographical facts. We have to be somewhat flexible in juggling the chronology of Jane Marple's life.

Thin and relatively tall, with white hair and blue eyes, Miss Marple stands and sits straight and upright. She sometimes wears tweeds and at other times Victorian-style lace and crepe dresses. When going out she usually puts on a fleecy coat with hat and gloves and takes along an umbrella, just in case.

Miss Marple health is fairly good, considering her age, but she suffers from arthritis and from time to time comes down with bronchitis or pneumonia. She doesn't much believe in doctors, preferring old-fashioned remedies such as camphorated oil and chamomile or tansy tea.

In temperament she is very brave and has a great curiosity, especially about people. She is extremely intelligent. Usually believing the worst about most people, she rarely accepts what they say as the complete truth.

Not a lot is known about Miss Marple's life before she reaches her 60s. It is thought that she came from a clerical family in a rural area of England and had one sibling, a sister. For a time, the two girls had a German governess and may have attended village schools.

At age 14, she visited London for the first time, staying at Bertram's Hotel. Bertram's probably was patterned after the very proper Brown's Hotel in Mayfair, which opened in 1837. She was to return there, likely in 1964, on a fortnight's vacation, as recounted in the novel *At Bertram's Hotel.* Today, Brown's is a five-star luxury hotel, part of a small chain of hotels in Britain, continental Europe and Russia. It counts among its many famous guests Rudyard Kipling and Winston Churchill.

At age 16, Jane Marple was sent to Florence, Italy, to finish her education. About the rest of her youth and middle age, we know little. There is some suggestion that she stayed at home and nursed her aging parents.

Although she has a maid or housekeeper and owns her own home, thanks probably to a small inheritance from her parents, she is not wealthy and sometimes has to depend on the generosity of friends or of her nephew, Raymond West, a successful author, for financial help. Raymond kindly pays for several nice vacations for his aunt, including to the Caribbean island of St. Honoré, perhaps based on Barbados (the BBC version of the novel *A Caribbean Vacation* was shot there), and for two weeks at Jane's beloved Bertram's Hotel in London.

As far as we know, Jane Marple has never worked at a regular job. She is not paid for her amateur detective work, except toward the end of her life, in *Nemesis,* when she receives, as a bequest in the will of Jason Rafiel the sum of 20,000 pounds (over $300,000 in today's money) to solve a mystery. She had met and worked with the wealthy businessman Rafiel on the Caribbean island of St. Honoré in *A Caribbean Mystery.*

Of course has never married, although when young she had many beaux and enjoyed parties and dancing. She knows more than one might think about romance and sex. Miss Marple enjoys gardening, until her rheumatism prevents her from doing much of it. She loves old-fashioned flowers such as snapdragons, sweet peas, hollyhocks and roses.

We first meet Miss Marple at meetings of the Tuesday Night Club, held in her drawing room and attended by Miss Marple, her nephew Raymond West, Sir Henry Clithering, a retired Commissioner of Scotland Yard, Joyce Lemprière, an artist, Mr. Petherick, a solicitor, and Dr. Pender, a clergyman.

The club discusses a series of unsolved crimes, and to everyone's amazement Miss Marple solves them all. This is the beginning of her career as crime expert in St. Mary Mead, her fame initially spread by Sir Henry and Mr. Petherick.

We then get to know Miss Marple better in the first novel, *Murder at the Vicarage,* narrated by the Reverend Leonard Clement of St. Mary Mead village.

Miss Marple's Digs: Many of the novels and stories featuring Miss Jane Marple, especially the earlier ones, are set in the fictional small village of St. Mary Mead, just outside the also fictional town of Much Benham, in the fictional county of Downshire, 12 miles from another fictional town, Market Basing and about 25 miles southwest of the real London. St. Mary Mead is about a dozen miles from the coast.

Presumably, Miss Marple learned much of her skill in solving mysteries by observing the residents of St. Mary Mead. Over the approximately four decades of the Miss Marple stories, a total of 16 murders took place in the tiny village, five by poisoning, two by shooting, two by strangling, two by drowning and five by other, unidentified means. Another four attempted murders occurred, along with eight cases of embezzling, five robberies and a number of other crimes. This crime rate, on a per-capita basis, is probably even higher than in Jessica Fletcher's Cabot Cove, Me.

In a map of St. Mary Mead that appeared in *Murder at the Vicarage,* published in 1930, most of the houses and shops in the village are along High Street, from the railroad station at one end to the Blue Boar tavern at the other.

Miss Marple's cottage, which fronts on High Street and backs on to an unnamed lane, sits between the large Queen Anne and Georgian houses of Dr. Haydock to the northwest and Miss Hartnell to the southeast. Immediately beyond Miss Hartnell's is Miss Weatherby's house. Nearby are several shops and the post office on High Street and the Vicarage on Vicarage Road. Two "great houses" at the edges of the village are Gossington Hall, the home of Colonel Bantry and Dolly Bantry, who later becomes a good friend of Miss Marple, and Old Hall, the home of the ill-fated Colonel Protheroe.

Miss Marple's drawing room contains three chairs, a large grandfather's chair by the fireplace hearth, a chair by the window and in later years an upright armchair that helps Jane's arthritic back. It also has a bookcase for Miss Marple's research books, a corner cupboard for glasses and a bottle cupboard for alcoholic drinks. There is a good-quality rug on the floor and a telephone, whose number in the early days was 35.

The bedrooms are upstairs, up an old-fashioned staircase with a sharp corner in the middle. Miss Marple's bed is fitted with cool linen sheets of high quality.

Out back is Miss Marple's flower and vegetable garden, with a small greenhouse and old stables. A jasmine hedge borders the gardens.

Later, although the heart of St. Mary Mead village doesn't change too much, the Development attracts a lot of new people to the area, and ugly new houses replace meadowlands.

In the BBC Miss Marple series starring Joan Hickson that brought all of the Marple novels to television, and which strived for authenticity, the Hampshire village of Nether Wallup in Southeast England is used as a stand-in for St. Mary Mead. With its thatched houses and Victorian cottages, Nether Wallup is considered one of the prettiest villages in England.

Dane Cottage on Five Bells Lane, Nether Wallup, is used as the home of Jane Marple. How times have changed since Miss Marple's day! In 2014, Dane Cottage, much renovated and refurbished, rented for 2,500 pounds ($4,000) a month and in 2015 the five-bedroom, two-story brick house with thatch roof was put up for sale for 785,000 pounds, then about $1,250,000.

In her later years, Miss Marple travels more outside St. Mary Mead, spending time touring England, visiting resorts on the coast, staying at London hotels and with old friends at their country homes and even going to the Caribbean.

Miss Marple's Drives: Spending much of her life in a small village, where nearly everything is in walking distance, Miss Marple does not need a car. The excellent British Rail system, with a station in St. Mary Mead, is available when she wants to travel far afield. So far as we know, Miss Marple never learned to drive. However, motorcars play important supporting roles in many of Christie's works. Often they break down, creating a plot complication. The most common make of car mentioned in Christie's work is Rolls-Royce, which is cited 27 times (two times the car is referred to as "Rolls Bentley.") From 1931, when Rolls-Royce bought the bankrupt Bentley, to well after Christie's death Bentleys were basically rebadged Rolls-Royce cars, the biggest difference being the radiator design).

Miss Marple's Drinks: Although Miss Marple drinks tea (without milk), she does not disdain the harder stuff. When friends come to visit, she opens her "bottle cupboard."

It contains not tea but a decanter of sherry, homemade cherry brandy made from a family recipe, whisky and soda water for the men, cowslip wine (a delicate light yellow wine, usually homemade from cowslip flowers, typically served in small flutes with biscuits) and damson gin.

The damson gin she makes herself, using fresh damson plums, which ripen in England in early September. Damson gin, a traditional drink in Britain, is similar to sloe gin. Sloe gin is made using another, more sour, type of plum, the blackthorn.

Here's how to make damson gin: Wash about one pound of damson plums and prick them with a needle to aid the absorption of the liquid. Soak the whole plums in a fifth (750 ml) medium-quality gin with about 5 ounces of sugar candy, or substitute 5 ounces of white granulated sugar, for at least three months. If you prefer a sweeter drink, you can add more sugar during the soaking process. The result is a liqueur with a beautiful garnet color.

Damson Gin Mystery Cocktail

3 oz. damson gin

(use homemade as above, or substitute a commercial brand such as Averell Damson Gin Liqueur)

½ oz. fresh lemon juice

½ oz. simple syrup (1 part sugar and 1 part water, mixed well)

½ of egg white from 1 egg

Put all ingredients in a cocktail shaker with ice. Shake and pour into a martini or other cocktail glass and sip.

About Author Agatha Christie and Miss Marple:

Miss Marple arguably was Agatha Christie's favorite creation. She tired of her other, equally famous character, Hercule Poirot, keeping him alive due only to popular demand, but she never seemed to tire of Jane Marple. *(For more details on Christie's life, see the chapter in this book on Hercule Poirot.)*

Miss Marple also was a favorite of movie and television producers. Margaret Rutherford, Helen Hayes, Angela Lansbury and Joan Dickson all portrayed Jane Marple in notable movies and television programs.

Margaret Rutherford, with her bulldog looks and squat build, looks nothing like the Marple of Christie's books, but she played the amateur sleuth as a bold, self-assured woman in four popular black-and-white British MGM productions of the early 1960s.

These include *Murder, She Said* (1961), based on *4:50 from Paddington*; *Murder at the Gallop* (1963), based on a Hercule Poirot novel, *After the Funeral; Murder Most Foul* (1964), also based on a Poirot novel, *Mrs McGinty's Dead;* and *Murder, Ahoy!* (1964), based on an original screenplay by David Pursall and Jack Seddon and not on a Christie work, although elements of the plot derive from the Christie novel *They Do It with Mirrors.*

As portrayed in these films, Miss Marple is in Milchester, a village a good deal larger than St. Mary Mead in the books. Denham, Buckinghamshire is where the first three Rutherford movies were filmed. In *Murder, Ahoy* Miss Marple spends most of her time on a naval training vessel in a coastal village. Location filming was in St. Mawes, Cornwall.

In this series of movies, Miss Marple has a good friend, the librarian Mr Stringer, who is played by Rutherford's real-life husband, Stringer Davis. All four movies were directed by George Pollock, and all used essentially the same memorable but irritating music by Ron Goodwin. Christie did not care for Dame Rutherford's take on Miss Marple.

Angela Lansbury (1925-), also English-born and best known for her long-lived television series *Murder, She Wrote (see the chapter on this television series)* did a turn as Miss Marple in the 1980 movie, *The Mirror Crack'd,* starring Elizabeth Taylor, Rock Hudson, Tony Curtis, Kim Novak and other Hollywood stars.

The acclaimed stage and screen actress Helen Hayes (1900-1993) played Miss Marple in three made-for-TV movies: *Murder Is Easy* (1982); *A Caribbean Mystery* (1983); and *Murder With Mirrors* (1985). Hayes' appearance is much closer to the Jane Marple of the Christie books than are Rutherford's or Lansbury's.

The best known, and often considered the best, portrayal of Marple is by English actress Joan Bogle Hickson (1906-1998) in the BBC series that aired from 1984 to 1992. Hickson had appeared on the stage in the 1940s in a Christie play, *Appointment with Death,* and at the time Christie wrote Hickson saying that she hoped Hickson would some day play Miss Marple.

The BBC series adapted all 12 Miss Marple novels for full-length TV movies, although not in the same order as the books' publication.

The Hickson Marple movies started with *The Body in the Library* in 1984 and ended with *The Mirror Crack'd from Side to Side* in 1992. The creators of the BBC series strived for authenticity and to accurately echo the Miss Marple books, in terms of setting and especially as regards the Jane Marple character. Most critics agree that they succeeded.

Also, iTV in Britain created a 23-episode television series that aired from 2004 to 2013, *Agatha Christie's Marple,* starring Geraldine McEwan (1932-2015) for the first 12 episodes through *Nemesis* in 2008 and then Julia McKenzie (1941-) beginning in 2008 for the remaining ones.

Although based on Christie's books and stories, the iTV series played somewhat fast and loose with the characters and plots, changing and adding elements, and Julia McKenzie in particular did not match Christie's descriptions of Miss Marple.

Miss Marple Novels by Agatha Christie

The Murder at the Vicarage (1930)
The Body in the Library (1942)
The Moving Finger (1943)
A Murder is Announced (1950)
They Do It with Mirrors, also titled *Murder with Mirrors* (1952)
A Pocket Full of Rye (1953)
4.50 from Paddington, also titled *What Mrs. McGillicuddy Saw!* (1957)
The Mirror Crack'd from Side to Side, also titled *The Mirror Crack'd* (1962)
A Caribbean Mystery (1964)
At Bertram's Hotel (1965)
Nemesis (1971)
Sleeping Murder (1976 but written around 1940)

Miss Marple Short Story Collections

The Thirteen Problems, also titled *The Tuesday Club Murders* (1932)
Miss Marple's Final Cases and Two Other Stories (1979)
All 20 Miss Marple stories are collected in *Miss Marple: The Complete Short Stories* (1985)

Notable Books About Miss Marple and Agatha Christie

Christie, Agatha, *An Autobiography* (1977). Christie reports not only her happy childhood and most of the key events in her life, but the author also provides insights on how she created Poirot, Marple and her other much-beloved characters. This is, however, a selective telling. The famous episode of her disappearance for 11 days is not even mentioned.

Hack, Richard, *Duchess of Death: The Unauthorized Biography of Agatha Christie* (2009). Arguably the best of the several unauthorized biographies of Christie, although much of it is rehashed from previous biographical works and Christie's autobiography, despite the author's claim that it is drawn from "5,000 previously unpublished letters ... and documents."

Hart, Anne, *The Life and Times of Miss Jane Marple* (1985), Charming "biography" of Jane Marple by a Nova Scotia writer who also authored a biography of Hercule Poirot *(q.v.)*.

Pendergast, Bruce, *Everyman's Guide to the Mysteries of Agatha Christie* (2004). Although attacked by some for alleged sloppy research and factual errors, we found this exhaustive, self-published 455-page work by Canadian Bruce Pendergast, which focuses on pointing out inconsistencies in the Christie works, to be useful.

THE DAILY NEWS, SATURDAY, DECEMBER 11, 1926

MRS. CHRISTIE DISGUISED.

Mrs. Agatha Christie as she was last seen (centre), and (on left and right) how she may have disguised herself by altering the style of her hairdressing and by wearing glasses. Col. Christie says his wife had stated that she could disappear at will if she liked, and, in view of the fact that she was a writer of detective stories, it would be very natural for her to adopt some form of disguise to carry out that idea.

DISARMI[...]
GERM[...]

"NOT COM[...]

BRITISH AD[...]
HOLD UP I[...]

From Our Special [...]

The agenda of the
League of Nations
finished, and to-morr
hoped, will be devot
sions regarding Leagu
man armaments. It
however, that a Sund
necessary.
The British, French,
and Belgian Foreign M
morning, and endeavo
outstanding difference
That, however, the
the Conference of

This is how The Daily News *of London reported the disappearance of Agatha Christie in 1926 – in her autobiography, Christie did not discuss the incident*

Hercule Poirot

From the Hercule Poirot books and short stories by Agatha Christie (1890-1976)

"Use your little grey cells, *mon ami.*"
Hercule Poirot, *The Mysterious Affair at Styles* by Agatha Christie

The famous Orient Express of Compagnie Internationale des Wagons-Lits during a halt at a border station at Switzerland – Photo by Murdockcrs

Hercule Poirot is the Belgian-born detective who uses his "little grey cells" to solve mysteries in 33 novels, a play and more than 50 short stories by Agatha Christie.

From the Poirot stories and novels, and from the book-length "biography" of Poirot, *The Life and Times of Hercule Poirot* by Anne Hart, we know that Poirot spent most of his professional life as a senior officer in the Belgium national police force, headquartered in Brussels. Having retired as the most renowned detective in Belgium, he came to England as a refugee in 1916, after Germany occupied his country during World War I.

As recounted in *The Mysterious Affair at Styles,* Christie's first novel, it was in the small village of Styles St. Mary, Essex, that Poirot solves his first case in England, the murder of the wealthy Mrs. Inglethorp at the Cavendish chateau of Styles.

Although French is his native language, Poirot speaks English fluently, albeit with an accent, except when extremely excited when he might lose some of his grasp of English syntax.

Poirot is adamant that as a refugee in, and a guest of, England, it is imperative that he and his Belgian compatriots should always speak English. Along the way, he also picks up a little Russian, some Arabic and other languages.

The Styles affair and a few other well-publicized early cases make Poirot's name in Britain. He moves to London, where he lives most of his life, except for a year early on in a house he bought in the village of King's Abbot and for a time in Monte Carlo on the French Riviera, until his death in 1974. Ill with heart disease and in a wheelchair, he dies, ironically enough, in Styles St. Mary, site of his first English case. This is recounted in Christie's last Poirot book, *Curtain* (1975). An obituary of Poirot was published on the front page of *The New York Times,* August 6, 1975. It is believed that this is the only time a fictional character received an obit in *The Times.*

Although by the calendar Poirot spends more than five decades as a private detective in England, in Poirot years he ages only by about two decades.

We know of Poirot's great accomplishments thanks to his own Watson, Captain Arthur Hastings, OBE. Hasting recounts Poirot's exploits in 26 stories and eight early novels, although he remains as Poirot's friend and confident for many years, but it is Hastings who establishes the narrative style that created the global audience for Christie's Poirot tales.

Hastings, we learn, had first met and got to know Poirot in Belgium before the first war, while Hastings was working for Lloyds of London. They are accidentally reunited in Styles, and after Hasting recommends the already aging detective to the Cavendish family, Poirot quickly takes over the case. Christie's narrator tells the long, rambling tale of how the affair at Styles was eventually resolved. Like Watson with Sherlock Holmes, Captain Hastings usually comes across as a well bred he was educated at Eton College but bumbling English gentleman, who nearly invariably fails to understand the clues that Poirot so quickly spots.

In later novels, Poirot's confidents include Ariadne Oliver, a London writer of successful mystery novels who may share some qualities with Agatha Christie herself, and Countess Vera Rossakoff, a Russian refugee. Countess Rossakoff, indeed, is more than a friend. She is the great romantic passion of Poirot's life. At one point, in *The Big Four,* he even contemplates proposing marriage.

Poirot's long-time secretary, the highly efficient Miss Felicity Lemon, is invaluable in helping Poirot manage his business and social affairs. Toward the end of his life, Poirot also engages a valet, George (whose last name is never revealed), to assist him in his domestic life.

Short, about five feet four inches, with a large, egg-shaped head and a curling, carefully tended and waxed black mustache, Poirot is notoriously fastidious in his personal habits and in his dress. While not OCD, he likes things to be orderly and arranged just so. He likes symmetry and dislikes dust and dirt. In the early part of his career as a private detective in England, he dresses like a dandy in the latest styles, but as he grows older, and perhaps a bit wider in girth, his clothing also grows out of date. He begins to affect a pince nez and usually wears shiny patent leather black shoes.

By the 1920s, taking some cases with large fees, Poirot becomes quite wealthy. Showing his Belgian thriftiness, he is careful with his money, not spending foolishly, watching his shillings and investing only in gilt-edged instruments. He apparently does not lose his money in the Great Depression.

Although Poirot comes to enjoy London and his comfortable luxury flat there, he fairly often visits English resorts or, by invitation, English country homes, and occasionally ventures abroad. His favorite destination is the French Riviera, but he also travels to Paris, where he likes to stay at the Ritz. He goes a few times back to his home country of Belgium, and to the Middle East, notably to Egypt in *Death on the Nile* and also to Syria and Iraq in *Appointment with Death*, *Murder in Mesopotamia* and other works. Agatha Christie's second husband was a noted archeologist who worked in the Middle East, and Christie accompanied him on a number of digs, becoming something of an expert herself.

Poirot's Digs: Poirot lives in several different places in London, some grander than others. The best known is called Whitehaven Mansions, a modernist Art Deco building believed to be in either Chelsea or Mayfair, where the detective has a large, third-floor luxury flat decorated with contemporary, angular furnishings. Poirot meets clients and conducts much of his detective business from his apartment. He does not maintain other offices. In the much-praised David Suchet Poirot television series, Charterhouse Square, Clerkenwell, London, is used for location shots of Whitehaven Mansions.

Poirot's Drives: In the city, Poirot usually goes by taxi, and for longer trips he sometimes hires a limousine with a driver. Poirot never drives himself, but briefly in the 1930s he owns a car, said to be a Messarro Gratz luxury car with a chauffeur (about this obscure motor car little is known), but he soon gives it up after finding it mechanically undependable. He does occasionally enjoy being driven in a Rolls-Royce or other fine car by a friend or client.

When he travels, Poirot much prefers to go by train, ideally on a luxury one such as *le train bleu*, as we know from *The Mystery of the Blue Train,* or in first class on the Orient Express (*Murder on the Orient Express*). He dislikes buses and airplanes and can only tolerate short trips by boat on quiet waters, as he suffers from *mal de mer.*

Poirot's Drinks: Poirot is not a heavy drinker of alcohol. He enjoys good French wines, and sometimes champagne, with meals. Poirot likes sherry and, after dinner, a Benedictine with a cup of black coffee. Especially as shown in films and on television, Poirot occasionally indulges in a Créme de Menthe, a sweet green liqueur made from mint leaves, or green Chartreuse, a 110 proof cordial made by Carthusian monks in France from a 400-year-old recipe using 130 different herbs and plants.

As a courtesy to his guests, Poirot keeps on hand whisky (Irish and Scotch) and soda, although Poirot himself detests whisky and soda and also British beer. In addition, he stocks brandy, sherry, port and a number of liqueurs and cordials, including, besides Benedictine, Créme de Menthe and Créme de Cacao.

More than anything, Poirot likes a glass of flavored syrup, especially *sirop de cassis* (black current syrup). During the workday, he frequently has cups of cocoa, alternating with coffee with several sugars or *tisane,* an herbal tea. Although he sometimes drinks regular tea, he never develops the British passion for it.

Poirot Green

2 oz. Créme de Menthe

Pour the Créme de Menthe liqueur into a small cocktail glass and serve.

About Author Agatha Christie and Her Hercule Poirot:

(See also the chapter on Miss Jane Marple.)

Who has not heard of Agatha Christie? She is best-selling novelist in history, with more than two billion of her books in print in more than 100 different languages. More than a billion copies in English alone have been sold. It is claimed that only the Bible and the works of Shakespeare have sold more copies.

Much also has been written about her. Besides her own autobiography, published posthumously in 1977, a memoir of her travels around the British Empire and a book about working at an archeological site in Syria, she has been the subject of a number of biographies, fictional treatments and biopics and other films.

Born into a wealthy family in the late summer of 1890 in Torquay, Devon, England, Christie was educated at home, at a girls' school in Torquay and at *pensions* and a finishing school in Paris. As a young adult, she spent several months with her mother in Egypt and set her first novel, *Snow Upon the Dessert,* in Cairo; the novel failed to find a publisher.

The would-be novelist met Archie Christie, who would become her first husband, at a dance in Devon. He was an army officer with the Royal Flying Corps. With the outbreak of World War I, and with Archie about to be sent to France, the couple married on Christmas Eve, 1914. During the war, Agatha Christie worked as a volunteer nurse and pharmacist's assistant in a hospital in Torquay. Christie's first and only child, Rosalind, was born in 1919.

A fan of Conan Doyle's Sherlock Holmes stories and Wilkie Collins' detective novels, in 1916 Christie tried her hand at the genre. She wrote her first detective novel, *The Mysterious Affair at Styles,* introducing Hercule Poirot. After being turned down by several publishers, it finally was accepted by The Bodley Head and published in 1920. Her second novel, *The Secret Adversary,* featuring detective couple Tommy and Tuppence, was published in 1922, and another Poirot novel, *Murder on the Links,* appeared in 1923. Initial sales of her detective novels were modest.

The Murder of Roger Ackroyd, with Poirot retired to the village of King's Abbot, was published in 1926 and received great critical attention due to its surprise ending. As is now well known, the guilty party is the narrator. This work remains controversial to this day.

Also in 1926, her husband Archie asked for a divorce so he could marry Nancy Steele, whom he had met earlier on the couple's round-the-world tour of Commonwealth countries. The couple quarreled, and Archie left to spend the weekend with his lover. That same evening, Agatha disappeared from her home. Her car was found abandoned, and a massive nationwide hunt was begun to find her. Christie's disappearance was featured in newspapers across Britain and in *The New York Times.*

Ten days later, Christie was finally found, registered as "Mrs. Steele," in a hotel in Harrogate.

Christie was diagnosed with depression and temporary amnesia, but many in Britain considered her disappearance a publicity stunt to boost sales of her novels. In her autobiography, Christie makes no reference to the incident, which has been the subject of books and movies.

The Christies divorced in 1928. In 1930, Christie married the Oxford-educated archeologist Max Mallowan, whom she had met earlier that year on a dig at Ur in Iraq. Mallowan took part in excavations in Iraq and Syria for the British Museum and British School of Archeology. Agatha accompanied her husband on some of the expeditions, writing about the Syrian digs in her 1946 book, *Come Tell Me How You Live.* She also used some of the Middle East settings in her stories and novels, including *Death on the Nile* and *Appointment with Death.*

Mallowan served in the Royal Air Force Reserve during World War II, rising to the rank of wing commander. During the war, Christie again worked in a hospital pharmacy, gaining knowledge of poisons that she put to use in her post-war novels. In this period Christie also wrote two novels, *Curtain* and *Sleeping Murder,* detailing respectively the final cases of Hercule Poirot and Miss Jane Marple. The completed novels were locked away and not published until near the end of Christie's life.

Following the war Mallowan became a professor at the University of London and was elected a fellow of All Souls College, Oxford. For his work in Middle Eastern archeology, Mallowan was knighted in 1968.

In the 1930s and 1940s, Christie's popularity and fame as a mystery writer was growing exponentially. In the early 1930s, three of her Poirot works were made into movies. Also during the 1930s, she published three of the most-admired and most popular Poirot novels: *Peril at End House* in 1932, *Murder on the Orient Express* in 1934 and *The ABC Murders* in 1935.

Although she murdered countless people in her stories, as a writer Christie seemingly could do no wrong. Her play, *The Mousetrap,* which began life as a 30-minute radio play titled "Three Blind Mice," opened in London's West End in on October 6, 1952, originally starring Richard Attenborough, and has run continuously ever since. It is the longest running play in modern history, with well over 25,000 performances in London. Its Toronto edition ran for 26 years and more than 9,000 performances, closing in 2004 as the longest-running play in North America.

Most of the 33 Poirot novels and 52 short stories have been adapted for the screen and television.

Austin Trevor, Tony Randall, Albert Finney and Peter Ustinov have played the Belgian detective in movies. The 1974 version of *Murder on the Orient Express,* with Finney as Poirot, was well received by critics and remains popular in television reruns.

A better appraisal is that this version is grossly overacted by its all-star cast, and Finney is irritating, at best, as an overweight and loud-mouthed Poirot.

On television, Peter Ustinov and, most notably, David Suchet, have portrayed Poirot. The ITV production, "Agatha Christie's Poirot" with Suchet as the detective, ran from January 1989 to November 2013, with a total of 70 episodes. ITV aired the show in Britain, and PBS and A&E aired it in the U.S. It is available on Netflix and through Amazon and also has been released on DVD.

Critics have acclaimed Suchet as the actor who best captures the character of Poirot. To prepare for the role, Suchet read every Poirot novel and short story, met with Christie's living family members and others who knew her and made extensive notes about Poirot's appearance, mannerisms and character. It is now nearly impossible to read a Poirot story without thinking of David Suchet as the detective.

The author herself grew increasingly tired of her famous Belgian detective. At one point, she called Poirot an "egocentric creep." By contrast, she remained fond of Miss Marple. However, because Poirot was so popular Christie kept him going, right up to *Curtain,* which she had written during World War II. Christie authorized the publication of Poirot's "final case" in 1975, just before her death, and it proved a great success.

In 1971, three years after her husband had been knighted, Christie became Dame Agatha Christie when she was named Dame Commander of the Order of the British Empire (DBE).

Christie died of natural causes on January 12, 1976, at her home in Oxfordshire, England. She was 85. After her death, some experts, using text analysis of her late works, which appeared less complex and used a smaller vocabulary than her earlier works, suggested that Christie may have suffered from early stage Alzheimer's.

In 2013, the Christie family authorized the release of a new Poirot story, *The Monogram Murders*, written by British author Sophie Hannah.

Hercule Poirot Novels by Agatha Christie

The Mysterious Affair at Styles (1920)
The Murder on the Links (1923)
The Murder of Roger Ackroyd (1926)
The Big Four (1927)
The Mystery of the Blue Train (1928)
Peril at End House (1932)
Lord Edgware Dies also published as *Thirteen at Dinner* (1933)
Murder on the Orient Express also published as *Murder in the Calais Coach* (1934)

Three Act Tragedy also published as *Murder in Three Acts* (1935)
Death in the Clouds also published as *Death in the Air* (1935)
The A.B.C. Murders (1936)
Murder in Mesopotamia (1936)
Cards on the Table (1936)
Dumb Witness also published as *Poirot Loses a Client* (1937)
Death on the Nile (1937)
Appointment with Death (1938)
Hercule Poirot's Christmas also published as *Murder for Christmas* and as *A Holiday for Murder* (1938)
Sad Cypress (1940)
One, Two, Buckle My Shoe also published as *Overdose of Death* and as *The Patriotic Murders* (1940)
Evil Under the Sun (1941)
Five Little Pigs also published as *Murder in Retrospect* (1942)
The Hollow also published as *Murder after Hours* (1946)
Taken at the Flood also published as *There Is a Tide* (1948)
Mrs McGinty's Dead also published as *Blood Will Tell* (1952)
After the Funeral also published as *Funerals are Fatal* (1953)
Hickory Dickory Dock also published as *Hickory Dickory Death* (1955)
Dead Man's Folly (1956)
Cat Among the Pigeons (1959)
The Clocks (1963)
Third Girl (1966)
Hallowe'en Party (1969)
Elephants Can Remember (1972)
Curtain (written about 1940, published 1975)
Black Coffee (adapted from 1930 play, novel published 1998)

Hercule Poirot Short Story Collections
Poirot Investigates (1924)
Murder in the Mews also published as *Dead Man's Mirror* (1937)
The Regatta Mystery and Other Stories (1939)
The Labours of Hercules (1947)
The Under Dog and Other Stories (1951)
The Adventure of the Christmas Pudding (1960)
Double Sin and Other Stories (1961)
Poirot's Early Cases (1974)
Problem at Pollensa Bay and Other Stories (1991)
The Harlequin Tea Set (1997)
While the Light Lasts and Other Stories (1997)
Hercule Poirot: The Complete Short Stories (1999)

Notable Books about Hercule Poirot and Agatha Christie

(Also see this section of the Miss Marple chapter.)

Hart, Anne, *The Life and Times of Hercule Poirot* (1990). As in her companion "biography" of Miss Marple, Anne Hart explores the life of the egg-headed Belgian detective as described in the Agatha Christie books (but as he appeared in film and television.)

Mallowan, Agatha Christie, *Come Tell Me How You Live: An Archeological Memoir* (1946). This is Christie's memoir of her times on digs in Syria with her archeologist second husband, Max Mallowan. It is particularly moving, given the horrific events in Syria today, including the destruction of some historic sites. It is one of only two books that she published under both her married names, Christie and Mallowan.

Lord Peter Wimsey

From the Lord Peter Wimsey series by Dorothy L. Sayers (1893-1957)

"As my Whimsey Takes Me"
Motto on the Wimsey family coat of arms

Lord Peter Death Bredon Wimsey first appeared as a minor character in an unpublished short story by Dorothy L. Sayers written in France in 1920. In the story, he is described as the younger son of a Duke: "Fair-haired, big nose, aristocratic sort of man whose socks match his tie. No politics."

When Sayers returned from France to London in the late summer of 1920, Lord Peter was on her mind as she sketched out the idea for a detective novel. In an article published much later, in 1936, titled "How I Came to Invent the Character of Lord Peter," Sayers says she does not remember inventing him at all. Rather, she says, when she was thinking of writing a detective story, Lord Peter just walked in "complete with spats" and applied for the job.

In his first public appearance in *Whose Body?* in 1923, Lord Peter's character, appearance and style are fully fleshed out, although over the course of 11 novels and many short stories some elements change. For example, in 1931 he comes to know Harriet Vane, an Oxford-educated mystery writer on trial for murder in *Strong Poison,* and finally marries her in *Gaudy Nights.*

Lord Peter is a straight-up aristocrat, the second son of the fictitious 15th Duke of Denver. Coming from a very old family, his ancestry can be traced back to the 12th-century knight Gerald de Wimsey, who went with King Richard the Lionheart on the Third Crusade. Wimsey is called Lord as a courtesy to the son of a duke. He is not a peer and has no right to sit in the House of Lords.

Wimsey is of average height and slim build, with fair, straw-colored hair and a beaked nose. Sayers is believed to have patterned his physical appearance after the poet Roy Ridley, whom she saw reading his Newdigate Prize-winning poem "Oxford" in 1913. Wimsey was born in 1890, making him 32 in *Whose Body?* By the time of the last Lord Peter novel, *Busman's Honeymoon,* he is said to be 45. He is both a scholar and an athlete, having been educated at Eton College and taking a first in modern history at Balliol College, Oxford, in 1912 while also being an outstanding cricket player for Oxford.

Daimler Double Six, the favorite motor car of Lord Peter Wimsey

Lord Peter served on the Western Front in World War I from 1914 to 1918 in the Rifle Brigade (The Prince Consort's Own), rising to the rank of major. He served both as a line officer and in intelligence. In 1918, near Caudry, France, he was severely wounded by an artillery shell. He suffered from shell shock (now known as PTSD) and was sent home to the family estate to recover. Lord Peter was taken care of by a sergeant with whom he served on the Western Front, Mervyn Bunter, who becomes his valet.

In addition to his hobby of criminology, Lord Peter is a bibliophile, with special expertise in inculabula, books printed in Europe before 1501. Wimsey is a talented pianist and is knowledgeable about classical music, especially Bach. He also knows good food and drink, especially fine wine, and is an expert on male fashion.

But don't think that Lord Peter is a typical rich British aristocrat. He is veddy British, or English, as Sayers would prefer to say, and he is wealthy (the source of his fortune is never made clear), but sometimes he pratters on cheerfully and says the first thing that comes to his mind, no matter whether pertinent or not. Many of his witticisms and jokes fall flat. Some of his mannerisms are mindful of P. G. Wodehouse's bumbling character, Bertie Wooster. His valet, Mervyn Butner, is patterned to a degree on Bertie's man, Jeeves. Sayers admitted to as much, because, she said, it entertained her.

"Oh, damn!" These are the first words spoken by Lord Peter in *Whose Body?* They are also Wimsey's last words in *Busman's Honeymoon.*

Whose Body? (1923) turns on the discovery of a naked, dead man in the bathtub of an architect. At first, the body is thought to be that of a wealthy financier, Sir Reuben Levy, but Lord Peter, in what was a rather risqué turn for the times, realizes it can't be, as Levy was an observant Jew yet the dead man is uncircumcised.

In the second novel, *Cloud of Witness,* Lord Peter rushes back from holiday upon finding his brother is accused of murdering their sister's fiancé. As Peter's brother is the current Duke of Denver, he is tried in the House of Lords, and Sayers consulted peers and other experts on how such a trial would be handled. It is up to Peter and his friend, Inspector Charles Parker of Scotland Yard, a continuing character in the series and later his brother-in-law, to discover what actually took place on the fateful night.

The third Lord Peter book, *Unnatural Death* (1927), involves the death three years earlier of an old lady suffering from cancer.

Using the investigative efforts of Kittie Climson, a spinster who works in Wimsey's typing bureau, Wimsey discovers the real cause of death was the insertion of a bubble of air from a hypodermic needle, but after the publication of the novel readers pointed out that the murderess injects the air into an artery, not a vein, which likely would have not caused death. Besides, it would have been nearly impossible to inject enough air to cause the death in the way Sayers described it.

After the first three novels, Sayers begins to hit her stride, with *The Unpleasantness at the Bellona Club* (1928). Bellona is one of Lord Peter's three clubs in London. A 91-year-old general is found dead in his armchair at the club. After much ado, Lord Peter determines the general had died from an overdose of digitalis.

The fifth novel, *Strong Poison,* introduces Harriet Vane, who is on trial for the poisoning of her former lover. Harriet Vane is in many ways Dorothy Sayers' alter ego, as Vane is an Oxford-educated mystery writer. After a retrial, Vane is found innocent due to the work of Lord Peter, who declares his love for her and proposes marriage, but Vane refuses.

The *Five Red Herrings* is set in Galloway, Scotland, and uniquely among the Lord Peter books depends on the exact locations of real places and actual train timetables. *Have His Carcase* brings Lord Peter to a seaside resort near Devon where Harriet Vane has discovered a dead body.

Most of the action in *Murder Must Advertise* (1933) takes place in an advertising agency, Pym's, very similar to Benson's where Sayers had worked.

Lord Peter, under an assumed name, takes a job at the agency as a copywriter – he turns out to be good at it, creating a successful ad campaign for a major client – to investigate the death of an agency employee. This is one of the most light-hearted of the Wimsey series and was popular with readers, although Sayers herself disliked the book.

The Nine Tailors involves a lengthy, complex and almost completely accurate explanation of church bell ringing. Although panned by some critics, including famously by the American literary critic Edmund Wilson in his essay "*Who Cares Who Killed Roger Ackroyd?*" it is a favorite of many Lord Peter readers, was one of best selling of her books and was named the best mystery novel of the 1930s by the British Crime Writers Association. Many consider it her most accomplished novel. One of the characters in the novel, the Reverend Mr Venables, is an affectionate portrait of Sayers' own father.

The penultimate Lord Peter novel by Sayers, *Gaudy Night* (1935) takes Harriet Vane and, later in the story, Lord Peter, back to their beloved alma mater, Oxford. Gaudy comes from the Latin *gaudium,* or merry-making. It is the Oxford name for a college reunion. The novel is unusual in the detective genre because it does not include a murder, although there are two attempts. At the end of the novel, Harriet finally accepts Peter's proposal of marriage.

The final Lord Peter book by Sayers, *Busman's Honeymoon,* was a novelization of a play of the same name by Sayers and Muriel St. Clare Byrne. (An unfinished Wimsey book, *Thrones, Dominations,* was much later completed by another British novelist, Jill Paton Walsh.) After their long-delayed marriage, Peter and Harriet go on a honeymoon to Talboys, an old farmhouse in Hertfordshire that Peter has given her as a wedding gift. As might be expected, the honeymoon turns into a crime story, as the former owner of the house is found dead in the cellar. A short story, "Talboys," published in 1942, is the last story Sayers ever wrote about Lord Peter. It is a lighthearted tale, and the only crime in it is the theft of peaches.

Lord Peter's Digs: Lord Peter lives in a luxury flat at 110A, Piccadilly, London, W1. Dorothy Sayers wrote, "After all it cost me nothing and at that time I was particularly hard up and it have me great pleasure to spend his fortune for him. When I was dissatisfied with my single unfurnished room I took a luxurious flat for him Piccadilly. When my cheap rug got a hole in it, I ordered him an Aubusson carpet."

Besides the carpet, the flat has a fireplace, bronze chrysanthemums and a grand piano, on which Lord Peter plays Scarlatti and Bach. This Piccadilly address is currently the Sheraton Grand Park Lane Hotel, which has a suite named for Lord Peter. In Wimsey's *Who's Who* listing, which appears in some of the novels, his residences also include the family manor house, Bredon Hall, Duke's Denver, Norfolk.

Lord Peter's Drives: Lord Peter's favorite motor car is a 12-cylinder ("Double-Six") Daimler four-seater, which he calls "Mrs Merdle" after a character in Charles Dickens' Little Dorrit who "hated fuss." The Daimler Double-Six engine was a V-12 manufactured by The Daimler Company Limited of Coventry, England, between 1926 and 1938 for their flagship cars.

Lord Peter's Drinks: Lord Peter is a man who appreciates a fine old port, an expensive sherry or a Napoleon brandy.

Lord's Brandy

Napoleon brandy, aged at least six years

Pour a generous serving of XO (Napoleon) brandy into a brandy snifter. Sip sitting beside a fireplace.

About Dorothy L. Sayers:

Dorothy Leigh Sayers (most pronounce it *Say-ers,* but Dorothy herself preferred *Sayrz*) is one of the most intelligent and most gifted of all mystery writers. Born June 13, 1893, Dorothy was the only child of Rev. Henry Sayers, a chaplain at Christ Church, Oxford, and headmaster of the Choir School, and Helen Mary (née Leigh) Sayers, the daughter of a solicitor. As a young child, her father taught her Latin, and she became fluent in French and German. Her Greek and Latin were good enough to pass an examination for college, and she sprinkled her books with bits of Latin. Later she became a scholar of medieval Italian. She was an accomplished violinist and pianist and sang beautifully as a contralto.

While at boarding school, she placed first in all of England in an examination for admission to Cambridge. However, given her father's ties to Oxford (besides being a chaplain there, he held an M.A. from that university), she decided to go up to Somerville College, a woman's college at Oxford.

At Oxford, which she loved all her life, she studied modern languages and medieval literature, had an active social life, danced, sang in the choir, wrote epic poetry, sculled and punted.

Sayers was one of the first women in history to receive degrees from Oxford. At the time, women could not earn degrees at Oxford, but she finished with first class honors in French. When the rules changed, in 1920, she was among the first women to be awarded a B.A. degree and also, as she had two years of postgraduate study at Oxford, received an M.A. (It wasn't until after World War II that Cambridge began offering degrees to women.)

Sayers was traveling in France when the war with Germany began. She tried to join the Red Cross, but was turned down as being too young. Sayers helped care for wounded and shell-shocked troops in England and lost many of her Oxford classmates to the war, but otherwise she played little to no role in the British war effort.

Her first published work was a volume in the Oxford Poetry series. *Op. I* came out in 1915. It included a series of 12 metrically interrelated poems, in a structure called a lay, on the beauty and enchantment of Oxford.

After short stints at teaching and working at a publishing company she spent a year in France as an assistant to Eric Whelpton, who was involved with a school at Verneuil. Sayers believed she was in love with Whelpton, but Whelpton had fallen deeply in love with another woman.

It was about this time that Sayers began to think about writing a mystery story. The character who would become Lord Peter Wimsey seems to have been based on Whelpton as well as on Charles Crichton, an old Etonian and ex-cavalry officer who also was also at Verneuil, and, at least in terms of appearance, on Roy Ridley, whom Sayers had seen at Oxford.

Both Crichton and Whelpton were well dressed, buying their suits on Savile Row. Whelpton in particular was widely traveled and knew the world of high society in London and Paris. His aristocratic family had a large manor house in Wales, and he was a connoisseur of fine wine and good food.

In 1920, Sayers returned to London. By this time, she had had several small volumes of poetry published, had taught school for four terms and had held several jobs, but she had little money saved and had difficulty finding a place to live. She did find work as a translator, being paid by the page, and with that and a small allowance from her family she settled in an unfurnished room at the top of a women's club at 36 St George's Square, Pimlico. Miss Pimlico, Lord Peter Wimsey's assistant, would live in a similar room on the top floor of a flat in the same square.

In 1921 she took a job as a high school teacher and moved to a room at 44 Mecklenburg Square. In her spare time, she continued working as a translator and also read books on criminology at the British Museum. It was here that she began writing her first Lord Peter Wimsey book, *Whose Body?* By November 1921, she had finished it and was having it typed, and she immediately began work on the second Wimsey novel, *Clouds of Witness.*

The early 1920s were a busy and turbulent time for Sayers, who was then in her late 20s. Dorothy got a job as a copywriter with an advertising agency in London, S. H. Benson, which paid her a steady four pounds a week, shortly raised to five and then to almost seven pounds (about $150 today). She moved again, to a flat in 24 Great James Street, where she would live the rest of her life. The flat had three rooms and a shared bath down the hall. The initial rent was 70 pounds a year (about $1,500 today).

Dorothy also had two love affairs, one with the Russian-born Jewish journalist and novelist John Cournos. His first novel, *The Mask,* won the Hawthornden Prize in 1919, and he went on to write more than two dozen novels, non-fiction books and collections. The relationship was unsatisfactory on both sides. Sayers wanted to get married and have children, but Cournos claimed to believe in the philosophy of free love. Their relationship would be portrayed in Sayers' Lord Peter novel *Strong Poison* in 1930 and in Cournos' *The Devil Is an English Gentleman*, published in 1932.

The second affair was with Bill White, almost the exact opposite of Cournos. White had no intellectual pretensions, road a motorcycle (later Dorothy would get her own) and worked as a car salesman and mechanic. The main result of this affair, likely Dorothy's first consummated sexual experience, was a child. Bill White and Sayers did not want to marry, but Dorothy decided to have the child anyway. She hid her pregnancy from her parents, most of her friends and even her ad agency associates. The child, a boy whom she named John Anthony, was born in January 1924 in a maternity home in Southbourne. (Sayers had taken a two-month medical leave from her ad agency job.) She arranged with a cousin and childhood friend, Ivy Shrimpton, to keep the child. Ivy was to prove a highly competent foster mother for John Anthony Sayers.

Sayers also had found publishers for her first Lord Peter Wimsey novel, *Whose Body.* In July 1922, Boni & Liveright offered to publish it in the United States, giving her an advance of $250 (about $3,700 today). It appeared in early 1923.

In England, the firm of T. Fisher Unwin published *Whose Body?* in 1923 and *Clouds of Witness* in 1926. That same year, the Unwin firm was merged into Ernest Benn Limited, which published *Unnatural Death* in 1927 and two additional Lord Peter novels.

Initial sales of the first Lord Peter novels were modest, and it was necessary for her to keep working as an advertising copywriter. She worked at Benson's until 1931, when her earnings from the Lord Peter books allowed her to quit her job, although her financial affairs remained less than ideal for most of her life. Among other clients, at Benson's she worked on the Guinness account, helping create the long-running campaign featuring zoo animals.

In 1925, Sayers met Oswold Arthur, who had for unknown reasons adopted the name Atherton Fleming and was called Mac Fleming. A Scot, Fleming had been married and had two daughters. Probably as a result of his experiences in the war, his marriage collapsed and his wife sued for divorce. When Sayers met Fleming, he was a reporter, on crime and car racing, for the newspaper *News of the World.* He also was a freelance writer and a photographer.

Mac and Dorothy were married in April 1926. By all accounts, it was a good partnership, at least in the early years. Mac helped Dorothy with her writing work, and Dorothy enjoyed going to the motor car races with Mac. Later, Mac fell ill with a variety of afflictions, including depression and moodiness, became unable to hold a job and depended on Dorothy for money.

Sayers also worked hard to provide financially for her son, John, continuing for a while at the ad agency by day and writing short stories, articles and novels at night. Although John never came to live with Mac and Dorothy, and Dorothy never publicly acknowledged him as her son, Mac finally formally adopted him (Dorothy's son later took the name Anthony Fleming), she did make sure he received a good education, paying for his education including at a top preparatory school. After working for the British government during World War II, he eventually took a first-class degree from Balliol, Oxford, Lord Peter's college, where ironically his tutor for a time was Roy Ridley, said to be the physical pattern for Lord Peter.

The Detection Club was formed in 1930 by a group of British mystery writers, including Dorothy L. Sayers, Agatha Christie, Freeman Wills Crofts, Ronald Knox, Hugh Walpole, G. D. H. Cole, Margaret Cole, E. C. Bentley, Henry Wade, H. C. Bailey and others The first president was G. K. Chesterton. There was a fanciful initiation ritual with an oath probably written by either Chesterton or Sayers.

The club held regular dinner meetings in London, put together and published a number of mystery short story collection, and members helped each other with technical matters. The members of the club agreed to adhere to a "code of ethics" in their writing to give the reader a fair chance at guessing the guilty party. It remains in existence to this day, with Martin Edwards, a British lawyer and crime writer, the current president.

About the time of the beginning of the Second World War in Europe, for reasons that are not completely clear, Sayers stopped writing mysteries. It wasn't exactly that she was tired of Lord Peter, who, she said, remained a real figure to her in her mind and indeed in some ways more real than her own life. In a letter to a fellow mystery author, she wrote, "As for writing detective stories – there are a thousand and one reasons why I can feel no desire for it; but the chief one is that, like Conan Doyle, I have been so much put off by being badgered to do it when I was wrapped up in other things that the mere thought now gives me a kind of nausea." She also complained that making more money just meant higher taxes and that she had concluded that detective stories had a bad effect on people, making them feel there was a neat solution to all problems.

About the same time, she also became a committed Christian. She wrote several religious plays and spoke and wrote publically on religious matters. She became quite well known in Britain as a commentator on the BBC and elsewhere on modern life and religion. Sayers also returned her professional attention to academic matters, including a major translation.

Sayers' fame rests on her Lord Peter Wimsey novels and stories written between the World Wars. Altogether, she wrote 11 Lord Peter novels and five collections of short stories. However, she considered her great life's work her verse translation of Dante's *Divine Comedy* from the medieval Italian, a job that occupied her for the last 14 years of her life. Sayers used Dante's rhyme scheme, *terza rima* (aba, bcb, cdc, etc.,) which is extraordinarily difficult as English has many fewer rhymes than Italian.

Sayers completed the translation of Cantica I, *Hell,* (published in 1949) and Cantica II, *Purgatory* (1955). She died in 1957 after suffering a stroke before completing the translation, but Cantica III, *Paradise,* was finally published in 1962, with additional translation by Barbara Reynolds, her friend and biographer.

Besides the novels and short story collections listed below, many of the Lord Peter novels and short stories have been made into radio programs, plays, films and television series.

The BBC made the novels into television series on two separate occasions. Five novels (*Clouds of Witness, The Unpleasantness at the Bellona Club, Five Red Herrings, Murder Must Advertise* and *The Nine Tailors)* under the umbrella title *Lord Peter Wimsey* ran between 1972 and 1975. Lord Peter was played by Ian Carmichael, with Bunter being played in all but one by Glyn Houston; Derek Newark played Bunter in *The Unpleasantness at The Bellona Club.* Edward Petherbridge played Lord Peter for BBC Television in 1987, in three of the four major Wimsey/Vane novels (*Strong Poison, Have His Carcase* and *Gaudy Night*) under the umbrella title *A Dorothy L. Sayers Mystery.* Harriet Vane was played by Harriet Walter and Bunter was played by Richard Morant. The rights to *Busman's Honeymoon* couldn't be arranged, and this Wimsey-Vane episode wasn't included in the series.

Lord Peter Wimsey Novels by Dorothy L. Sayers

Whose Body? (1923)
Clouds of Witness (1926)
Unnatural Death (1927)
The Unpleasantness at the Bellona Club (1928)
Strong Poison (1931)
Five Red Herrings (1931)
Have His Carcase (1932)
Murder Must Advertise (1933)
The Nine Tailors (1934)
Gaudy Night (1935)
Busman's Honeymoon (1937)

Lord Peter Wimsey Novels by Jill Paton Walsh

Jill Paton Walsh is an English novelist and children's book author who was selected to complete an unfinished manuscript by Dorothy Sayers and then did three Lord Peter novels on her own.

Thrones, Dominations (1998; unfinished Sayers manuscript completed by Walsh)
A Presumption of Death (2002)
The Attenbury Emeralds (2010)
The Late Scholar (2014)

Lord Peter Wimsey Short Story Collections

Lord Peter Views the Body (1928)
Hangman's Holiday (1933)
In the Teeth of the Evidence (1939)
Striding Folly (1972)
Lord Peter (1972

Notable Works on Dorothy L. Sayers

Clarke, Stephen P., *The Lord Peter Wimsey Companion* (2002). The OCD guide to every last detail in the Lord Peter books. Unfortunately, this is now a rare and out-of-print book that goes for $300 and up from used booksellers.

Reynolds, Barbara, *Dorothy L. Sayers, Her Life and Soul, a Biography* (1993). By Sayers' friend who finished Dorothy's translation of the *Divine Comedy,* this is arguably the best-informed biography of the writer.

THE PROFESSIONALS

William Hopper and Raymond Burr as Paul Drake and Perry Mason in the long-running television series

The Professional Detectives we've collected here are, to be truthful, a varied and motley bunch. Criminal attorney **Perry Mason** and his private investigator **Paul Drake** are a mixed couple, a famous lawyer who in the course of trials solved murders, proved his clients innocent and found the real murderer; this almost always required the footwork of PI Paul.

Charlie Chan, whom his creator Earl Derr Biggers based on a real Cantonese police detective in Honolulu, but who in the many B movies made about him was most often on his own.

Adrian Monk, the dysfunctional OCD detective, is one of the most television's most original characters. **Ellery Queen,** the hybrid creation of two cousins, was once incredibly famous in books, magazines, films and TV, although Queen's fame has faded some today.

Nero Wolfe and his wisecracking assistant Guy Friday, **Archie Goodwin,** were the creations of the prolific, highly intelligent Rex Stout (Stout's IQ was thought to be at least 180).

In their own ways, all of these are professionals, not amateurs. They almost always accept fees for their work, and they all spend their working lives as detectives, if only as in the case of Nero Wolfe to support his hobbies of eating well and growing orchids.

Charlie Chan

From the Charlie Chan novels by Earl Derr Biggers (1884-1933) and the Charlie Chan movies

"At night all cats are black."
– Charlie Chan

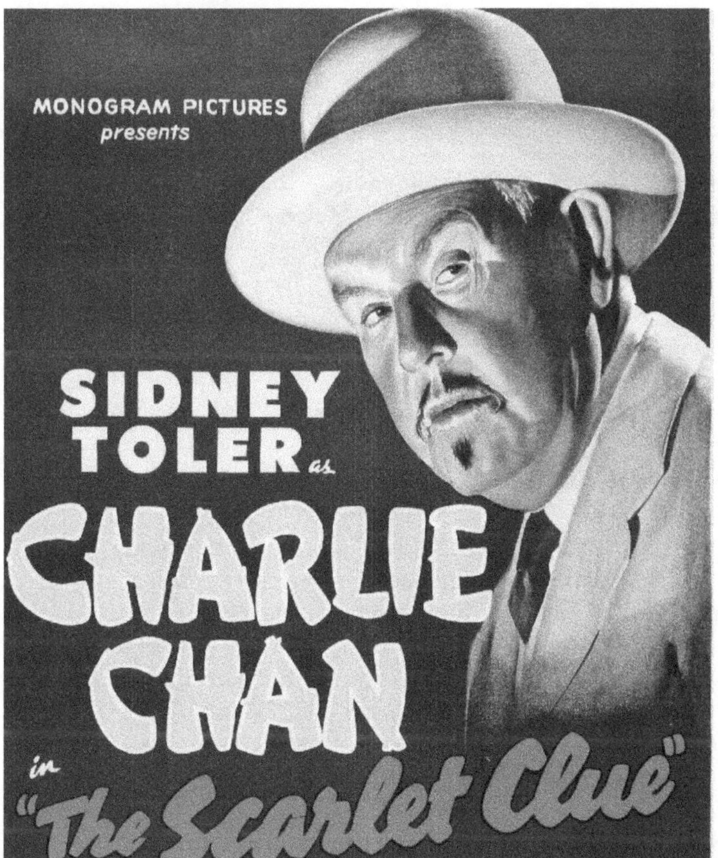

Sidney Toler as Charlie Chan, from Monogram movie poster for The Scarlet Clue

There are many different Charlie Chans. The public was introduced to one Charlie Chan in Earl Derr Biggers' 1925 novel, *The House Without a Key*. In this first Chan novel, Chan plays a fairly minor role, not being introduced until Chapter VII. Chan is presented as a Cantonese detective on the Honolulu police force, sent to investigate the murder of a former Boston Brahmin who has been living in Hawaii for many years.

Chan is described as "huge" and a "grotesque figure." While some in the victim's family are skeptical of having a Chinese policeman working on the case, he is described as "the best detective on the force" and as someone who always gets his man.

As in many of the Chan books and movies, Charlie, whose first language is Cantonese, speaks in a kind of elevated pidgin English, speaking in the present tense, dropping plurals and with nouns and verbs often not in agreement. The Chinese language is very different from English – for example, verbs don't have tenses (time adverbs are used to indicate past, present and future.) Thus, it is often difficult for Chinese speakers to learn to speak English fluently, and vice-versa. The first words Charlie speaks in *The House Without a Key* are "No knife are present in neighborhood of crime." However, as the Biggers' series of Charlie Chan novels progresses, Charlie's English improves, rising at times to eloquence.

Always, there are his aphorisms, which have been described as pseudo-Confucian:

"The man who is about to cross a stream should not revile crocodile's mother."

"He who feeds the chickens deserves the eggs."

"Admitting failure like drinking bitter tea."

"Always happens - when conscience tries to speak, telephone out of order."

In *The House Without a Key,* Charlie says he is no newcomer to the islands, that he has been here 25 years. He enjoys the respect of his coworkers and of his superior, a captain of detectives.

The House Without a Key was first made into a 10-part serial silent film of the same name in 1926, featuring the Japanese-American George Kuwa as Chan, and then again in 1933, as *Charlie Chan's Greatest Case*, starring Warner Oland.

In the second Charlie Chan novel, *The Chinese Parrot* (1926) Charlie travels from Hawaii to the California desert. Working under cover as a "houseboy," Chan solves a number of crimes. While in California, he learns he is a new father, his wife having given birth to their 11th child. Like *Key*, this novel was made into two movies, a silent and a talkie, but both are now considered lost. The third Chan novel, *Behind That Curtain,* also is set in California and involves a Scotland Yard detective pursuing a cold case murder of a London solicitor.

Then there were the fourth, fifth and sixth novels, ending with Ke*eper of the Keys* in 1932. They piled up large royalties for Biggers, who with them was able to buy a large house in Southern California.

However, Charlie Chan really came to prominence in the Charlie Chan movies made from the early 1930s to the late 1940s. The first Charlie Chan in the "talking pictures" was Warner Oland, born in 1879 as Johan Verner Olund in the Swedish village of Bjurholm. Olund immigrated to America with his parents, Anglicized his name and attended drama school in Boston. Among Oland's claims to fame is that he was featured in the first commercial talkie, *The Jazz Singer*, with Al Jolson. Olund played a Jewish cantor.

Olund had played the sinister Fu Manchu in several silent films and talkies, so the Swede was the natural Aryan choice to play the Chinese detective. Biggers himself commended Oland to Fox Studios as a likely choice for Chan. Olund didn't disappoint. He read Chinese history and philosophy and even studied the language to ready himself for the part.

Fox's 1931 production of *Charlie Chan Carries On* was a popular and critical success. Biggers himself was pleased by Olund's characterization. He told a friend, "after all these weary years, they have got Charlie right on the screen." Fox then bought the film rights to Biggers' novel, *The Black Camel* and adapted it for the screen. This movie was filmed later in 1931 on location in Honolulu, where both Olund and Biggers met Chang Apana, the Honolulu police detective widely believed to have been the original inspiration for Charlie Chan.

After two more films based on Biggers' work (one lost), Biggers would not permit Fox to have screenwriters create new scripts for Charlie Chan movies. Following Biggers' death in 1933, Fox negotiated with Biggers' wife, Eleanor Biggers, and bought some rights to the Chan character. The studio quickly made a series of inexpensively produced Charlie Chan movies starring Warner Olund including *Charlie Chan in London, Charlie Chan in Paris* and the controversial *Charlie Chan in Egypt.* In *Charlie Chan in Egypt,* Chan is paired with the African-American comedian, Lincoln Theodore Monroe Andrew Perry, whose stage name was Stepin Fetchit. Perry always played the caricatured lazy, shiftless "darkie." While his roles were demeaning to black people, he was a highly sought-after actor, appearing in 26 movies between 1929 and 1935. At the time of the *Egypt* movie, he was at the height of his fame. Perry, who had been born in Key West to West Indian immigrants, was the first black actor to make a million dollars from Hollywood films.

In 1935, Fox merged with Twentieth Century pictures, becoming Twentieth Century-Fox. The merged studio continued to use Warner Olund as the key figure in their mystery movie franchise.

Olund's salary continued to climb, eventually to $20,000 a picture (the equivalent of at least $350,000 today.) Olund's work on the Chan films was so lucrative Olund was able to buy a house in Beverly Hills, a ranch in California, another 7,000-acre ranch in Mexico and a house in Massachusetts.

Unfortunately, unlike Charlie Chan, who didn't drink, Olund had a serious problem with alcohol. At first, the studios encouraged Olund to take a drink before filming, which gave him a relaxed, smiling countenance that worked with the Charlie Chan character. As time went on, however, his drinking increased. On some occasions he missed stage calls, forgot lines or fell asleep during filming. In 1938, while filming *Charlie Chan at Ringside,* he walked off the set and disappeared. After hospitalization and rehab, he recovered enough that the studio signed him to do additional Chan movies, but later in 1938 he traveled to Europe and died, at age 57, at his mother's home in Sweden.

Despite Olund's death, Twentieth Century-Fox wanted to continue to make Charlie Chan movies. Most cost less than $250,000 to make and usually grossed more than $1 million ($4 million and $18 million, respectively, in today's dollars). At three Chan movies a year, this was a nice profit for the time.

The studio auditioned more than 30 actors for the Chan role. The winner was Sidney Toler. Toler (1874-1947) was a Missouri-born Hollywood veteran who before he stepped into the role of Charlie Chan had been in some 50 films, mostly in character and supporting roles. He also was a well-regarded comedy actor on Broadway.

Filming began almost immediately on *Charlie Chan in Honolulu,* which had been scripted for Warner Olund. Another change that happened at this time is that Number One Son Lee, played by the Shanghai-born American actor Key Luke, was replaced by Number Two Son Jimmy, played by Sen Yung, a San Francisco-born actor of Chinese heritage.

Toler brought a somewhat sharper edge to the Chan character. His sarcasm, often directed toward his son Jimmy, and opinions were in contrast to the more easy-going style of Olund's Chan.

Over a period of four years, Toler made 11 Charlie Chan movies for Twentieth Century-Fox. In 1942, following the filming of *Castle in the Desert,* one of the Chan movies with the highest production values – it was directed by Harry Lachman, earlier a noted post-Impressionist painter in Paris and set in a Spanish Revival style villa in Death Valley – the studio canceled the series, along with several other B-movie series, in great part due to the impact of World War II.

Toler saw the value of the Chan character and was able to purchase the rights to the character from Biggers' widow, Eleanor Biggers Cole, who still had an interest in the copyrights. Failing to negotiate a production and distribution deal with major studios, Toler went to Monogram Pictures, a low-budget studio.

Under Monogram, the production values of the Charlie Chan movies suffered, especially initially, as the budgets were less than one-half of what they had been with Twentieth Century-Fox. The movies gradually improved, and the later Monogram pictures with Toler, such as *The Chinese Cat*, *The Shanghai Cobra*, and *Dark Alibi*, did well.

Some of the Monogram movies featured the popular Mantan Moreland, who played Birmingham Brown as a chauffeur and assistant to Charlie. Although not as bad as the Stepin Fetchit character, Brown was portrayed as a stereotypical black man. However, he brought a popular comedic side to the Monogram movies. Altogether, Moreland appeared in 15 Charlie Chan movies. Monogram also replaced Number Two Son Jimmy with Number Three Son Tommy, played by Benson Fong, an actor born in California of Chinese heritage.

Toler was diagnosed with intestinal cancer in 1946 and died in early 1947. Monogram continued the series with six more Charlie Chan movies starring Roland Winters, a Boston-born actor.

Most fans consider Winters' portrayal of Chan as the weakest of all. His *Docks of New Orleans* (1948) is considered by some the worst Chan movie of all time. In part this was not Winters' fault. It was partly due to the low Monogram budgets and the fact that the series, having been running for more than two decades, was getting tired. The last Winters/Chan movie, Cha*rlie Chan and the Sky Dragon,* appeared in 1949.

Charlie's Chan's Digs: In several of the Biggers books and in some films, Charlie Chan lives in Honolulu, where he is a member of the Honolulu police force.

In the films, Chan travels the globe, appearing in major cities in the United States, Europe, Asia and elsewhere. While he sometimes consults with the U.S. government or local police departments, he generally acts on his own as an independent private detective.

Charlie Chan's Drives: Most of the time, Charlie takes taxis, public transport or is driven by officials or clients for whom he is working. Birmingham Brown (as noted, played by Mantan Moreland) is his chauffeur in many of the Monogram Chan movies.

Charlie Chan's Drinks: Charlie was a teetotaler. If not drinking tea, he might have a sarsaparilla soft drink.

About Author Earl Derr Biggers and Charlie Chan Movies:

Earl Derr Biggers was born August 26, 1884, in the little Ohio town of Warren near the Pennsylvania state line, not far from Akron and Canton. He grew up in comfortable conditions. Early on Biggers aspired to become a writer. He was an avid reader of comic strips, wrote boyish adventure stories and founded a monthly magazine at his local high school.

After high school, Biggers left the cornfields and mills of Ohio for the more rarified atmosphere of Harvard. There, he became a member of the Signet Club, a prestigious literary society with quarters on Dunster Street, near the edge of Harvard Square. Among its members were T. S. Eliot, whose time at Harvard overlapped a little with that of Biggers – Diggers was class of 1907, Eliot 1910 – Robert Frost, Wallace Stevens, Norman Mailer and John Updike. Diggers also was a member of the Harvard *Lampoon.*

Following Harvard, Biggers worked as a reporter for the *Cleveland Plain Dealer,* where he didn't last long, and as a drama critic at the Boston *Traveller,* from which he was fired when the evening newspaper was purchased in 1912 by the Boston *Herald.*

Without a regular job, Biggers tried his hand at writing a mystery. It took him only three months to finish the book. In 1913, *Seven Keys to Baldpate* was published by Bobbs-Merrill, where Biggers had briefly worked as a manuscript reader. Against all odds for a novice writer, *Seven Keys* was a great success. George M. Cohan purchased rights to the melodrama, and the play ran for 320 performances on Broadway. Over the years, it was made into a movie seven times.

Biggers continued to find success writing. He authored several more Broadway plays and sold short stories to the "slicks," including the *Saturday Evening Post* and the *Ladies' Home Journal.*

Exhausted by work, in 1920 Biggers took a vacation to Hawaii, where he stayed for three months in a cottage on Waikiki beach. It was in Honolulu that some, notably Yunte Huang, a professor of English at the University of California at Santa Barbara who formerly taught at Harvard, believe Biggers found the inspiration for his Chinese detective. In his 2010 book, *Charlie Chan, The Untold Story of the Honorable Detective and His Rendezvous with American History,* Huang makes a convincing case for that origin of Biggers' Chan.

Sergeant Chang Apana was a slim, short (only 5 feet tall) veteran of the Honolulu police. He was one of the few Chinese on the force, most of the rest being Hawaiians, along with a few *haoles* (whites). A former cowboy on a cattle ranch in Hawaii, Chang Apana was known for being honest and incorruptible, and he wielded a leather whip to clean up the gang-ridden streets of Honolulu.

Biggers himself, in a 1932 letter to the *Honolulu Advertiser,* acknowledged that the real-life Apana was an inspiration for the fictional Charlie Chan.

What about the origin of the name Charlie Chan? It may have been simply created out of the ether by Biggers, or it may have been adapted from the Hawaiian detective's name, Chang. Possibly it came from the name of the owner of a laundry in Akron during Biggers' time in Ohio, Charlie Chan.

In any case, Charlie Chan made his debut in *The House Without a Key,* published in 1925. Although Chan was only a secondary character in that novel – his first words, in pidgin English, are "No knife are present in neighborhood of crime" – the public demanded to hear more about this Chinese detective.

Biggers wrote five more novels featuring Charlie Chan. They were the inspiration for almost four dozen Charlie Chan movies, including three early silent films, 16 starring Warner Oland, 21 starring Sydney Toler and six starring Roland Winters. Most were B movies turned out by studios on a small budget, but nearly all made money. Despite the fact that not a one starred a Chinese actor as Charlie Chan, many were popular in China.

After suffering a heart attack, Biggers died in a Pasadena, Calif., hospital on April 5, 1933, at age 48.

Charlie Chan Novels by Earl Derr Biggers

The House Without a Key (1925)
The Chinese Parrot (1926)
Behind That Curtain (1928)
The Black Camel (1929)
Charlie Chan Carries On (1930)
Keeper of the Keys (1932)

Charlie Chan Movies

Early Films

The House Without a Key (1926) with George Kuwa as Charlie Chan

The Chinese Parrot (1927) with Kamiyama Sojin as Charlie Chan (considered lost)

Behind That Curtain (1929) with E. L. Park as Charlie Chan

With Warner Oland as Charlie Chan

Charlie Chan Carries On (1931)
The Black Camel (1931)
Charlie Chan's Chance (1932)
Charlie Chan's Greatest Case (1933)

Charlie Chan's Courage (1934) (considered lost)
Charlie Chan in London (1934)
Charlie Chan in Paris (1935)
Charlie Chan in Egypt (1935)
Charlie Chan in Shanghai (1935)
Charlie Chan's Secret (1936)
Charlie Chan at the Circus (1936)
Charlie Chan at the Race Track (1936)
Charlie Chan at the Opera (1936)
Charlie Chan at the Olympics (1937)
Charlie Chan on Broadway (1937)
Charlie Chan at Monte Carlo (1937)

With Sidney Toler as Charlie Chan
Charlie Chan in Honolulu (1938)
Charlie Chan in Reno (1939)
Charlie Chan at Treasure Island (1939)
Charlie Chan in Panama (1940)
Charlie Chan's Murder Cruise (1940)
Charlie Chan at the Wax Museum (1940)
Murder Over New York (1940)
Dead Men Tell (1941)
Charlie Chan in Rio (1941)
Castle in the Desert (1942)
Charlie Chan in the Secret Service (1944)
Charlie Chan and the Chinese Cat (1944)
Charlie Chan in Meeting at Midnight (1944)
The Jade Mask (1945)
The Scarlet Clue (1945)
The Shanghai Cobra (1945)
The Red Dragon (1945)
Dark Alibi (1946)
Shadows Over Chinatown (1946)
Dangerous Money (1946)
The Trap (1946)

With Roland Winters as Charlie Chan
The Chinese Ring (1947)
Docks of New Orleans (1948)
Shanghai Chest (1948)
The Golden Eye (1948)
The Feathered Serpent (1948)
The Sky Dragon (1949)

Charlie Chan also appeared in a number of radio series, in *The New Adventures of Charlie Chan* television series (1957-58) starring Carrol Naish, in the 1981 comedy/mystery film *Charlie Chan and the Curse of the Dragon Queen* starring Peter Ustinov, in comic books and in other media.

Notable Works on Charlie Chan

Berlin, Howard M., *The Charlie Chan Film Encyclopedia* (2000). Everything you ever wanted to know about Charlie Chan in films, including the most detailed trivia.

Hanke, Ken, *Charlie Chan at the Movies: History, Filmography, and Criticism* (1984). The first attempt at providing detailed information on the Charlie Chan films. Hanke provides plot summaries, casts and personally rates and reviews the films.

Huang, Yunte, *Charlie Chan, The Untold Story of the Honorable Detective and His Rendezvous with American History (2010).* Dr. Hunte, a professor of English at the University of California, Santa Barbara, provides a cultural history of Charlie Chan, tying the iconic detective and his creator with the story of the Chinese in America, never avoiding the issues of racism and anti-immigrant attitudes that Chan and others faced. It is the most literate and best work on Charlie Chan.

Perry Mason and Paul Drake

From the Perry Mason novels by Erle Stanley Gardner (1889-1970) and the original Perry Mason show on CBS (1957-1966)

"You're not like most of these criminal attorneys. You don't want just to get the client off. You try to dig out the truth. I like that. That's what I want."

– Addison Balfour to Perry Mason in *The Case of the Lucky Loser*

Perry Mason, of course, is a trial attorney, not a private detective, but as crafted by his creator, Erle Stanley Gardner, who was himself an attorney, Perry's *modus operandi* is to get his client off by solving the murder and identifying the murderer, as a detective does. Mason's favorite private investigator, Paul Drake, stands out in this collection of great PIs because unlike the other detectives he rarely is involved directly in solving a murder. Instead, Drake's job, which he performs with remarkable efficiency, is getting information for his clients, and especially the "Chief," Perry Mason.

Mason, in the books, of which there are 86 published between 1933 and 1973, is described as a large, broad-shouldered man with a "granite jaw" and "wavy hair." In the long-running *Perry Mason* television show, Mason is played by Raymond Burr, who had slimmed down from a high of 340 pounds to 200 pounds to try out for the role, losing the final 60 pounds just before the screen tests. Burr later regained much of this weight. During casting for the TV series, when Gardner saw Burr, he reportedly exclaimed, "That is Perry Mason!"

The Canadian-born Burr was a regular on radio in the 1940s and appeared in a number of films in the 1950s, most notably *A Place in the Sun* with Elizabeth Taylor (1951) and Alfred Hitchcock's *Rear Window* with Jimmy Stewart and Grace Kelly (1954). He also played the reporter in *Godzilla, King of the Monsters!* (1956).

Burr may have been perfect for the Mason role, but his personal history wasn't always so perfect.

After his death in 1993, it was discovered that his claims to have been in the U.S. Navy in World War II and wounded at Okinawa weren't true. Burr, who was gay, also apparently fabricated stories about past marriages, athletic achievements, his education and other matters. Perhaps some of the false or unverifiable details of his private life were created to give him public cover in that homophobic period.

Publicity still shows Perry (Raymond Burr) with Della Street, played in the television series by Barbara Hale

In the Perry Mason novels, Paul Drake, head of the Drake Detective Agency, is described as tall, with drooping shoulders, slim, with a florid expression, protruding and somewhat glassy eyes and often a sullen expression. He chews gum and enjoys a hearty meal and a drink.

The Paul Drake most of us know is the one from the *Perry Mason* television series that ran from 1957 to 1966. The TV Drake is William Hopper, son of the movie star and gossip columnist Hedda Hopper. He is tall, thin, with a full head of prematurely gray hair. Drake likes to drive a Ford Thunderbird convertible and has an eye for an attractive woman. He often greets Perry's confidential secretary, Della Street, with a breezy, "Hello, Beautiful!"

Self-admittedly laid-back and not too ambitious, Hopper tried out for the Perry Mason role but later said he was glad he didn't get it, claiming that he wouldn't have been able to pull it off. He says he played the Paul Drake character "his way," quite differently than how Drake appeared in the novels.

Della Street is Perry's confidential secretary. Originally, Gardner describes Della as being around 27 years old, quietly efficient, fast on her feet and trim with chestnut hair. In the early Perry Mason novels, Gardner presents Perry and Della as being, at the very least, on the edge of a romantic relationship. The two exchange kisses and physical embraces. Perry several times proposes marriage, but Della always turns him down. However, in later novels and in the television series, there is only a hint of anything beyond a professional relationship.

A number of Gardner's associates have said they believe that Della is based on Gardner's long-time real life secretary, Jean Bethell, born Agnes Hellene Walther. Erle married Jean in 1968, after the death of his first wife, Nat, from whom the author had been separated for some 30 years. Others, however, including Jean herself, thought that the character was drawn from several different women that Gardner knew.

In early movies and radio shows, Della was played by a series of different actresses, nearly a dozen altogether. However, the Della Street most people think of is the one made famous by Barbara Hale in the *Perry Mason* television series and in 30 TV movies after the series ended. Hale, born in DeKalb, Ill., in 1922, was a successful film actress in the 1940s and early 1950s, playing lead roles opposite Robert Young, Jimmy Stewart, Robert Mitchum, James Cagney and Rock Hudson.

Perry's chief antagonist in most of the novels and television shows is LA District Attorney Hamilton Burger. Burger first appears in Gardner's sixth Mason novel, *The Case of the Counterfeit Eye,* in 1935. As with the other characters in the series, the district attorney's character was defined by television. William Talman played Burger in the *Perry Mason* show. Before the Mason show, Talman, born in Detroit in 1915, was a Broadway actor. He starred as a psychopathic killer in Ida Lupino's 1953 film noir, *The Hitch-Hiker.*

It has often been noted that Hamilton Burger – one screenwriter thought that the name was a private joke made up by Gardner and tried to change his name – is the most unsuccessful district attorney in history. He nearly always lost to Perry Mason in court hearings and trials.

Two of his trials as prosecutor did result in a guilty verdict – in *The Case of the Terrified Typist* and *The Case of the Deadly Verdict* – but those victories proved short-lived. Asked how a district attorney could keep his state job if he lost so many trials, the executive producer of the television series, Gail Patrick Jackson, noted that although Mr. Burger may have lost nearly all the trials on Saturdays, the night the show was broadcast for its first five seasons, that he won his trials on Mondays, Tuesdays, Wednesdays, Thursdays and Fridays. (The program was moved to Thursday nights in 1962 for its last four seasons.)

Ironically, William Talman was fired from the TV show in March 1960, when he was charged with lewd conduct after police found him at a party where most of the guests were nude and marijuana was being smoked. Although the charges were dropped in June, Talman, claimed to be in violation of his contract's morals clause, remained *persona non grata* at CBS and with executives of the *Mason* show from March until December 1960, when he publicly apologized and was reinstated as the DA in *The Case of the Fickle Fortune.*

Homicide cop Lieutenant Arthur Tragg, who arrests many of the suspects Perry Mason ends up defending and getting off, is portrayed in the novels as a fairly young man, but in the television series he is much older. On TV, he is played by Ray Collins, born in Sacramento, Calif., in 1889, the same year as Gardner. Collins, in his late 60s when the *Mason* show began, was an accomplished veteran actor, long associated with Orson Welles. He was in many of Welles' Mercury Theatre stage, film and radio productions, including "The War of the Worlds" radio program, in which Collins plays three roles including the broadcaster who describes the destruction of New York from his position on a rooftop. Collins also appeared in Welles' famed *Citizen Kane* (1941) and in more than 75 other movies including *The Best Years of Our Lives* (1946) and with Cary Grant in *The Bachelor and the Bobby-Soxer* (1947).

Lt. Tragg is the DA's right-hand man. In many of the *Perry Mason* program episodes he sits at the prosecutor's table in the courtroom, which would be highly uncommon in a real trial situation. By the early 1960s, suffering from emphysema and memory loss, Collins was in poor health. His last appearance on the television show was in *The Case of the Disappearing Camera,* filmed in October 1963 and broadcast in January 1964, although as a special courtesy to him his name appeared on the show's credits through the end of the eighth season in May 1965. Collins died in July 1965. Lt. Tragg's replacements on the show were Lt. Andy Anderson (Wesley Lau) and Lt. Steve Drumm (Richard Anderson).

In the Gardner novels, Perry Mason typically shows up early in the story and is the dominant character through the fact-gathering period, courtroom trial and the discovery of the true murderer. However, in the television series, the arc of most of the stories is changed, so that the featured murder and its background story are established first, and Perry Mason usually doesn't have much of a role until the preliminary hearing or the murder trial. Especially in the novels, the courtroom scenes are detailed with meticulous precision and with careful attention to trial procedure and the rules of evidence.

This excerpt from *The Case of the Terrified Typist* (1956) is an example of the typical courtroom jousting that goes on for many pages in every Mason book, always sounding totally authentic:

"You go by the name of Yvonne Manco?" Mason asked.

"Yes."

"You have another name?"

"No."

"You were really married to Munroe Baster, were you not?"

"Yes, but now that I am a widow I choose to keep my maiden name of Yvonne Manco."

"I see," Mason said. "You don't want to bear the name of your husband?"

"It is not that," she said. "Yvonne Manco is my professional name."

"What profession?" Mason asked.

There was a moment's silence, then Hamilton Burger was on his feet. "Your Honor, I object. I object to the manner in which the question is asked. I object to the question. Incompetent, irrelevant, and immaterial."

Judge Hartley strokes his chin thoughtfully. "Well," he said, "under the circumstances I'm going to sustain the objection. However, in view of the answer of the witness – However, the objection is sustained."

"You were, however, married to Munroe Baxter?"

"Yes."

"On shipboard?"

"Yes."

"Before that?"

"No."

"There had been no previous ceremony?"

"No."

"Are you familiar with what is referred to as a common law marriage?"

"Yes."

"Have you ever gone by the name of Mrs. Baxter?"

"Yes."

"Prior to this cruise?"

"Yes."

"As a part of this plot which you and Munroe Baxter hatched up, he was to pretend to be dead. Is that right?"

"Yes."

"With whom did the idea originate?" You or Munroe Baster?"

"With him."

"He was to pretend to jump overboard and bed dead, so he could smuggle in some diamonds."

"Yes. I have told you this."

"In other words," Mason said, "if at any time it should be to his advantage, he was quite willing to pretend to be dead."

"Objected to as calling for the conclusion of the witness as already asked and answered," Hamilton Burger said.

"Sustained," Judge Hartley said.

Mason, having made his point, smiled at the jury.

After all, Gardner had been a practicing trial attorney for two decades, and in his many Perry Mason books he is the widely acknowledged master of presenting courtroom dialogue and drama. In addition, when the books made the transition to television, the *Perry Mason* show's first producer, Ben Brady, had earlier practiced as an attorney in New York, story editor Gene Wang had graduated from law school and executive producer Gail Patrick Jackson had attended law school in Alabama before becoming a movie actress.

Although some rules of trial procedure have changed since the books were written, and rules may vary from court to court, Gardner did such as good job with the presentation of the trials that readers were fascinated by the details of the courtroom testifying and the minutiae of trail procedure. When the Mason novels finally went out of print, Ankerwyke, the publishing division of the American Bar Association, in 2015 took up the gavel and republished some of Gardner's books.

Many have remarked that in the television series the set-up for the stories often involves attractive young women, few of whom went on to notable careers in broadcast or film. According to several sources, including Jim Davidson in his *The Perry Mason Book: A Comprehensive Guide to America's Favorite Defender of Justice,* this was because Ben Brady, the CBS producer on the first three years of the *Perry Mason* program, had an eye for good-looking starlets and pushed to hire them, even if their acting talent was minimal.

Los Angeles is the main setting for all of the Perry Mason novels and television programs, although parts of the books and TV shows take place elsewhere. The city of Los Angeles together with the rest of Los Angeles County during Erle Stanley Gardner's working life was, as today, a major national population center.

In 1930, Los Angeles became the first city in the West to crack the list of the top five cities in the country in terms of population. LA then had about 1.2 million residents, compared with 7 million in New York, 3.4 million in Chicago, 2 million in Philadelphia and 1.6 million in Detroit. As the decades passed, LA's population grew rapidly, and by the 1960s and 1970s it ranked behind only New York and Chicago. As will be explored in more detail below, both Perry and Paul have offices in Downtown Los Angeles. The situation has changed now, and Downtown LA is becoming an increasingly popular entertainment and residential area, but at the time of the books and television shows it was mostly a daytime business destination, nearly deserted after dark.

Perry does not usually spell out his hourly fee, but on a murder case his usual retainer is at least $2,000 to $2,500, and the cost of his fees, not including expenses, for defending a murder charge, is $5,000 or more. In today's dollars, depending on the date of the case, the actual cost in today's dollars would be much greater. For example, $5,000 in 1935 would be around $80,000 today. In *The Case of the Lucky Loser,* published in 1956, Perry quotes his day rate at $500, more than $4,000 today. In that same case, a wealthy business offers Perry a fee of $100,000, more than $800,000 in current dollars (the fee is later rescinded). In *The Case of the Howling Dog* (both the novel and a Warner movie based on it that came out in 1934), a client leaves a $10,000 retainer check, the equivalent of around $180,000 in today's dollars. Over the course of the nearly four decades of Perry Mason books, radio shows and the television show, prices obviously changed, including Perry's fees. As the novels were republished again and again over the years, prices for such things as telephone calls and a cup of coffee were adjusted, although not always consistently.

It is not clear what Paul Drake charges, but on a single case, *The Case of the Bigamous Spouse,* the Gardner novel published in 1961, Perry Mason shells out $1,250 in detective fees, equivalent to over $10,000 in today's dollars.

Perry's and Paul's Digs: In most of the Perry Mason novels, Perry Mason and the Drake Detective Agency have offices on the same floor of the Central Utilities Building at Central and Clark streets in Downtown Los Angeles. (In some early Perry Mason novels, Drake's offices are on the floor below.) According to the description in several of the novels, Paul's offices are to the right as you get off the elevator, while Perry's are farther along the hall around a bend.

In the novels, Perry's offices are rectangular in shape, with a reception area behind the sign that reads "Perry Mason—Lawyer—Entrance." The reception is staffed by Della and Gertie. The law library and Perry's clerk's office are directly behind the reception area, and to the left is a workroom with file cabinets and space for at least two typists. Perry's large office is to the right of the entrance, with Perry's desk, a safe, a secretarial desk, a high-backed leather chair for clients (and for Paul), a bust of Sir William Blackstone, the 18th century British jurist on whose head Perry pitches his hat. There is a back door to Perry's office, frequently used by Paul Drake, who has a coded knock, which varies over time, to let Perry know who is at the door.

Paul's offices are utilitarian, and cluttered with telephones. At one point, he employs two women who run his office, Mabel and France, along with a stenographer, Ruth. At times, according to the Gardner books, Paul has a secretary, a night operator and a couple of typists, plus a stable of freelance operatives. The Drake Detective Agency offices are described as having a long narrow corridor, flanked by doors of cubbyhole offices where Paul's operatives interview witnesses, conduct polygraph tests and prepare reports.

In the *Perry Mason* television series, Perry and Paul's offices are in the Brent Building. The exterior of the Brent Building is represented by a high-rise building at 550 South Flower Street at the corner of 6th and South Flower in Downtown Los Angeles. The real 12-story, welded steel, marble-clad building was originally constructed in 1956 as the corporate headquarters of Superior Oil. It was the first all-welded steel office building in Los Angeles. Superior Oil is now a part of ExxonMobil. During the filming of the Perry Mason show, this building in 1963 became the Southern California headquarters of The Bank of California. Today, it is The Standard, a 207-room hotel in Downtown LA. The hotel opened in 2002, with the addition of a rooftop swimming pool and a redesigned two-story lobby formerly occupied by the bank office. In 2003, the building was placed on the National Register of Historic Places as an example of mid-20th century California modern architecture.

The layout of Perry Mason's office, on the ninth floor, Suite 908 of the Brent Building, changes during the course of the television series and subsequent TV movies. However, the office has a reception area, with an area for the receptionist, Gertie. The reception area leads to Della's windowless private office, off of which is the law library.

The largest office, which is entered through Della's office, belongs to Perry. There also is a back door by which Paul Drake often enters. Paul again uses a special knock to alert Perry that it is he. The knock varies over time but typically involves a series of long and short knocks. As in the novels, when Paul is in Perry's office, he usually lounges in the client chair, an oversized leather affair, with his leg carelessly draped over the arm.

Interior scenes of the *Mason* show were filmed on the 20th Century-Fox Western Avenue studio lot, and most exteriors were filmed at Fox Studios in Westwood or the Fox Movie Ranch in Malibu Canyon. Later episodes in the series were filmed at CBS LaBrea Studios in Hollywood.

Perry's and Drake's Drives: In the original television series, Perry himself most often is seen driving a new model Cadillac convertible, but he also drives a Lincoln Continental convertible, a Ford Sunliner convertible, a Ford Galaxie 500 and other cars. Paul drives a variety of different cars, including a 1957 and a 1965 Corvette convertible and a Buick. Most often, however, his ride is a Ford Thunderbird convertible. He has a Thunderbird from the 1957, 1958, 1960, 1961, 1962, 1963, 1964 and 1965 model years. His favorite seems to be the 1958 Thunderbird convertible, California license PXY 260, which he drives in several seasons of the show.

Paul is an early adaptor of mobile phone technology. He gets one in the mid-1960s, as recounted in the 1965 novel *The Case of the Beautiful Beggar*. Perry is impressed, but more importantly the use of car phones by Paul and his operatives means that in the days before cell phones they did not have to abandon a tail to find a pay phone to report their whereabouts. Paul's car phone number is PD 1246.

Perry's and Paul's Drinks: As portrayed in the books and on television, Perry is not a big drinker. He sometimes has a glass of champagne or other wine and occasionally a cocktail, but when he goes to dinner – and often he is so busy he doesn't take time to dine out – he usually has coffee along with a steak and potato. In the first of the Perry Mason novels, *The Case of the Velvet Claws* (1933), Perry orders a bottle of whiskey from the bellboy at the Hotel Ripley, even though prohibition is still in effect at the time.

In the 1964 television episode *The Case of the Careless Kidnapper* Perry suggests to Della that it's time to go to a nightclub, drink champagne and dance to dawn. In the novels, Perry keeps a bottle of rye in his office for Paul. At restaurants Paul sometimes orders a beer. In the 10th Mason book, *The Case of the Dangerous Dowager* (1937), Paul has a couple of drinks – Scotch and sodas – with Della.

Champagne is featured in a number of the Mason novels and TV shows. Sometimes, Della breaks out a bottle of champagne to celebrate winning a case. In one television episode, Perry suggests that he and Della go out and drink champagne and dance all night. In at least two of Perry's cases, the 1958 TV episode *The Case of the Lonely Heiress* and the 1960 episode *The Case of the Madcap Modiste,* victims are allegedly poisoned while drinking champagne, in the former through the introduction of prussic acid through the cork of a champagne bottle and in the latter from a pill taken with champagne.

Perry's Poisoned Champagne Cocktail

3 oz. champagne
2 dashes Angostura bitters
1 sugar cube
¼ oz. cognac

Put two dashes Angostura bitters on a sugar cube and drop it into champagne flute. Add the cognac. Gently pour chilled champagne into the flute. If desired, garnish with orange slice. Note: It's not really poison!

About Author Erle Stanley Gardner:

Erle Stanley Gardner was born in Malden, Mass., in 1889, the second of three sons of a self-taught civil engineer and his wife, both from New England families of long standing. His mother's family claimed to have come over on the *Mayflower,* and his father said he was descended from a line of Nantucket sea captains. When the future author was around 10, the family moved west to Oroville, Calif., then a rough gold-mining town, where there was another civil engineering job waiting. The boy, who usually spelled his name Earl or Earle until he was in high school, generally was a good student, although due to disputes with his school principal he was suspended several times.

After graduating from Oroville (now Palo Alto) High School, Gardner briefly attended Valparaiso University in Indiana, intending to study law, but left after only a few weeks. He then began reading law in various lawyers' offices in California.

In those days, neither undergraduate college work nor a law degree was required for admission to the California bar, and indeed there was an active debate in the profession on whether a formal legal degree or an apprenticeship produced a better lawyer. Still today in California, and in a handful of other states, an apprenticeship can be substituted for *a juris doctor* degree. Now in California the apprenticeship program has formal requirements for supervision with periodic reports and exams over a minimum of four years.

Gardner took the California bar exam in 1911, passed it and became an attorney at age 21. He rented an office in Merced, Calif., and hung out his shingle. Gardner soon moved to Oxnard in Ventura County, where he practiced law for 20 years. Like most small-town lawyers, Gardner had a varied practice, involving business and contract law, family law, civil disputes and some criminal cases. He later said he didn't like the routine practice of law but did enjoy trial work, especially trying cases in front of a jury.

Gardner married Natalie "Nat" Talbert in 1912, and in 1915 the young attorney became a partner the established law practice of Frank Orr in the town of Ventura, the county seat of Ventura County. Orr handled the corporate side of the practice, and Gardner did the trial work, winning most of his cases with his courtroom dramatics and strong self-confidence. Although Frank Orr remained the Gardner family attorney for the rest of his life, the initial partnership was only for about two years, as Gardner was talked into joining a longtime friend's manufacturers' agent business, traveling around the West and Midwest. Gardner's sales career lasted about three years. In 1921, after a period of post-war success, the business went broke, and Gardner returned to his law practice in Ventura with Frank Orr.

About the same time, Gardner began trying to become a writer, thinking that if his law practice ever failed, as his sales career had, he would have a backup profession. Gardner attempted to break into the pulps, but at first had little success in placing stories. In 1923, he finally sold a story to *Black Mask*. He was paid $160. With that sale, Gardner was launched in his career as a paid professional writer. He continued to practice law by day and to bang out stories on his typewriter at night. After a full day at the office, after dinner he would work on his pulp stories until 1 or 2 am. It was grueling work, and success came slowly.

After two or three years of trying to invent characters and plots, Gardner came up with what he later said was one of his most useful and successful ideas. He invented a "plot machine," a cardboard wheel with spokes radiating from the center.

Some of the spokes had brief character sketches, some had story situations and others had unexpected complications and conflict development. When Gardner revolved the spokes, where the characters, situations and conflicts came together often would suggest a plot.

Using the plot machine, Gardner claimed he could come up with a new plot in 30 seconds. While critics call his writing pedestrian, Gardner always has been considered a genius at plotting. In his novels, Gardner purposefully avoided long narrative descriptions. He justifiably felt that his readers wanted action and crisp dialogue and that descriptions of places or characters only slowed down the action.

It was also about this time that Gardner began dictating his stories, instead of writing them in longhand or, in his two-fingered style, on a typewriter. He began dictating his stories at night to his legal secretary, Jean Bethell. Although dictation allowed Gardner to work fast, sometimes churning out a complete novel plus several short stories or articles a month, his practice of dictating sometimes means that narrative elements and dialogue are repeated several times in slightly different ways, and other errors creep in. Readers also may feel that the Gardner stories are unnecessarily wordy, as if the author was still being paid by the word.

Gardner set for himself the goal of writing 100,000 words a month, a long short story or short novelette every three or four days. In 1925, Gardner found a New York agent, Robert Thomas Hardy, to represent him. The next year, 1926, Gardner and his agent sold 97 of Gardner's stores, including 26 to *Black Mask* and 15 to another pulp, *Top Notch.* He made more than $6,000 that year from his writing, at least $90,000 in today's dollars.

By the early 1930s, although Gardner was making almost $20,000 a year from his pulp writing, more than $350,000 in today's money. However, Gardner's agent Hardy was urging the author to do a novel, with the possibility that the novel would be serialized for big money in one of the "slicks" such as the *Saturday Evening Post* or *Collier's.* Gardner, still busy with his law practice and in writing for the pulps, at first demurred.

Gardner did write the book-length *The Log of a Landlubber* about his yacht trip to Alaska, but Hardy was never able to place it as a book. *Landlubber* was eventually serialized in the magazine *Pacific Motor Boat.*

Finally, Gardner came up with two mystery novels, originally titled *Reasonable Doubt* and *Silent Verdict.* Both were turned down by the slicks for serialization.

In late 1932, agent Hardy took drafts of Gardner's first two novels to Thayer Hobson, president of the publishing firm of William Morrow and Company, which had been established in 1926. This would eventually become one of the great publishing relationships of the 20th century.

After total rewrites of Gardner's first two novels, with the lawyers in each of the books combined into the Perry Mason character, William Morrow published the first Mason novel, *The Case of the Velvet Claws*, in March 1933 and *The Case of the Sulky Girl* in September of that year. Although the characters would evolve over the years, the initial books introduced most of the main characters including Perry, Della and Paul.

Gardner at this time was podunking – now usually called boondocking – in his campers and trailers in the desert. He wrote at a terrific pace. At one point, in an eight-day period he dictated three novelettes and almost all of a novel. Gardner called his camp wagon train, complete with his wife, Nat, and three secretaries – all sisters, Jean Bethell, Ruth (Honey) Moore and Peggy Down – to handle the dictation, typing and editing, his "Fiction Factory" on wheels. Later, his secretarial staff grew to number five. At times, he completed four to eight books a year, plus non-fiction articles, novelettes and short stories.

The lawyer-author remained with what had become the law firm of Sheridan, Orr, Drapeau and Gardner until the success of *The Case of the Velvet Claws,* set at the historic Pierpont Inn near the law firm, and other early Perry Mason novels. In 1937, he moved to Temecula, Calif., buying a ranch. He made the ranch, called Rancho del Paisano, his primary home for the rest of his life.

Over the course of his working life, the prolific writer produced 86 Perry Mason novels from 1933 to 1973. The last five Perry Mason novels were published after the author's death in 1970. Also, Gardner wrote 29 Bertha Cool and Donald Lam novels published under the pseudonym A. A. Fair, along with a total of 17 other novels, most under pseudonyms, and 15 non-fiction books, primarily about travel in Mexico. In addition, he published scores of short stories, novelettes and non-fiction articles. He typically knocked out a million words or more a year.

In the 1940s, Gardner expanded his reach with a contract deal with the new Pocket Books company for publishing his books in inexpensive paperback format. Under the 1940 contract, Gardner was guaranteed $100,000 a year in royalties, the equivalent of $1.7 million today.

By 1960, Gardner had sold more than 100 million copies of his books in Pocket Book format alone.

According to Alice Payne Hackett's *Seventy Years of Best Sellers,* a study of best-selling books from 1895 to 1965, only 151 mystery books during that period sold more than a million copies. Of these, 91 were written by Erle Stanley Gardner, either under his own name or under the pseudonym A. A. Fair.

Gardner was founder and member of the Court of Last Resort (later the Case Review Committee) from 1948 to 1960, a real-life association of crime experts and investigators who reopened cases wherein a person might have been falsely convicted. His nonfiction account of this organization's cases won him the 1952 Fact Crime Edgar Alan Poe Award from the *Mystery Writers of America,* an organization he helped found. In 1961, he won the Grand Master Award from the *Mystery Writers of America.*

A number of Perry Mason movies were filmed in the 1930s and 1940s, including six Warner Bros. products starting with *The Case of the Howling Dog* in 1934 with Warren William as Mason. William starred in a total of four Mason movies in the 1930s, including the 1936 film version of the original novel in the series, *The Case of the Velvet Claws.* The Warner series ends with *The Case of the Stuttering Bishop* in 1937, with Donald Woods playing Perry. Gardner was unhappy with most of these screen versions of his books.

In the 1940s, the Perry Mason books reached a new market through radio. In October 1943, the "Perry Mason Show" went on the air, initially as a 30-minute daytime soap opera. The Mason radio show stayed on the air for 12 years, with a total of 3,221 shows and a variety of different actors playing Perry, Della and Paul, the last broadcast airing on December 30, 1955.

By the 1950s, radio was in eclipse and television became the dominant medium. Gardner received a number of offers from television producers, but remembering the failure of most of the Mason movies, he turned down the offers. In television, the author was determined to control all of the rights and to have approval on scripts and key actors. To that end, Gardner formed Paisano Productions, named after his Rancho del Paisano in Temecula.

Gardner lucked upon Gail Patrick, a former minor movie star who was married to Corney Jackson, a J. Walter Thompson vice president in charge of the giant ad agency's Hollywood office. Patrick, who usually was credited on the show as Gail Patrick Jackson, turned out to be the ideal executive producer for the show.

Patrick, along with the show's first producer, Ben Brady, were instrumental in casting Raymond Burr as Perry, Barbara Hale as Della, William Hopper as Paul, William Talman as District Attorney Hamilton Burger and Ray Collins as homicide detective Arthur Tragg. Patrick also helped craft the style of the show and kept watch on its many scriptwriters, including notables such as Stirling Silliphant. Gardner himself took a keen interest in the television show and was often involved, if at a distance, in making changes in scripts. He, along with many other behind-the-scenes people, made a cameo appearance as the judge in the last *Perry Mason* episode.

The *Perry Mason* show debuted on CBS on September 21, 1957. It was an instant success and in its Saturday night slot was one of the top-ranked shows on television for almost nine years, through 271 episodes, until its last broadcast on May 22, 1966.

Perry Mason has aired in syndication in the United States and internationally ever since its cancellation, and the complete series has been released on DVD. A 2014 study found that Netflix users rate Raymond Burr as their favorite actor, with Barbara Hale number seven.

A second television series, *The New Perry Mason* starring Monte Markham, ran from 1973 to 1974. Also, 30 Perry Mason made-for-TV movies aired from 1985 to 1995, with Raymond Burr reprising the role of Mason in 26 of them.

Throughout much of his career, despite his high productivity and earnings that placed him near the top of writers of his time, Gardner had trouble staying ahead of the game financially. Occasionally he had to seek advances from his main publisher, William Morrow.

The reason wasn't so much that he didn't earn enough; rather, it was that he spent too much. Gardner traveled the West in his "camper," an early version of a recreational vehicle, and sometimes had a caravan of two or three campers and trailers. He bought land in several parts of the Western U.S. and Mexico so that he could podunk in his campers on his own properties. Eventually the ranch he bought in Temecula grew to some 3,000 acres with more than two dozen buildings. Gardner routinely had several full-time secretaries working for him, along with household and ranch staff, and even after he and Nat separated, he continued to pay many of her bills. He had many friends whom he hosted and entertained graciously. Gardner also traveled extensively in Latin America, the South Pacific and elsewhere.

Erle, who some called a "natural born bachelor," and his wife, Nat, separated in the early 1930s. They remained married until Nat's death in 1968 but never lived together again. The couple had one child, Grace, born in 1913. Not long after Nat's death, Gardner married his long-time secretary, Jean Bethell. Some noted that this is what fans of Gardner long had wanted Perry Mason to do, to tie the knot with his confidential secretary Della Street.

Gardner died on March 11, 1970, of cancer. At the time of his death, Gardner was the best-selling author in America.

Perry Mason Novels by Erle Stanley Gardner

All of the Perry Mason novels began with "The Case of ..." making them immediately identifiable as part of the Gardner oeuvre.

The Case of the Velvet Claws (1933)
The Case of the Sulky Girl (1933)
The Case of the Lucky Legs (1934)
The Case of the Howling Dog (1934)
The Case of the Curious Bride (1934)
The Case of the Counterfeit Eye (1935)
The Case of the Caretaker's Cat (1935)
The Case of the Sleepwalker's Niece (1936)
The Case of the Stuttering Bishop (1936)
The Case of the Dangerous Dowager (1937)
The Case of the Lame Canary (1937)
The Case of the Substitute Face (1938)
The Case of the Shoplifter's Shoe (1938)
The Case of the Perjured Parrot (1939)
The Case of the Rolling Bones (1939)
The Case of the Baited Hook (1940)
The Case of the Silent Partner (1940)
The Case of the Haunted Husband (1941)
The Case of the Empty Tin (1941)
The Case of the Drowning Duck (1942)
The Case of the Careless Kitten (1942)
The Case of the Buried Clock (1943)
The Case of the Drowsy Mosquito (1943)
The Case of the Crooked Candle (1940)
The Case of the Black-Eyed Blonde (1944)
The Case of the Gold-Digger's Purse (1942)
The Case of the Half-Wakened Wife (1945)
The Case of the Borrowed Brunette (1946)
The Case of the Fan Dancer's Horse (1947)

The Case of the Lazy Lover (1947)
The Case of the Lonely Heiress (1948)
The Case of the Vagabond Virgin (1948)
The Case of the Dubious Bridegroom (1949)
The Case of the Cautious Coquette (1949)
The Case of the Negligent Nymph (1950)
The Case of the One-Eyed Witness (1956)
The Case of the Fiery Fingers (1951)
The Case of the Angry Mourner (1951)
The Case of the Moth-Eaten Mink (1952)
The Case of the Grinning Gorilla (1952)
The Case of the Hesitant Hostess (1953)
The Case of the Green-Eyed Sister (1953)
The Case of the Fugitive Nurse (1954)
The Case of the Runaway Corpse (1954)
The Case of the Restless Redhead (1954)
The Case of the Glamorous Ghost (1955)
The Case of the Sun Bather's Diary (1955)
The Case of the Nervous Accomplice (1955)
The Case of the Terrified Typist (1956)
The Case of the Demure Defendant (1956)
The Case of the Gilded Lily (1956)
The Case of the Lucky Loser (1957)
The Case of the Screaming Woman (1957)
The Case of the Daring Decoy (1957)
The Case of the Long-Legged Models (1958)
The Case of the Foot-Loose Doll (1958)
The Case of the Calendar Girl (1958)
The Case of the Deadly Toy (1959)
The Case of the Mythical Monkeys (1959)
The Case of the Singing Skirt (1959)
The Case of the Waylaid Wolf (1960)
The Case of the Duplicate Daughter (1960)
The Case of the Shapely Shadow (1960)
The Case of the Spurious Spinster (1961)
The Case of the Bigamous Spouse (1961)
The Case of the Reluctant Model (1962)
The Case of the Blonde Bonanza (1962)
The Case of the Ice-Cold Hands (1962)
The Case of the Mischievous Doll (1963)
The Case of the Stepdaughter's Secret (1963)

The Case of the Amorous Aunt (1963)
The Case of the Daring Divorcee (1964)
The Case of the Phantom Fortune (1964)
The Case of the Horrified Heirs (1964)
The Case of the Troubled Trustee (1965)
The Case of the Beautiful Beggar (1965)
The Case of the Worried Waitress (1966)
The Case of the Queenly Contestant (1967)
The Case of the Careless Cupid (1968)
The Case of the Fabulous Fake (1969)
The Case of the Murderer's Bride (1969)
The Case of the Crimson Kiss (1971)
The Case of the Crying Swallow (1971)
The Case of the Irate Witness (1972)
The Case of the Fenced in Woman (1972)
The Case of the Postponed Murder (1973)

Notable Works on Perry Mason and Erle Stanley Gardner

Davidson, Jim, *The Perry Mason Book: A Comprehensive Guide to America's Favorite Defender of Justice* (2014). An obsessively detailed review of Everything Perry Mason, including lists of all of the Mason short stories, novels and individual radio and television shows, complete with all actors, producers, directions, writers and locations. It even includes the license numbers of cars used by key Perry Mason characters and, where known, their fictional telephone numbers and street addresses.

Hughes, Dorothy B., *The Case of the Real Perry Mason, A Biography* (1978). The only book-length Erle Stanley Gardner biography, by a mystery writer and the mystery book critic for the *Los Angeles Times.*

Adrian Monk

From the TV series co-created by Andy Breckman and related novelizations

"It's a gift, and a curse."
Adrian Monk from the *Monk* television show

Adrian Monk is the psychologically challenged detective played by the award=winning actor Tony Shalhoub. The series originally appeared on the USA Today network beginning in 2002. The highly successful show continued for 125 episodes over eight seasons, ending in mid-2009. The series remains in syndication and on streaming services. Following the early success of the television show, the Monk character appeared in 15 novels written by Lee Goldberg and then in four novels by Hy Conrad.

Monk's backstory is that he was a homicide detective with the San Francisco Police Department, high achieving despite some psychological issues, including obsessive-compulsive disorder and a personality disorder that may have been on the autism scale. When his beloved wife, Trudy, is killed by a car bomb, Monk has a nervous breakdown and is discharged from the police force.

After being a recluse for three and a half years, never leaving his house, Monk is helped by his psychiatrist, Dr. Charles Kroger, played during the first six seasons of the show by Stanley Kamel, and by his nurse and assistant, Sharona Fleming, played by Bitty Schram, to partly recover. He becomes a private detective and frequently serves as a consultant to the SFPD.

Monk's obsessive-compulsive disorder and his many phobias and fears (312 by Monk's own count), while a major problem in his private life, often are extremely useful in his professional life. It is claimed that he never fails to solve a case, except that of the murder of his wife, which is resolved in the series' last episode. He is extraordinarily focused on details, including those that escape other detectives, and he has what amounts to a photographic memory.

The OCD detective is able to function mainly due to the help of his nurse-assistant Sharona. After Sharona leaves to go back to her husband in New Jersey in the third season, she is replaced by another assistant, Natalie Teeger, played by Traylor Howard in the rest of the series. Sharona practices a kind of tough love with Monk. Natalie is less pushy than the loud, outgoing Sharona, and she is more deferential, occasionally to the point of being passive-aggressive, and calls him "Mr. Monk."

Adrian Monk is also supported by Captain Leland Stottlemeyer (Ted Levine), who formerly was Monk's partner when Monk was on the police force. Stottlemeyer has become head of the homicide division of the SFPD. He frequently stands up for Monk and uses him as a consultant on difficult murder cases.

Lieutenant Randy Disher (Jason Gray-Standford) is a well-meaning but sometimes naive and ineffectual assist to Captain Stottlemeyer. It all ends well, however, as in the eighth season he begins a relationship with Sharona. In the series finale he moves to New Jersey to live with Sharona and becomes chief of police of the town of Summit.

Other continuing characters include Kevin Dorfman (Jarrad Paul), Monk's irritating upstairs neighbor, a talkative accounting and budding magician, from season 2 until season 7, when he is killed. Dr. Charles Kroger (Stanley Kamel) is Monk's wise and helpful psychiatrist for the first six seasons. After the actor died of a heart attack in 2008, he is replaced on the show's last two seasons by actor Héctor Elizondo, who plays psychiatrist Dr. Neven Bell, who looks and sounds remarkably like Monk's first shrink. Harold Krenshaw (Tim Bagley) is a fellow patient of Monk's psychiatrists and often tries to outdo Monk in everything. Ambrose Monk (John Tururrow) is Monk's brother. He has a serious case of agoraphobia and seldom leaves his house.

Although Monk is a brilliant detective, his obsessive-compulsive behavior ("he has more tics than a junkyard dog," one promo for the show claims) and many phobias make working or even being with him a trial for his friends and co-workers. Most scenes are partly played for comedic effect, but the program has its share of violence – the scene in "Mister Monk and the 12th Man" where a toll-booth taker is dragged to his death by a motorist-killer is unforgettable – and pathos, especially on the many occasions when Monk recalls his wife Trudy.

Monk co-creator and head writer Andy Breckman has always claimed that he based Shahloub's character on Sherlock Holmes. "Quick, brilliant, analytical ... [with] an encyclopedic knowledge of a dozen unconventional and assorted subjects, from door locks to horticulture to architecture to human psychology," Beckman has been quoted as saying about Monk. Breckman also said he based Monk's brother Ambrose to some extent on Holmes' brother Mycroft. Of course, hundreds if not thousands of detectives over the years have been based on Arthur Conan Doyle's famous character.

Monk was so popular that a long series of books was written to take advantage of the success of the television show. The first 15 books were by Lee Goldberg, a screenwriter on the *Monk* show, and the last four by Hy Conrad, co-executive producer and screenwriter for the TV program. All of the novels are narrated by Natalie Teeger. Several of the books were the basis for episodes of the *Monk* TV show.

Monk's Digs, Drives and Drinks: In the television series, Monk lives in San Francisco, first in an apartment and later in a house. He doesn't drive; Sharona or Natalie drive him everywhere. Monk rarely drinks alcohol (in one episode, he does accidentally drink a little wine, with hilarious results). His drink of choice is bottled water, and the only brand he will drink in the first five seasons of the TV show is Sierra Springs, a real brand based in Sacramento and sold mostly in California and the West. After this, he switches to a fictitious brand, Summit Creek.

About Monk Co-Creator and Head Writer Andy Breckman:

Andrew Ross Breckman was born in Philadelphia March 3, 1955, grew up in a middle-class Jewish family in Haddonfield, N.J. (his father was an engineer and him mother a homemaker who did community theater), attended a Quaker high school for a while and dropped out of Boston University during his freshman year. After moving to New York in the early 1980s, he went on the folk music and comedy circuits. He later recorded a couple of now-forgotten folk music albums. His idols, he says, were Bob Dylan, Loudon Wainwright and Randy Newman, who wrote the title song, "It's a Jungle Out There," for the *Monk* show used in seasons 2 to 8. Newman's song won the 2004 Emmy for Best Main Title Music. During the first season an instrumental intro by songwriter Jeff Beal performed by guitarist Grant Geissman also won an Emmy for Best Main Title Music.

A writing gig on an obscure NBC show for teens called *Hot Hero Sandwich* brought him to the attention of the *David Letterman Show,* and Breckman wrote sketches for Letterman's first two seasons. From Letterman, Breckman moved on to *Saturday Night Live.* He was a writer there from 1981 to 1987. In the late 1980s through the 1990s, he wrote screenplays, including scripts for 1994 comedy *I.Q.*, with Walter Matthau as Einstein, *Sgt. Bilko* with Steve Martin in 1996 and the 2001 chase comedy *Rat Race.* Since 1992, he has co-hosted a weekly one-hour call-in comedy show, "Seven Second Delay," on WFMU Radio in Jersey City, N.J.

When veteran producer David Hoberman approached Breckman with the idea for a TV show about an OCD detective, Breckman jumped at the idea, even though he had mostly done comedy before, not crime shows. Hoberman, who has claimed that he himself is OCD, in a newspaper interview said, "Like Monk, I couldn't walk on cracks and had to touch poles. I have no idea why – but if I didn't do these things, something terrible would happen." After a stint at Metro-Goldwyn-Mayer, Hoberman helped bring back a production company he had previously established, Mandeville Films, and has produced a number of films with Disney Studios, including *Honey, I Shrank the Kids, The Shaggy Dog* and *The Muppets.* Over the course of his career, Hoberman has produced more than 40 movies.

Hoberman and Breckman pitched the *Monk* show to ABC, which turned it down, but USA Network agreed to do it.

Breckman, whose titles on the show included executive producer and head writer, lives with his second wife, Beth Landau in Madison, N.J. During the life of the *Monk* series, he flew to Los Angeles once a month.

About Tony Shalhoub:

The best decision Breckman and Hoberman made was to choose Tony Shalhoub for the role of the OCD detective.

Anthony Marcus Shalhoub, one of 10 children of a Lebanese immigrant family, was born October 9, 1953, in Green Bay, Wisc., and grew up there. His father was a meat peddler who drove a refrigerated truck and sold to area groceries. Later he opened a grocery store in downtown Green Bay. Shalhoub remains a Green Bay Packers fan and has season tickets. He earned a degree in drama from Southern Maine University and attended graduate school in drama at Yale.

Shalhoub spent four seasons with the American Repertory Theater in Cambridge, Mass., before moving to New York, where he got a number of roles in Off-Broadway and Broadway productions. He was nominated for a 1992 Tony for his featured role in Conv*ersations with My Father,* the Pulitzer Prize-nominated play by Herb Gardner. It was also in a Broadway play where he met his wife, the actress Brooke Adams.

In the 1990s, Shalhoub had a number of roles, mostly supporting ones, in television series and movies. His biggest TV gig was as an Italian cab driver for six seasons in the sitcom *Wings.* After that he snagged roles in two Coen brothers films, played the sleazy pawn shop owner, Jack Geebs, in *Men in Black* and *Men in Black 2* and a Cuban-American businessman in *Primary Colors.*

Shahloub's biggest film role was in 1998's thriller *The Seige,* in which he co-starred with Denzel Washington and Bruce Willis.

In 1999, Shalhoub starred as the horror novelist Ian Stark in the NBC comedy series *Stark Raving Mad.* Start is rather odd and is obsessed with playing practical jokes. Stark's editor, Henry McNeeley, played by Neal Patrick Harris, has a number of phobias and may well be OCD. The series, which ran for 22 episodes, ended in April 2000. Shahloub's role in this short-lived but fairly successful comedy may have contributed to his selection for the role of Adrian Monk.

As noted, the idea for the OCD defective detective had been bandied about for several years, first with ABC, which could never get the right people in place. Originally, Michael Richards, who played Kramer in *Seinfeld*, was considered for the role.

Around 2000, there were some personnel changes at USA Network, and one of the ABC execs came to USA, Jackie de Crinis, and brought the Monk idea with her, along with a script she had worked on, "Mr. Monk and the Candidate."

At USA, a number of actors, including Henry Winkler, Dave Foley and John Ritter, were considered, but none seemed exactly right for the role. Jeff Wachtel, executive vice president of original programming at USA Network, had three actors in mind that he thought would be good for the starring role: Stanley Tucci, Alfred Molina, and Tony Shalhoub. Tucci and Molina had other commitments, and in fact Shalhoub did as well – he had recently completed a pilot for another network and was temporarily prohibited from signing on with USA until a decision on the pilot had been made. (That pilot was never picked up, so Shalhoub became available.) Wachtel, David Hoberman and Andy Breckman wanted Shalhoub and pitched him strongly for the part. Shalhoub liked the idea, so Breckman expanded the existing de Crinis script into a pilot, in collaboration with Shalhoub, who became co-producer on the pilot along with Breckman and Hoberman. The *Monk* pilot did well, and USA Network commissioned the first season of 12 episodes, plus the pilot.

In addition to the starring role, Shalhoub also was the co-producer of 13 episodes on *Monk* in 2002 and an executive producer on the remaining 112 episodes from 2003 to 2009.

Over the course of the series, Shalhoub won three Emmys as Outstanding Lead Actor in a Comedy Series (2003, 2005 and 2006) and a 2003 Golden Globe award for Best Performance as an Actor in a Television Series.

Monk always did well in the cable TV ratings, and its final episode in 2009 was ranked the highest watched hour-long cable TV program in history up to that time, with 9.4 million viewers tuned in. An episode of *The Walking Dead* out pulled it in 2012.

In 1993 Shalhoub and his wife Brooke Adams bought a Mediterranean style house in the Windsor Square area of Los Angeles, where they and their two adopted children lived. They sold the house in 2016. Since the late 1990s, Adams and Shalhoub also have owned a 5,500-square-foot "cottage" on six acres near Chilmark Pond on Martha's Vineyard.

Notable Works about Monk

Erdmann, Terry J. and Block, Paula M., *Monk: The Official Episode Guide* (2006). This is the ultimate guide for the *Monk* TV series fan, at least for the first four seasons. It has detailed episode-by-episode descriptions of the plots and characters of each episode. It is filled with detailed inside information, as the writers did extensive interviews with writers and actors. They also had access to the sets and scripts.

Ellery Queen

From the Ellery Queen novels and short stories by Frederic Dannay (1905-1982) and Manfred Bennington Lee (1905-1971) and the Ellery Queen movies and radio and television programs

"It was wrong. It was like arresting the gun for murder."
– Ellery Queen, *The Player on the Other Side*

"Ellery Queen" Daniel Nathan (left) and Emanuel Lepofsky

Ellery Queen was a fictional amateur detective *and* fictional mystery writer created by two cousins in Brooklyn – Frederic Dannay, a pseudonym of Daniel Nathan, and Manfred Bennington Lee, a pseudonym of Emanuel Benjamin Lepofsky.

The fictional detective, Ellery Queen, is also the fictional author of the books he writes, if you can get your mind around that. However, Ellery Queen does not usually narrate the books, which are generally told by an omniscient narrator in the third person. The precedent for this unusual approach of the author and main character having the same name was the "Nick Carter, Master Detective," series of dime novels, produced from the 1880s by a variety of writers using the Nick Carter pen name for Street and Smith Publications.

Confused yet? It gets even more confusing, when you throw in the fact that the cousins later licensed the Ellery Queen name to other writers, who turned out mysteries "written by Ellery Queen," but which did *not* feature the fictional Queen.

Ellery Queen appeared in 30 novels by Dannay and Lee, under the Ellery Queen pen name. If you include Ellery Queen novels partially or completely ghost-written by other authors the number is much larger.

The cousins also were prolific historians, anthologists and editors of mystery fiction, publishing numerous collections of Sherlock Holmes and other detective fiction.

In addition, Frederic Dannay, with a little help from his cousin, created a hugely popular detective magazine, *Ellery Queen's Mystery Magazine*, which is still published today. There were also nine English-language Ellery Queen movies in the 1930s and 1940s, and others in the 1970s. As well, many Ellery Queen shows were on radio in the 1930s and 1940s.

The fictional Ellery Queen often worked, in an unofficial capacity, with his father, New York Police Inspector Richard Queen, who sometimes appeared as his uncle instead of his father. Inspector Queen, and even his boss, the New York Commissioner of Police, frequently seek Ellery Queen's help in solving tough crimes, such as identifying the serial killer, the Cat, in *Cat of Many Tails* (1949), so the Ellery Queen works have elements of both the amateur sleuth and the police procedural.

Ellery Queen arguably was the best-known name in mystery during the 1930s to the early 1950s. Ellery Queen novels and short story collections sold in the tens of millions. While less read today, many of the Ellery Queen novels are well written and are excellent examples of the genre. Queen is probably due for a comeback.

In the early days of television, an Ellery Queen show appeared in 1950-1952, returned briefly in 1954 and again in 1958-59, mostly on ABC, with a variety of actors playing Queen.

In 1975, another Ellery Queen television series starring Jim Hutton as an excellent Ellery ran for one season on NBC. Hutton died of cancer the year after the show was canceled.

Now, let's refocus on the Ellery Queen, the famed but fictional amateur detective and mystery writer:

We first meet Ellery Queen in *The Roman Hat Mystery,* written in 1927 but not published until 1929. Its style echoes that of S. S. Van Dine's *Philo Vance* novels.

In at least the early novels and stories, Ellery is presented as a snobbish Harvard graduate, an intellectual with a private income who solves mysteries because he enjoys the challenge. His mother is said to be a wealthy New York aristocrat married to an earthy New York City police officer, Richard Queen. Inspector Queen's assistant is Sergeant Thomas Velie. In the early works, Ellery is married and has a child, but in later books and stories he is a bachelor with occasional romantic interests.

The first Ellery Queen novels and stories follow the classic "puzzle" style of W. S. Van Dine and what would soon be seen as the golden age of mystery writing. These puzzle mysteries are also called "locked-room mysteries" although many don't involve an actual locked room. But this style of detective story presents a series of clues to the reader, supposedly in a "fair play" way so that everything the detective learns are also available to the reader, although red herrings and false solutions make figuring out the solution more difficult for the reader.

The early Ellery Queen works novels employed a "challenge to the reader," a page near the end of the book that sets out the main clues and challenges the reader to solve the mystery. Later Queen novels dropped this challenge. This same technique reappeared in the 1970s TV series starring Jim Hutton, as near the end of the show Hutton breaks the "fourth wall," the imaginary wall at the front of the stage or on a screen set. Ellery turns and speaks to the camera, noting that all the clues have been shown and asking the viewer if he or she can solve the mystery.

The Chinese Orange Mystery (1934), the eighth Ellery Queen novel, is worth noting because it has one of the strangest set-ups in mystery history. Most of the story takes place on the 22nd floor of a Manhattan hotel, where are located the offices and apartment of Donald Kirk, a wealthy publisher, socialite and collector, and of Kirk's sister, wheelchair-bound father and his father's nurse. One autumn afternoon, an ordinary looking man comes to the hotel seeking to see Kirk. Kirk's secretary tells him he isn't it, but the man elects to wait.

Over the course of an hour, several other people drop by, and then Kirk and his friend Ellery Queen show up. They find everything in the room turned upside down or inside out. Pictures and clocks on the walls are turned around, lamps are standing on their shades, the rug is turned over. The unknown visitor is dead, and every article of his clothing – shirt, suit jacket, shoes and so on – is on him backwards. Two African spears are thrust up his trouser legs, with the spearheads out at the waist. Chinese orange (tangerine peels) are in a fruit bowl.

What would you make of that? Without giving away the solution, we'll note that it involves the old rope trick.

Over the course of late the 1920s to 1960s when the Ellery Queen books and stories were mostly written, Ellery Queen, his life story and his relationships change significantly. In later books and stories, Ellery Queen becomes more empathetic and less the intellectual snob, although he remains very observant, smart and logical.

Works in the middle and later Ellery Queen periods become less focused on classic mystery puzzles, loosening the formula and providing more opportunity for character development and new plot twists.

Ellery Queen's Digs: In some Ellery Queen books and stories, the father and son share a bachelor apartment in a three-story brownstone at West 87th Street in Manhattan.

At one point, Ellery moves to Hollywood, working on movie scripts. Then, as recounted in three novels, Ellery lives in the small town of Wrightsville, N.Y. He sometimes returns to that rural retreat for vacations in later days. After the Hollywood and Wrightsville periods, Ellery returns to Manhattan and to his bachelor apartment with his father.

Ellery Queen's Drives: Over the course of the many Ellery Queen novels and short stories, including those licensed to other writers, Ellery Queen drives or is driven in many different vehicles.

In the likeable 1975-76 television show starring Jim Hutton, set inn the 1940s, Ellery's personal car in some shows is 1938 Packard Six Club Coupe. In other scenes Ellery is seen driving a DeSoto De Luxe, probably a 1946 model.

Ellery is sometimes portrayed as being a poor driver. He also often is picked up in a police car assigned to his father.

Ellery Queen's Drinks: While not a teetotaler, Ellery is not a big drinker. In one novel, when offered a Scotch he goes so far as to turn it down!

About Frederic Dannay and Manfred Bennington Lee:

The men who called themselves Frederic Dannay and Manfred B. Lee were born in 1905, nine months and five blocks apart, in Brooklyn's Brownsville district. The two, whose birth names were, respectively, David Nathan and Manford Leposky, were distant cousins, both of Russian Jewish heritage.

The Nathan family moved to Elmira, N.Y., when David was a baby and the young-writer-to-be spent the first 12 years of his life in the small Upstate town where Mark Twain had spent many summers. The Leposky family remained in the tenements of Brownsville. In 1917 the Nathan family moved back to Brooklyn, and soon the two cousins developed a close relationship, much like brothers. They went to high school together.

Manny Leposky then went to college at NYU, hoping to obtain graduate degrees and teach in college, but he was told by his NYU advisor that a Jew had little hope of getting tenure at any New York university. This was when he changed his name to the most un-Jewish name he could think of, Manfred Bennington Lee. He began working writing press releases for Pathé Pictures.

David Nathan dropped out of high school, to help support his family. Later he took some courses at the Arts' Students League but decided he would never be more than a second-rate artist. He then decided to try to pursue his interest in writing, taking the name Fredrick Dannay, the first name in honor of the composer Chopin and the second the first part of his birth name.

It was thanks to a magazine writing contest that the two cousins were launched on their careers as mystery writers. *McClure's Magazine* announced a contest for the best mystery novel, with a prize of $7,500, representing $5,000 for serial rights to the novel and $2,500 as an advance on the book edition. The two cousins decided to try for the prize. They came up with the pen name of Ellery Queen – Ellery was the name of Lee's best friend in Elmira, and Queen was suggested by a deck of cards – and together wrote what would become *The Roman Hat Mystery*.

This first Ellery Queen mystery was much influenced by the best-known detective character of the day, Philo Vance, created by art critic Willard Huntington Wright writing under the pen name S. S. Van Dine. The Wright/Van Dine novels such as *The "Canary" Murder Case* and *The Bishop Murder Case* are little read today, but they were wildly popular in the 1920s, and indeed these books played an important role in the development of the "puzzle" mystery genre perfected by Agatha Christie, John Dickson Carr, Ellery Queen and other writers of what would be called the "Golden Age" of mystery fiction.

All the submitted manuscripts had been given to the Curtis Brown literary agency, which represented both *McClure's* and the book publisher, Stokes. In 1929, the two cousins were told in confidence that their entry had won the prize. They were overjoyed, because the prize money, the equivalent of $100,000 or more in today's dollar, would have allowed them to become full-time writers. In what seemed at the time to be a cruel twist of fate, a short time later *McClure's Magazine* failed financially and was taken over by another magazine, *The Smart Set.* Editors of *The Smart Set* decided to award the prize to another entry.

However, Stokes still liked the Ellery Queen submission and agreed to publish *The Roman Hat Mystery*, with a total advance of just $400 (the equivalent of around $5,000 today). The debut novel, a puzzle mystery that involved a fast-acting poison, tetra ethyl lead, a little-known component of gasoline, ended up selling about 8,000 copies, good sales for a first novel. This delighted and encouraged Dannay and Lee, although they kept their day jobs in advertising and public relations. They began working on their second Ellery Queen, *The French Powder Mystery,* which was published in 1930. That was followed by *The Dutch Shoe Mystery* in 1931.

At this point, encourage by their literary agent, the two cousins decided to quit their regular jobs and become full-time writers. Working full time, they figured they could write four 90,000-word novels a year. However, that would be more Ellery Queen novels than the market could bear, so they started a second series featuring Drury Lane, an eccentric former Shakespearean actor turned amateur sleuth, who had left the stage due to deafness. The cousins wrote four Drury Lane novels under the pen name Barnaby Ross, starting with *The Tragedy of X.*

One of the best of the early Ellery Queen novels, *The Greek Coffin Mystery,* came out in 1932. In that same year, thanks to popularity of the Ellery Queen novels, Columbia University School of Journalism invited "Ellery Queen" to lecture on mystery writing. Manny Lee did the lecture, wearing a black mask to disguise his identity. About the same time, Frederic began speaking in public as Barnaby Ross, also wearing a mask. The two appeared together at lectures across the country, disguised as competing mystery writers.

Also in 1932, the two cousins began writing short stories featuring Ellery Queen. The next year, they started a magazine, *Mystery League,* to publish their own stories and those of other writers. *Mystery League* lasted for only four issues, but it gave the writers an entree to and an education in magazine publishing.

The Chinese Orange Mystery (1934) with its strange upside-down, backwards set-ups book sold well and made more money for the cousins than any Ellery Queen novel before, in part because it appeared in *Redbook* magazine, but it was not much appreciated by critics who thought the solution was outlandish. However, it has shown up on several top ten "best locked-door mystery" lists.

After *The Chinese Orange Mystery* and *The Spanish Cape Mystery* (1935), the next books in the Ellery Queen *oeuvre,* starting with *Halfway House* in 1936, moved away from the puzzle approach of the early novels patterned on Van Dine's novels, putting more emphasis on characterization and on romance. Near the end of his life, Frederic Dannay admitted this was an intentional effort to become more commercial, with the view of making highly remunerative sales to the slick magazines and to the movies. But it also had the effect of loosening up the format and allowing the cousins to do different kinds of mystery stories.

Ellery Queen Novels by Frederic Dannay and Manfred Bennington Lee

(Does not include ghost-written or licensed works.)

The Roman Hat Mystery (1929)
The French Powder Mystery (1930)
The Dutch Shoe Mystery (1931)
The Greek Coffin Mystery (1932)
The Egyptian Cross Mystery (1932)
The American Gun Mystery (1933)
The Siamese Twin Mystery (1933)
The Chinese Orange Mystery (1934)
The Spanish Cape Mystery (1935)
The Lamp of God (a novella, 1935)
Halfway House (1936)
The Door Between (1937)
The Devil to Pay (1938)
The Four of Hearts (1938)
The Dragon's Teeth also published as *The Virgin Heiresses* (1939)
Calamity Town (1942)
There Was an Old Woman also published as *The Quick and the Dead* (1943)
The Murderer is a Fox (1945)
Ten Days' Wonder (1948)
Cat of Many Tails (1949)
Double, Double (1950)
The Origin of Evil (1951)

The King is Dead (1952)
The Scarlet Letters (1953)
Inspector Queen's Own Case (1956, only brief appearance by Ellery Queen)
The Finishing Stroke (1958)
Face to Face (1967)
The Last Woman in His Life (1970)
A Fine and Private Place (1971)

Ellery Queen Short Story Collections by Frederic Dannay and Manfred Bennington Lee

(Does not include ghost-written or licensed works.)
The Adventures of Ellery Queen (1934)
The Ellery Queen Omnibus (1934)
The Ellery Queen Omnibus (1936)
Ellery Queen's Big Book (1938)
The New Adventures of Ellery Queen (1940)
More Adventures of Ellery Queen (1940)
Ellery Queen's Adventure Omnibus (1941)
The Wrightsville Murders (1942)
Ellery Queen's Mystery Parade (1944)
The Case Book of Ellery Queen (1945)
The Case Book of Ellery Queen (1949)
Calendar Of Crime (1952)
QBI: Queen's Bureau of Investigation (1955)
The Hollywood Murders (1957)
The New York Murders (1958)
The XYZ Murders (1961)
The Bizarre Murders (1962)
Queens Full (1966)
QED: Queen's Experiments In Detection (1966)
The Best Of Ellery Queen (1985)
The Tragedy Of Errors (1999)

Notable Works on Ellery Queen

Nevins, Francis M., *Ellery Queen: The Art of Detection* (2013). The best overview of the creators of Ellery Queen. In 1974, Nevins wrote an earlier book, *Royal Bloodline: Ellery Queen, Author and Detective,* which provided some material for the later book.

Nero Wolfe and Archie Goodwin

From the Nero Wolfe novels by Rex Stout (1896-1975)

"I am nobody's friend. How much can you pay?"
Nero Wolfe, in *Fer-de-Lance* by Rex Stout

Nero Wolfe, as portrayed by artist Carl Mueller in 1940

Nero Wolfe is the supersized, eccentric detective genius in more than 70 novels and novellas by Rex Stout. Wolfe was born in Montenegro, the small Balkan country in Southwestern Europe, bordered by the Adriatic Sea, Croatia, Serbia, Albania and Bosnia and Herzegovina. He speaks English fluently, along with six or seven other languages including his native one, a dialect of Serbo-Croatian.

Wolfe would prefer to spend all his time with his orchids, reading or eating and only takes cases when his bank balance falls too low.

Nearly everything we know about Nero Wolfe comes through the first-person narrator of the Wolfe stories, Archie Goodwin.

Goodwin is Wolfe's legman, errand boy, secretary, front man and occasional chauffeur. He is a licensed private detective who, when we first meet him in the first Wolfe novel, *Fer-de-Lance,* has been working for Wolfe for seven years. Archie, a high school grad in his mid-30s, is street smart, quick with a wisecrack, good with his fists, and he packs a pistol, sometimes a .32, sometimes a .38, sometimes both. He has an eye for good-looking women. His steadiest romantic companion is Lily Rowan, a wealthy socialite, but neither appears to have any interest in marriage.

Goodwin is as integral to the Nero Wolfe stories as Wolfe himself. Archie's appeal as a down-to-earth narrator, a foil to the foppish, pretentious, domineering and smugly brilliant Wolfe, doubtless is one of the keys to the series' continued popularity.

Wolfe is in his mid-40s and never ages throughout the five decades of the saga. The detective is highly knowledgeable about food, enough so to lecture on cooking to two groups of leading chefs, and enjoys eating three large meals every day, at fixed times. He has breakfast in his yellow silk pajamas in his bedroom, lunch usually at 1:15 and dinner at 7:30, sometimes 8. Wolfe only occasionally goes out to a restaurant, to Rusterman's, a white-tablecloth restaurant owned by his friend Marko Vukcic.

His meals at home are prepared by his long-time chef, Fritz Brenner. Wolfe especially enjoys shad roe, pressed duck, lamb, grouse and crab, and almost anything with lots of butter, cream and eggs, but he can also appreciate common American dishes such as chili, spareribs or cornbread. (See *The Nero Wolfe Cookbook* by Rex Stout, published in 1973.)

Today physicians would call Wolfe morbidly obese, although given the increase in the girth of a many Americans in recent decades, some of the frequent references to the detective's unusual size sound an odd note to current readers. Not particularly tall, Wolfe's weight is given variously from about 285 pounds (one-seventh of a ton) to 390 pounds. Once trim and in good condition when he was younger, when he was involved in intelligence work, Wolfe says, "I carry this fat to insulate my feelings."

The portly detective dislikes being touched and avoids shaking hands. He is a notorious misogynist who believes most women are prone to hysteria. The Wolfe household is run something like a men's club.

Wolfe's Digs: Wolfe lives in a luxurious three-story brownstone on West 35th Street in New York. He only rarely leaves the brownstone.

The exact street number is given in 10 different versions, perhaps to confuse Wolfe's enemies. The brownstone has a full basement made into living quarters for some of Wolfe's live-in staff and a roof top greenhouse for Wolfe's highly valuable collection of 10,000 orchids. His live-in gardener, Theodore Horstmann, helps Wolfe tend the orchids. Wolfe nearly invariably spends four hours a day with his orchids. His office is on the first floor, with a specially made chair to hold his bulk comfortably, a desk and chair for Archie, a red chair for clients and yellow chairs for others. Wolfe's living quarters are on the second floor. There is a small elevator generally reserved for his private use. Archie Goodwin lives rent-free in the West 35th brownstone, on the floor above Wolfe's living quarters.

Wolfe's Drives: Wolfe owns a Heron motorcar, a fictitious brand that may have been suggested by the stylized heron mascots or hood ornaments of Cadillac and LaSalle cars of the time. Rex Stout owned and drove Cadillacs.

Wolfe's Drinks: Although Nero Wolfe claims expertise in fine wines and brandies, his great love and regular drink is beer. And a lot of it.

Wolfe generally drinks five or six quarts of beer a day, a dozen or so bottles, with his first beer taken at 11 am. In the initial novel, set as Prohibition was ending, Wolfe buys bootleg beer by the keg, but after the repeal of Prohibition his chef Fritz Brenner brings a selection of 49 kinds of beer for Wolfe to taste. Out of all of them Wolfe chooses Remmer beer as his favorite. Remmer is a light lager originally brewed by the Wilhelm Remmer company in Bremen, Germany. The Remmer brewery was merged into Beck's. It is unclear how Fritz is able to keep Remmer in stock, as even before World War II Remmer primarily was distributed by Beck's only in Germany, but the Swiss-born Fritz doubtless has his sources.

The first recorded words of Nero Wolfe, in *Fer-de-Lance,* are "Where's the beer?" The narrator of the Wolfe novels, Archie Goodwin, is not much of a drinker. He has an occasional cocktail but prefers a cold glass of milk.

Wolfebier

Waldhaus Spezial Gold

At 11 a.m., open, preferably with a gold bottle opener, and pour a bottle of light German lager or pilsner beer in a glass. Wolfe's favorite beer was Remmer, produced for the domestic German market by the Beck brewery, but since that brand is no longer produced, you can substitute a beer such as Waldhaus Spezial Gold or Hoepfner Krausen or even Beck's regular lager. Drink in five gulps. Repeat throughout the day and evening, until you have consumed five to six quarts.

About Author Rex Stout:

Born in Indiana of devout Quaker parents and raised in Kansas, Rex Todhunter Stout was a child prodigy, with an IQ of at least 180. He taught himself to read at 18 months, and by age 4 he had read the entire Bible twice. By age 11 he had read all of the books in his father's library, about 1,200 of them including the works of the 18th century greats Addison, Pope, Swift, Johnson and Steele. From the library he also consumed Bacon's *Essays*, Plutarch's *Lives,* Gibbon's *Rise and Fall of the Roman Empire,* Bulfinch's *Mythology,* 10 volumes of Macaulay and many more classics, along with slightly lighter fare by Dumas, Twain, Hugo, Kipling and Walter Scott. Stout also was a child arithmetic prodigy, able to do complex computations in his head, and was a state spelling bee champion. Between the ages of 7 and 12 he read all of Shakespeare's plays and memorized every one of the Bard's 154 sonnets. Stout's biographer, John McAlfer, writes that even in his 80s Stout could recite the sonnets word for word.

Stout dropped out of high school and enlisted in the Navy, where he briefly served as a yeoman on President Theodore Roosevelt's yacht. After two years in the Navy, Stout worked at a variety of menial jobs. He attended the University of Kansas for a short time. In 1910, Stout sold three poems to *The Smart Set,* a respected literary magazine, and over the next several years sold more than 40 stories and serialized mystery novels to leading magazines of the time.

Then, in 1916 at age 30, having tired of writing, with his brother, Bob, he helped invent and develop a savings and bookkeeping system for public school children, called the Educational Thrift System. ETS eventually was adopted by school systems in more than 400 cities in 30 states. That same year Stout married Fay Kennedy of Topeka, Kan. This first marriage ended in divorce.

The royalties from ETS provided Stout with money and leisure to travel and to become involved in progressive intellectual movements of the day, including the establishment of the American Civil Liberties Union. In the late 1920s, Stout took up serious writing again, authoring his first published book, *How Like a God,* published by Vanguard, a publishing firm that he helped to found.

However, the stock market crash of 1929 and the beginning of the Great Depression wiped out much of Stout's savings. To make money and to support his new wife, Pola Weinbach Hoffman, an Austrian designer, he turned again to writing, turning out several not very successful novels.

In 1934, his first Nero Wolfe novel, *Fer-de-Lance,* was published, and in 1935 *The League of Frightened Men* came out. These first two Nero Wolfe books are widely considered among the best of 20th century mysteries. They also sold well. From 1934 to his death in 1975, Stout wrote 33 Nero Wolfe novels along with about 40 Wolfe novellas and short stories.

With the success of the Wolfe *oeuvre* Stout became a gentlemen farmer on a 58-acre estate in Brewster, N.Y., north of New York City, anchored by a 14-room hilltop house he designed and helped construct, with the advice of architect Lawrence Kocher. Kocher was a colleague of Bauhaus founder Walter Gropius and among other notable buildings designed the Studies Building at Black Mountain College, the noted experimental college near Asheville, N.C. Stout remained active in liberal causes, helping found *The New Masses* magazine. Stout severed his association with the magazine after he realized it was only a mouthpiece for the U.S. Communist Party. In the 1950s, Stout was called before the House Un-American Activities Committee and was investigated by the FBI for his alleged communist-front associations. Stout, for his part, said he "hated communists" and later supported the Vietnam War. He served as president of the Authors League and of the Mystery Writers of America. In 1959, Stout received the MWA's Grand Master Award.

After the death of Stout and his widow, the Stout estate commissioned seven Nero Wolfe books by Robert Goldsborough, published from 1986 to 1994. The Goldsborough series resumed in 2012, with three additional Wolfe novels published to date.

Nero Wolfe has appeared in many film, radio and television productions. Rex Stout himself believed that Charles Laughton would make the best Wolfe, but the actor never played him. Columbia Pictures made the first two novels in the series, *Fer-de-Lance* and *The League of Frightened Men* into motion pictures in 1936 and 1937 respectively. The first starred Edward Arnold as Wolfe; the second, Walter Connolly. Lionel Sander played Archie Goodwin in both movies. After these films, Rex Stout declined to sell any more of his novels to Hollywood.

There were several radio Nero Wolfe productions. Of all of them, Stout preferred the 1950-51 series on NBC with Sydney Greenstreet as Wolfe.

Numerous television versions of the Nero Wolfe novels have appeared over the years, both in the U.S. and internationally.

Arguably the best series is from the A&E Network, featuring Maury Alan Chaykin as Wolfe and Timothy Hutton as Goodwin, airing starting in 2001 with a kind of test pilot show in 2000.

In a nod to the radio mystery series of the 1930s and 1940s, A&E used an ensemble cast of the same actors, frequently showing up as different characters from week to week. Some viewers were confused by this repertory style, with, say, the actor playing a murder victim in one episode reappearing the next week as a Wolfe client. However, the program, titled *A Nero Wolfe Mystery,* received a warm reception from critics.

Nero Wolfe Novels and Novella Collections by Rex Stout

Fer-de-Lance (1934)

The League of Frightened Men (1935)

The Rubber Band (1936)

The Red Box (1937)

Too Many Cooks (1938)

Some Buried Caesar (1939)

Over My Dead Body (1940)

Where There's a Will (1940)

Black Orchids (1942) (contains "Black Orchids" and "Cordially Invited to Meet Death")

Not Quite Dead Enough (1944) (contains "Not Quite Dead Enough" and "Booby Trap")

The Silent Speaker (1946)

Too Many Women (1947)

And Be a Villain (1948)

Trouble in Triplicate (1949) (contains "Before I Die," "Help Wanted, Male" and "Instead of Evidence")

The Second Confession (1949)

Three Doors to Death (1950) (contains "Man Alive," "Omit Flowers" and "Door to Death")

In the Best Families (1950)

Curtains for Three (1951) (contains "The Gun with Wings," "Bullet for One" and "Disguise for Murder")

Murder by the Book (1951)

Triple Jeopardy (1952) (contains "Home to Roost," "The Cop-Killer" and "The Squirt and the Monkey")

Prisoner's Base (1952)

The Golden Spiders (1953)

Three Men Out (contains "Invitation to Murder," "The Zero Clue" and "This Won't Kill You") (1954)

The Black Mountain (1954)

Before Midnight (1955)

Three Witnesses (1956) (contains "The Next Witness," "When a Man Murders" and "Die Like a Dog")

Might as Well Be Dead (1956)

Three for the Chair (1957) (contains "A Window for Death," "Immune to Murder" and "Too Many Detectives")

If Death Ever Slept (1957)

And Four to Go (contains "Christmas Party," "Easter Parade," "Fourth of July Picnic" and "Murder Is No Joke") (1958)

Champagne for One (1958)

Plot It Yourself (1959)

Three at Wolfe's Door (contains "Poison à la Carte," "Method Three for Murder" and "The Rodeo Murder") (1960)

Too Many Clients (1960)

The Final Deduction (1961)

Homicide Trinity (contains "Eeny Meeny Murder Mo," "Death of a Demon" and "Counterfeit for Murder") (1962)

Gambit (1962)

The Mother Hunt (1963)

Trio for Blunt Instruments (contains "Kill Now—Pay Later," "Murder Is Corny" and "Blood Will Tell") (1964)

A Right to Die (1964)

The Doorbell Rang (1965)

Death of a Doxy (1966)

The Father Hunt (1968)

Death of a Dude (1969)

Please Pass the Guilt (1973)

A Family Affair (1975)

Death Times Three (posthumous; contains "Bitter End," "Frame-Up for Murder" and "Assault on a Brownstone") (1985)

Nero Wolfe Novels by Robert Goldsborough

After the death of Rex Stout's widow in 1984, the Stout estate approved the continuation of the Nero Wolfe series by journalist and advertising man Robert Golsborough. Goldsborough was faithful to the Stout works, although he updated some of material to fit the times.

Murder in E Minor (1986)

Death on Deadline (1987)

The Bloodied Ivy (1988)

The Last Coincidence (1989)

Fade to Black (1990)

Silver Spire (1992)

The Missing Chapter (1994)

Archie Meets Nero Wolfe (a prequel) (2012)

Murder in the Ballpark (2014)

Archie in the Crosshairs (2015)

Stop the Presses! (2016)
Murder, Stage Left (2017)

Notable Books about Rex Stout and Nero Wolfe:

Baring-Gould, William, *Nero Wolfe of West 35th Street* (1982). A "biography" of Nero Wolfe, it also includes a chronology of cases and a sometime controversial illustration of the floor plan of Wolfe's brownstone.

McAleer, John A., *Rex Stout: A Biography* (1977). Early and comprehensive (over 670 pps.) biography of Stout.

TOUGH GUYS

Humphrey Bogart and Lauren Bacall sent the sparks flying in The Big Sleep, based on the novel by hardboiled writer Raymond Chandler

We confess: Of all the detectives in this book, we love the tough guys the best.

Most, but not all, of the tough guys here are of the famed "hardboiled detective" school. This was pioneered in the 1920s by Carroll John Daly. It's generally accepted that the first hardboiled detective story was Daly's "The False Burton Combs," published in 1923 in *Black Mask* magazine, the famous pulp magazine.

The hardboiled genre was popularized by Dashiell Hammett, who in five novels and a number of short stories done over a period of only a few years in the late 1920s and early 1930s changed the course of detective fiction for decades. Hammett's hardboiled private eye **Sam Spade** appeared in one novel, *The Maltese Falcon,* and, most famously, in the 1941 movie of the same name starring Humphrey Bogart and with screenplay and direction by John Huston. Many critics say the novel is a masterpiece of the detective genre, and the film is widely considered the best detective story on celluloid.

The hardboiled detective was perfected by Raymond Chandler in the form of his famous character, **Philip Marlowe,** and by Dr. Ross Macdonald (he held a PhD) with his complex detective character, **Lew Archer.** All three – Spade, Marlowe and Archer – were denizens of the state of California.

After World War II, another tough guy sprang on the scene, the brutal **Mike Hammer,** a creation of the unexpectedly religious Mickey Spillane. In cheap paperbacks sold in drugstores and other non-traditional places, Mike Hammer enjoyed incredible sales, at one point having a majority of the top 10 fiction best sellers published from the late 19th to mid-20th century. Hammer changed the reading habits of the American public, or at least of a part of it.

Later, mostly in the 1970s and 1980s, two wonderful tough guy characters came to public attention, the "salvage consultant" **Travis McGee,** who drives an old Rolls-Royce customized pickup and lives on a boat in Fort Lauderdale. John D. MacDonald created McGee and featured him in 21 novels. About the same time, the maverick (yes, pun intended) **Jim Rockford** entertained millions on television in *The Rockford Files.*

Finally, perhaps the toughest of the tough guys, **Spenser,** arose in Boston and Cambridge, fathered by Robert B. Parker, another PhD and former college professor. Spenser is our favorite detective, and we're happy this noble knight and his code of chivalry have been continued after Dr. Parker's death by Ace Atkins.

Lew Archer

From the Lew Archer series of novels by Ross Macdonald (1915-1983)

"We are all underground men, making a brief transit from darkness to darkness."

Ross Macdonald/Kenneth Millar

Private eye Lew Archer is the central character in 18 novels and a collection of short stories by Kenneth Millar, writing as Ross Macdonald.

Archer is a hard man to get to know. Bits of his life story are sprinkled here and there throughout the novels, but in the typical Archer novel the private detective is the low-key narrator. Moody, thoughtful and sometimes morose, he is more like a psychologist who observes, asks questions and makes occasional observations than a go-get-'em PI who uses his fists and guns.

The little we know about Archer: He was born in Long Beach, Calif., and went to primary school in Oakland. In his youth he was, he admits, a thief and a gang member. He admits that a brief attempt at college didn't work for him. After service in Army intelligence in World War II, he reforms and joins the Long Beach police department, working his way up to detective sergeant, from which he either departs on his own or is fired (he tells the story both ways.) In any case, he leaves the department and gets his private detective's license, opening an office on Sunset Boulevard in Los Angeles. He marries but is soon divorced by his wife. Archer has occasional flings, but romance is not a driving force for him. Neither is money. In the first novel he get $50 a day; in his prime he gets $100 a day plus expenses. In some cases he declines an advance or shrugs off an attempt to pay him.

Southern California is his beat. Many of the novels are set in Los Angeles, though in later novels he has moved a bit north to Santa Barbara, or Santa Teresa as it's called in the novels. Occasionally he travels to another state or to Canada or Mexico to track down a lead.

Archer is six feet, two inches tall and weighs around 190 pounds. He has dark hair and blue eyes. A heavy smoker for much of his life, he can still handle himself well in fights, although he frequently is the victim, being badly beaten up many times over the course of the series. This PI doesn't usually carry a gun, but when he needs to he prefers a police pistol, usually a .38 Special revolver, or sometimes a .32 or .38 automatic.

The detective ages through the series, roughly paralleling the age of the author, beginning at about age 35 in the first Lew Archer novel, *The Moving Target.* By the last novels, he is close to 60. Many readers think of him as looking like Paul Newman, who played him in two movies, the first in 1966. By the later novels, he may look more like Brian Keith, who played him in a short-lived 1970s television series.

The Archer novels usually begin slowly. Typically, Archer takes what seems to be an ordinary missing person or find-my-wife/husband case, but the PI gradually uncovers layers of misinformation and lost pathways in the maze. This often leads back to a long-ago relationship or a terrible secret involving the main characters and reveals the true facts of the current mystery.

Archer's Digs: For much of his career, Archer works out of a small rented office on Sunset Boulevard in Los Angeles.

Archer's Drives: Lew Archer, although part of the automobile culture of Southern California, drives nondescript cars, including an old Chevrolet convertible and an Oldsmobile. He prefers big American cars.

Archer's Drinks: Unlike some other PIs of the time, Lew Archer isn't a particularly heavy drinker. On the other hand, many of the detective's clients and suspects are hard drinkers. When Archer has a drink, it usually is bourbon, Scotch or a gin and tonic. Archer rarely specified a specific brand. Sometimes, he asks for a double but rarely has more than one or two. Occasionally Archer will have a beer, usually Bass or Black Horse Ale.

Archer's G&T

2 oz. gin

Angostura bitters

Twist of lime

Schweppes tonic water

Fill highball glass with ice cubes. Add gin, a couple of splashes of bitters and fill with tonic water. Squeeze twist of lime into drink and use the twist for a garnish.

About Author Kenneth Millar/Ross Macdonald:

Ross Macdonald is usually considered the last of the "Big Three" originators of the hard-boiled school of detective fiction. Some critics consider him a better, or at least more sophisticated, writer than Dashiell Hammett or Raymond Chandler.

Certainly, with his PhD from the University of Michigan Macdonald is more erudite than either, and his Lew Archer novels are more psychologically complex, with echoes of both Proust, Macdonald's favorite author, and Dostoevsky. Macdonald, however, admits his direct debt to both Hammett and Chandler. He took the name of his best-known character from Hammett – Miles Archer was Sam Spade's murdered partner in *The Maltese Falcon* – and to some degree patterns Archer after Chandler's Philip Marlowe. Macdonald was believed to be deeply disappointed that Chandler did not like the younger writer's work.

Born Kenneth Millar December 13, 1915, in Los Gatos, Calif., Millar spent his early years in the San Francisco area. After his father, a sea captain, abandoned his family when Millar was five, Millar spent the rest of his childhood and his adolescence shuttled around to a series of family members. He once said he had lived in 50 different homes. Some of his relatives were in Canada, and Millar attended schools and college in that country. It was at the University of Western Ontario that Millar met his future wife, Margaret Sturm, who was to herself become a noted mystery author, writing as Margaret Millar.

After marrying Sturm, Millar taught high school English and enrolled, first part-time and later full-time, as a graduate student at the University of Michigan. At one point, he studied under the poet W. H. Auden. Millar's PhD dissertation was on the psychological aspects of Coleridge criticism. During graduate school and also during service as a Naval officer in the Pacific Theater in World War II, Millar began writing and publishing novels. His early novels were psychological in style and usually contained an Oedipal theme.

After the war, Millar joined his wife and young daughter in Santa Barbara, called Santa Teresa in his novels (in his wife's novels, the city is called San Felice or Santa Felicia, where they lived the rest of their lives.

In 1949, Millar's first Lew Archer novel, *The Moving Target,* was published. To avoid confusion with his now well-known writer wife, he adopted a pseudonym, first John Macdonald, which then of course created confusion with John D. MacDonald. Then Millar began writing under the name Ross Macdonald. Even with this change, all their lives the two writers were confused with each other.

Eventually, Millar/Macdonald authored 18 Lew Archer novels and one collection of Archer short stories. The last novel, *The Blue Hammer,* came out in 1973.

Many critics consider *The Galton Case* (1959) and *The Underground Man* (1971) as the best books in the series. Dark, complex and deeply interwoven with psychological threads, with plots that are difficult to summarize and often repetitive, Macdonald's novels, in the author's own words, remind us that "we are all underground men, making a brief transit from darkness to darkness."

Although during his working lifetime Macdonald never received an Edgar or other top award for mystery writing, the Private Eye Writers of America in 1982 awarded Macdonald, then deeply in dementia and unable to accept it himself, its first Lifetime Achievement Award.

Lew Archer was featured in several Hollywood films and television show. Paul Newman starred as Archer (called Harper in the Newman movies) in two successful films, *Harper* from Macdonald's first Archer novel, *The Moving Target,* in 1966 and *The Drowning Pool* from the novel of the same name in 1975. A made-for-TV movie, *The Underground Man,* starred Peter Graves.

Archer, a 1975 NBC series staring Brian Keith as Lew Archer, lasted only six episodes. The 2008 season of the TV show, *Californication,* had a character named Lew Ashby, loosely based on singer and songwriter Warren Zevon, who was a great fan of Ross Macdonald's work.

In his early 60s, Macdonald began suffering from early on-set Alzheimer's disease. He died in the summer of 1983 at age 67 in Santa Barbara.

Lew Archer Novels by Ross Macdonald

The Moving Target (1949)
The Drowning Pool (1950)
The Way Some People Die (1951)
The Ivory Grin (1952) (also published as *Marked for Murder*)
Find a Victim (1954)
The Barbarous Coast (1956)
The Doomsters (1958)
The Galton Case (1959)
The Wycherly Woman (1961)
The Zebra-Striped Hearse (1962)
The Chill (1964)
The Far Side of the Dollar (1965)
Black Money (1966)
The Instant Enemy (1968)
The Goodbye Look (1969)
The Underground Man (1971)

Sleeping Beauty (1973)
The Blue Hammer (1976)

Notable Works on Ross Macdonald

Marrs, Suzanne and Nolan, Tom (eds.) *Meanwhile There Are Letters: The Correspondence of Eudora Welty and Ross Macdonald (2015).* Letters in the 13-year-long correspondence between Macdonald and Welty.

Nolan, Tom, *Ross Macdonald: A Biography* (1999). The definitive biography of Macdonald.

Mike Hammer

From the Mike Hammer series by Mickey Spillane (1918-2006)

"I don't give a hoot about reading reviews. What I want to read is the royalty checks."

Mickey Spillane

Mickey Spillane was the Donald Trump of his time – semi-illiterate, phony and a favorite of the underclass

Mike Hammer is the ultimate 20th century tough guy private eye. Indeed, he's so ready to knock someone's teeth out or plug them in the gut with a round from his .45 pistol that he is almost a parody of the hardboiled shamus.

Self-righteous, politically incorrect, misanthropic and often a misogynist, Hammer follows his own simplistic code, dispensing his version of justice as judge, jury and executioner as he sees fit.

The pattern is set in Mickey Spillane's first Hammer novel, *I, the Jury,* published in July 1947. To avenge the murder of his friend Jack Williams, who gave up his arm to save Mike in a jungle battle in World War II, Hammer fights his way through a number of other murders and murder-attempts until, in the end, he finally realizes – no spoiler alert needed here, as the ending is known so well that Jack's killer is in fact Hammer's own bride-to-be, a beautiful, drug-dealing psychiatrist. Hammer kills his fiancée, who has stripped naked in a last futile attempt to seduce him, with a single .45 shot, just below her belly button.

Violence permeates the tales. The first six Mike Hammer novels, ones published from 1947 to 1952 that make up the "classic" Hammer genre (five more were published later, not counting the nine by Max Alan Collins published after Spillane's death), average around ten killings per book. That doesn't include the other forms of violence that seem to appear anytime Hammer is around. When Hammer questions a possible suspect, or almost anyone who might know something, he follows the "beat'em up first, ask questions later" approach. Hammer uses his fists like, well, hammers to slug a guy in the gut so hard he vomits, to break a nose or loosen teeth or to slam the heads of two wise guys together so violently that they fall unconscious to the floor.

Hammer is loosely based on the real-life Texas Ranger and gunfighter, Frank Hamer, who was best known for tracking down and killing Bonnie Parker and Clyde Barrow in an ambush in Louisiana in 1934.

A World War II vet who had seen action in the Pacific, Hammer stands a little over 6 feet tall – he never says specifically – and usually weighs 190 pounds, but at one time he hit 200 and another fell to 168. His eyes are a mottled blue. One of his conquests says of him, "You're so ugly you're beautiful." Hammer is usually a good dresser, wearing custom-tailored suits. In bad weather he wears a trench coat. Although a heavy smoker (he usually smokes Lucky Strikes, unfiltered of course), a hard drinker – mostly rye, bourbon and beer – bad at some sports such as tennis and not a guy to work out, he is in good enough shape and savvy enough about street brawling to win nearly every fight.

Hammer normally carries a Colt M1911A1, a semi-automatic, magazine-fed, recoil-operated 45-caliber pistol that was, in several slightly changed versions, standard issue in the U.S. Armed Forces from 1911 (hence the original model designation of M1911) to 1986, from World War I to the Vietnam War.

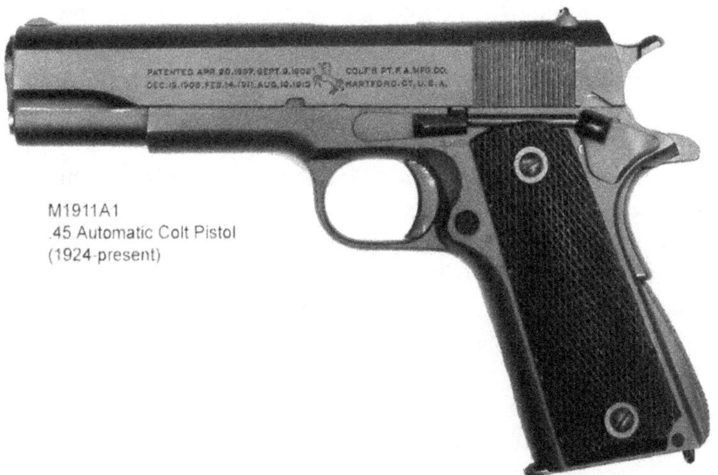

Colt semi-automatic .45 carried by Mike Hammer

The M1911A1 was first employed in 1924. A magazine in the butt of the pistol holds seven cartridges. When used against a human target, this .45, even with a standard 230-grain ACP cartridge with full metal jacket, is known for its stopping power. The large diameter bullet, leaving the muzzle at 830 feet per second, creates a large, deep wound channel that lowers blood pressure rapidly.

The PI loves guns and has a number of others, including a .25, a .32 and a .30 Luger. In *One Lonely Night* he uses a machine gun to kill more than 20 Commie agents.

For reasons that may not be clear to most readers, Mike Hammer is irresistible to nearly every woman he meets. They fall for him like a ton of mid-century bricks. It must be his caveman, tough-guy image. Hammer isn't opposed to a quick one with a "nymphomaniac" dame or broad, even if he's already in love and engaged to be married. With "good girls," though, Hammer wants to save sex to after the wedding. He maintains a flirtatious relationship with his shapely secretary, Velda.

At the risk of being anachronistic, politically Hammer is somewhere to the right of Steve Bannon, Politically incorrect? He could give Donald Trump lessons. He's always ready to make fun of "fruits," "pansies" and "queers." Maids, bartenders, elevator operators and porters are easily identified by their dialect, full of "mistah" and "yassuh" and comments such as "De police gennimuns in de front room was 'specting you."

If that's not clear enough, Hammer points you to a "high yellow" or a "coal-black." There's a dope peddler, a filthy crook, a corrupt politicians or a dirty Commie under nearly every block of granite in Hammer's Manhattan.

Hammer's Digs: Mike Hammer maintains a two-room office in the Hackard Building in Manhattan. It is staffed only by his curvaceous secretary, Velda, who also holds a PI license. The outer room has a desk for Velda and two captain's chairs and a bench for clients. Hammer's office has a battered desk, a leather swivel chair, a leather couch and a wash basin. The building may be nondescript, but it's in a good location, and it has private parking in the basement.

Hammer's Drives: In classic novels from the late 1940s and early 1950s, Hammer drives what he often refers to as a "jalopy" or a "heap." But under the hood, the car has been fitted with a powerful engine. From *I, the Jury:* "From the outside it looked like any beat-up wreck that ought to be retired, but the rubber was good and the engine better. It was souped up to the ears. I've had it on the road doing over a hundred and the pedal was only half down. Henry [Hammer's mechanic] pulled the motor from a limousine that had the rear end knocked in and sold it to me for a song. Whenever a mech saw the power that was under the hood, he let out a long low whistle. In its own way it was a masterpiece."

Hammer's Drinks: Mike Hammer likes brown booze – Scotch and soda, bourbon straight up, rye and soda. The brand seems unimportant. He drinks beer, sometimes by the case, and doesn't seem to care what kind it is. In *The Girl Hunters,* published in 1962, after a Hammer hiatus of 10 years, Hammer admits to having been on a seven-year drunk.

In the 11 Hammer novels by Spillane, Mike Manner visits scores of bars, restaurants and watering holes. Most frequently, he goes to the Blue Ribbon on 44th Street in Manhattan, a real-life establishment (now closed, although several other places still open have similar names) that served German food and where Spillane's picture was displayed on the wall, along with photos of many other celebrities. He also visits fictional dives, including the Hi-Ho Club, Clover Bar, Bowery Inn and Zero Zero Club.

Hammerhead Rye and Soda

2 oz. Old Overholt Rye

Soda to taste

Put ice cubes in an old-fashioned class. Add the rye and enough soda to float the rocks. Ask bartender to bring you one every 15 minutes.

About Author Mickey Spillane:

Frank Morrison "Mickey" Spillane was born in Brooklyn on March 9, 1918. His father was an Irish Catholic bartender and his mother, of Scottish descent, was a Protestant, so he was baptized twice.

Mickey Spillane grew up in Elizabeth, N.J., a tough working-class town. He was a voracious reader and claims to have read all of Melville's works by the time he was 11 years old. After graduating from Erasmus Hall High School, he somehow made his way to Fort Hays State College (now University) in Hays, Kansas, where he played football and was on the college's swim team.

Spillane soon left college and worked at a series of odd jobs, including a stint with Ringling Bros. Barnum & Bailey Circus and as a salesman for Gimbels department store.

Spillane had been trying to sell short stories since his high school days. While at Gimbels he was referred by a fellow salesman, Joe Gill, to Joe's brother, Ray Gill, who wrote for Funnies, Inc., a comic book publisher. Soon Spillane was doing story treatments and outlines for some of the major comic book characters of the 1940s, including Batman, Superman and Captain Marvel.

When the Japanese attacked Pearl Harbor in 1941, Spillane enlisted in the U.S. Army. As a part of the Army Air Corp, he became a fighter pilot but spent most of his time in the service as a domestic flight instructor, although some sources claim he flew some military missions but never saw combat. While stationed as a flight instructor at Greenwood Army Airfield in Greenwood, Miss., he met and married his first wife, Mary Ann Pearce, in 1944. The couple would eventually have four children. Spillane was discharged in 1946 as a captain and returned to New York. He resumed his work writing comics.

As Spillane recounts it, the couple had some property in Newburgh, N.Y., about 60 miles north of New York City and wanted to build a house on it. To get the money, Spillane tried his hand at writing a novel. By some accounts, writing it took only nine days and by others 19 days, but in any case he finished what would be *I, the Jury* very quickly. It featured what Spillane had originally tried to peddle as a comic book featuring Mike Danger, but that had been rejected.

At the suggestion of his comics mentor, Ray Gill, he sent the novel to E. P. Dutton. Dutton was reluctant to buy it but decided it was worth a gamble, as if nothing else it could be published at low cost as a paperback pulp novel.

Coming out in July 1947, as a hardback Dutton book, it had modest initial sales. But when it appeared as a Signet paperback Spillane's debut novel quickly became a strong seller. Signet, a new publishing nameplate that was established in 1948 by Dutton and marketed under the slogan "Good Reading for the Masses" in some 85,000 outlets, including drugstores and grocery stores, in the U.S. and Canada.

By the time the book was adapted into a United Artists 3-D movie in 1953, it had gone through 33 printings and had sold 3,500,000 copies. It eventually went on to sell more than 8 million copies, all but a few thousand in paperback.

Spillane quickly followed up with five more Mike Hammer sequels, *Vengeance Is Mine* and *My Gun is Quick* in 1950, *The Big Kill* and *One Lonely Night* in 1951, and *Kiss Me, Deadly* in 1952. *Kiss Me, Deadly* reportedly became the first detective novel to reach *The New York Times* bestseller list.

Unfortunately for Spillane, his Hammer novels, while written in a cinematic style, did not do well as movies. The movie version of *I, the Jury,* did mediocre box office. *Kiss Me, Deadly* in 1955 grossed less than three quarters of a million. *My Gun Is Quick* in 1957 did less than $400,000. In the fourth and last movie on the United Artists contract, *The Girl Hunters*, released in 1963, Spillane himself played Mike Hammer. Despite a lot of promotion, and decent acting jobs by Spillane and actors Lloyd Nolan and Shirley Eaton, the movie again failed, grossing less than $1 million. For some reason, the Mike Hammer novels didn't translate well to celluloid. As a curiosity piece, *Ring of Fire* (1954) Spillane is unique: Spillane was cast as himself, a mystery writer, who is hired by Clyde Beatty to track down a killer who is sabotaging the Clyde Beatty Circus. In this movie, Mike Hammer is played by George Stang, the Texas Ranger on whom the Hammer character is partly based. Like the other Spillane/Hammer movies of the time, this one also bombed at the box office.

All the Mike Hammer novels, especially the classic ones published between 1947 and 1952, follow the same formula. They are short, typically around 30,000 words. They use short sentences, averaging around 10 words. The typical word has only four letters. Textual analysis shows that typical chapter reads at the fourth- to fifth-grade level, understandable by the average 11-year-old.

The Hammer novels are written in the first person. The writer is skilled in the sense that a graffiti artist or a comic book writer, which Spillane was, is skilled. Yet they have a powerful energy.

As Max Allan Collins and James L. Taylor put it in their 1984 biography of Spillane, *One Lonely Knight,* Spillane's writing has the primitive power of a Grandma Moses painting.

The novels' first-person narrator is opinionated, and most of his opinions about other people are negative. He is judgmental. He lives in a world of corrupt public officials, fat, weak men, cops who try to do a good job but often fail due to the loopholes of laws or to their own weaknesses, nymphos, pansies and stupid frat boys. Hammer doesn't shy from making racist and misogynist comments. He is violent, frequently engaging in beatings and fights and killing bad guys with his Colt .45 semi-automatic. When he kills, he expresses no regrets. He smokes, he drinks, he shoots.

Plotting in the Mike Hammer books and short stories is simple. Hammer typically comes upon a murder, often of a woman, and spends the rest of the book beating up suspects, or killing them, until it finally dawns on him which of the remaining suspects is the killer. At that point, Hammer usually kills the killer. Many of the plots are ridiculously unbelievable. For example, in *I, the Jury,* one of the bad guys enrolls as a student at many different colleges, using plastic surgery to keep himself looking youthful, to recruit co-eds into a prostitution ring.

Absurd as the plots may be, as primitive as the writing is, the formula works. At one time in the 1980s, seven of the top 10 best selling novels of all time were by Mickey Spillane. His books have sold at least 225 million copies worldwide, and the total continues to grow.

Although not widely recognized by critics, a major factor in the success of the Mike Hammer novels was the cover illustrations on the Signet paperback editions. The bold illustrations, which always featured beautiful women, usually partially undressed, often in poses of helplessness and in several cases suggesting bondage, bordered on being soft porn. Lu Kimmel (1905-1973) created the cover paintings for *My Gun Is Quick*, *Vengeance Is Mine*, *One Lonely Night* and *The Long Wait.* The original painting for the cover of *One Lonely Night*, a half-naked woman strung up by her wrists, for many years hung on a wall in Spillane's house in Murrells Inlet, S.C. Kimmel also did pulp covers for many other writers of the time, including John Dickson Carr. He did covers for Signet, Gold Medal Books and other paperback imprints. The cover art for *Kiss Me, Deadly* was by James Meese, another prolific creator of covers featuring beautiful women for paperback books and men's magazines in the 1940s and 1950s.

The classic Hammer books were written in the late 1940s and early 1950s, along with one non-Hammer novel, *The Long Wait,* in 1951.

In 1952, Hammer converted to the Jehovah's Witness religion and stopped writing Hammer or other novels almost a decade. He didn't publish again, other than short stories and non-fiction mostly for men's magazines, until the early 1960s. A Mike Hammer novel, *The Girl Hunters,* came out in 1962. While he published other Hammer books, and a total of 22 novels in all, plus several collections of short stories, Spillane's reputation, such as it is, was mostly made from his early Hammer books. They make up at least two-thirds of his total book sales.

Why Spillane stopped writing novels during much of the 1950s, when he was at the height of his success, remains a matter of speculation. In part it likely was due to his conversion to the Jehovah's Witness religion. Spillane took his religion seriously, remaining a Witness until the end of his life. He even took on the duty required by the religion of spreading the word door-to-door, handling out the *Watchtower* magazine and other tracts.

The fact that his Mike Hammer books were savaged by serious literary critics probably also played a part. From almost the beginning, the reviews of his Hammer novels were almost universally negative. *The New York Times* reviewers called his work "repellant" and "overheated, unbelievable, disorganized." The *Saturday Review* said his work was "lurid" and "immature." There were also highly negative reviews in *Harper's, Time,* the *New Republic* and many other respected publications of the period.

Even Ogden Nash piled on with a short attack poem:

"The Marquis de Sade
Wasn't always mad.
What addled his brain
Was Mickey Spillane."

Although Spillane claimed to not pay attention to the critics, he kept copies of many reviews posted in his office.

Spillane himself, in a 1962 interview with Gay Talese, claims he had become "stale." In the article Spillane says, "The impact that Hammer made on the public was fantastic, and I couldn't keep up with him. I had to lay off for a while."

Although Spillane did not write another Hammer novel until *The Girl Hunters* in 1962, he kept his name alive with numerous reprints of his Hammer novels and short story collections, with magazine work and with movies and television series.

Even after the advent of word processors and computers, Spillane banged out his books and other work on old manual typewriters, usually using yellow paper.

Spillane's first marriage ended in 1962. In November 1965, Spillane married his second wife, nightclub singer Sherri Malinou. After that marriage ended in divorce in early 1983, he married Jane Rogers Johnson in October 1983.

Spillane had moved to a rambling two-story house right on the water in Murrells Inlet in 1954. He had first seen Murrells Inlet from the air when flying over it as a flight instructor during World War II.

Some claim that Spillane and his first wife, Mary Ann, were the first yankees to move Murrells Inlet. At that time, it was a tiny fishing village. Today, the town has about 9,000 residents, claims to be the "Seafood Capital of South Carolina" and is known for its golf courses. It is part of the Grand Strand of Myrtle Beach, one of the major tourist areas in the South, which has a metropolitan population of around half a million and attracts more than 17 million visitors a year. Spillane's home, valued at over $800,000 then, was destroyed by Hurricane Hugo in 1984. Spillane and his third wife, Jane, rebuilt a on the same location, a large three-story house with a wrap-around deck.

Mickey Spillane's Mike Hammer was a syndicated television series in 78 half-hour black-and-white episodes starring Darren McGavin as Hammer that ran in 1958 and 1959. *TV Guide* called it "easily the worst series on TV." As noted, five of Spillane's novels were made into movies in the 1950s, although none achieved much commercial success. Bill Eliot played Mike Hammer in *I, the Jury* (1953). A non-Hammer Spillane novel, *The Long Wait* (1954), starred Anthony Quinn as John McBridge. In *Ring of Fear* (1954), Spillane himself plays himself, while Texas Ranger George Stang plays Mike Hammer. Ralph Meeker starred as Hammer in *Kiss Me Deadly* (1955). In *My Gun Is Quick* (1957), Robert Bray plays Mike Hammer.

During the 1950s, there also was a Mike Hammer radio series, "The Mickey Spillane Mystery: That Hammer Guy" with Larry Haines (later of *F Troop*) and Ted De Corsia as Hammer. Also, a daily comic strip, "From the Files of ... Mike Hammer," was syndicated in 1953 and 1954, written by Spillane, Ed Robbins and Joe Gill and drawn by Ed Robbins.

After Spillane resumed writing Hammer novels with 1962's *The Girl Hunters* (which was made into a 1963 movie featuring Spillane himself as Mike Hammer), a number of other Spillane novels were made into films and TV movies.

Most notably, Stacy Keach played Mike Hammer in a 1984-1985 series on CBS TV, *Mickey Spillane's Mike Hammer*. The series was 24 hour-long episodes. It received good critical and popular reaction, but the show ended prematurely after Keach was arrested in England for possession of cocaine and sent to Reading Prison for six months.

Prior to the show's release, Keach also played Hammer in two CBS made-for-television movies, *Mickey Spillane's Murder Me, Murder You* (1983) and *More Than Murder* (1984) and later, in 1986, *The Return of Mickey Spillane's Mike Hammer.* In 1987, Keach rehashed his role in a follow-up TV series, *The New Mike Hammer,* which ran for 20 episodes before being cancelled due to poor ratings.

Although Spillane continued to write and publish in the 1960s, 70s, 80s and 90s, perhaps he was best known by the general public in his later years for his appearances in television commercials, especially for Miller Lite beer. Miller's ad agency, McCann Erickson, introduced the new lower-calorie brew in 1973 in commercials featuring retired New York Jets running back Matt Snell. Miller rolled out the brand nationally in 1975. The agency then hired Mickey Spillane and got actress Lee Meredith to appear with him in a series of ads promoting the brand. Many of the commercials featured Spillane dressed in a trench coat, looking like his hero Hammer. Spillane continued to do Miller Lite commercials, which also featured other celebrities and sports figures, until the mid-1980s. He also did national TV ads for Lifebuoy soap and other products.

Spillane died July 17, 2006, at his home in Murrells Inlet of pancreatic carcinoma.

From the obituary of Mickey Spillane by Ann Wroe in *The Economist:*

"On days like this, the weather sat over Manhattan like a lid on a boiler. But the cab was cool. Mike Hammer jumped in, directed the driver to Midtown, and watched the city slide by.

"He had heard of Mickey Spillane's death on the TV news as he took a shower. Sad, and hard to believe…Hammer could hear his voice now, a snarl of contempt for the writers who thought his books were repulsive and illiterate. What the hell, they sold. He was maybe the most popular writer ever. A literary type once complained to him that seven of his books were among the ten top sellers of all time. 'Lucky I only wrote seven books,' growled Mr. Spillane."

The Mike Hammer Novels

I, the Jury 1947
My Gun Is Quick 1950
Vengeance Is Mine 1950
One Lonely Night 1951
The Big Kill 1951
Kiss Me, Deadly 1952
The Girl Hunters 1962
The Snake 1964

The Twisted Thing 1966
*The Body Lovers*1967
Survival...Zero! 1970
The Killing Man 1989
Black Alley 1996

The Mike Hammer Novels "by Mickey Spillane" with Max Alan Collins

These Mike Hammer novels are based on uncompleted manuscripts, plot lines and notes left by Spillane. Collins, Spillane's friend, literary executor and the co-author of a 1984 biography of Spillane, wrote most of the text of the posthumous Mike Hammer novels.

The Goliath Bone 2008
The Big Bang 2010
Kiss Her Goodbye 2011
Lady, Go Die! 2012
Complex 90 2013
King of the Weeds 2014
Kill Me, Darling 2015
Murder Never Knocks 2016
The Will To Kill 2017

Notable Books on Mickey Spillane and Mike Hammer

Collins, Max Allan and Traylor, James L., *One Lonely Knight, Mickey Spillane's Mike Hammer* (1984). This is the only full-length biography of Spillane. Max Allan Collins, Spillane's friend and literary executor as well as the "co-author" of a series of posthumous Mike Hammer novels, paints Spillane is the best possible terms.

Spillane, Jane, *My Life with Mickey* (2014). This short memoir by Spillane's third wife concentrates on their life in Murrells Inlet.

Stang, Jack Jr., *The Real Mike Hammer* (2012). Self-published ebook by the son of Jack Stang, the Texas Ranger who was said to be the model for Mike Hammer.

Philip Marlowe

From the Philip Marlowe series of novels by Raymond Chandler (1888-1959)

"A real gimlet is half gin and half Rose's Lime Juice and nothing else. It beats martinis hollow."

– Terry Lennox in *The Long Goodbye* by Raymond Chandler

If Dashiell Hammett created and popularized the hard-boiled detective – Sam Spade and the Continental Op – Raymond Chandler perfected him in the character of Philip Marlowe.

Philip Marlowe is the first-person narrator of seven novels and several dozen short stories by Raymond Chandler. Although Chandler does not tell the reader much about Marlowe the person, we learn a little about him: Marlowe was born in 1906. He finished two years of college in Oregon, either at Oregon State or the University of Oregon. Before becoming a private eye, he worked as an insurance investigator and as an investigator for the Los Angeles County District Attorney's Office, from which he was fired for insubordination.

About six feet tall and 190 pounds, he has dark hair and brown eyes. Marlowe usually wears a trench coat and a hat and has only one good suit. He smokes Camels and sometimes a pipe. He is a heavy drinker.

Marlowe has never been married, but many women find him attractive. His sex life, generally unsatisfactory, is a series of one-night stands. A few critics, citing his frequent homophobic slurs, claim that underneath his rugged exterior he likely is a closeted homosexual. Most critics, however, see Marlowe as a man who would like to find love but has difficulty in establishing relationships with women because he tends to idealize and romanticize them.

Tough talking and cynical on the surface, underneath Marlowe is basically kind and decent. He despises pretense, cruelty and corruption. Like many other of the great detectives of fiction, Marlowe is a knight-errant seeking to aid the helpless and to right the wrongs of a corrupt society. In *Playback,* in response to a question from the heroine of the novel about how a hard man can be gentle, Marlowe says, "If I wasn't hard, I wouldn't be alive. If I couldn't ever be gentle, I wouldn't deserve to be alive."

In *The Big Sleep,* which was published in 1939. Marlowe is summoned to the home of General Sternwood. The general wants Marlowe to deal with an attempted blackmail of one of his daughters, Carmen, by a bookseller named Arthur Geiger. Sternwood's other daughter, Vivian, would also play a role in the story.

Marlowe investigates and finds that Geiger's bookstore is actually a lending library for pornography. The PI stakes out Geiger's house and sees Carmen enter. Marlowe hears screams, followed by gunshots. Marlowe goes in the house and finds Geiger dead and Carmen drugged and naked, in front of an empty camera. He takes Carmen home, but when he returns to Geiger's house Geiger's body has been removed. A little later, Marlowe stakes out the bookstore and finds that the inventory is being moved to Joe Brody's house. Brody had earlier blackmailed Carmen.

Marlowe then finds Brody with Agnes, the clerk at the bookstore. Carmen arrives, forces her way in with a gun and demands the pornographic photos taken of her, but Marlowe makes her leave. From Brody, Marlowe learns that Geiger was blackmailing Carmen; the family chauffeur, Owen Taylor, didn't like it, so he killed Geiger, then took the film of Carmen. Brody had followed the chauffeur, knocked him out and took the film. Suddenly, Brody is shot dead. Marlowe gives chase and catches Geiger's male lover, who shot Brody because he thought he had killed Geiger.

This is only part of the complex series of double-crosses and dirty secrets that Marlowe discovers.

Chandler's novel was made into a noted movie in 1946, directed by Howard Hawks and starring Humphrey Bogart as Marlowe and Lauren Bacall as Vivian. A classic of the film noir genre, the movie version differs in some ways from the novel – for example, in the film references to homosexuality are eliminated and the porno book store is an antiquarian bookshop – but the two share a highly convoluted plot. Two versions of the movie were actually filmed, with sections reshot to highlight the real-life relationship between Bogart and Bacall.

Marlowe's Digs: Like many other fictional private dicks of his time, Marlowe's beat is Los Angeles, He lives in a cheap sixth-story apartment and works out of a small office on Hollywood Boulevard in Los Angeles, where he keeps a bottle of bourbon in his desk drawer for clients and for his own use. Making only $25 a day, later increased to $40, plus expenses, he can't afford a secretary or even an answering service. He'll take almost any kind of detective work except divorces.

Marlowe's Drives: Marlowe drives a Chevrolet or an Oldsmobile, a convertible when he can afford one. He carries a Smith & Wesson .38 special in a shoulder holster but also keeps a Luger pistol in his car.

Philip Marlowe's Drinks: Like his creator, Raymond Chandler, Philip Marlowe is a heavy drinker. Before dinner, he usually has a couple of double Gibsons (a vodka martini with cocktail onions rather than olives). At home he drinks Scotch or Four Roses whiskey with ginger ale. However, the drink probably most associated with him is the Gimlet, of which his client Terry Lennox is fond.

Lennox Gimlet

1 ½ oz. gin

1 ½ oz. Rose's Lime Juice

Put gin and Rose's in a shaker with ice. Shake until chilled. Strain and serve straight up in a chilled martini glass. Some contemporary drinkers prefer their gimlets with two parts gin (preferably Bombay Sapphire) to one part Rose's.

Marlowe Double Gibson

3 to 4 oz. vodka

½ oz. dries vermouth

Cocktail onions

Put the vodka and vermouth in a shaker with ice. Shake until chilled. Strain and serve straight up in a chilled martini glass. Garnish with a couple of cocktail onions.

About Author Raymond Chandler:

Today, Raymond Thornton Chandler is widely considered among the most important writers of detective fiction in history. His work is taught in colleges and universities, many serious critical studies and several biographies have been written about him. A number of PhD dissertations (including one by Robert B. Parker, creator of Spenser) focus on his work.

Yet, his early books received relatively little notice, did not sell very well and if reviewed at all were usually panned. It is said that only 17 people attended his funeral.

Chandler was born July 23, 1888, in Laramie, Wyo. (some sources give his place of birth as Chicago), and spent his early years in Chicago and Nebraska. After his parents divorced at age eight, his mother moved to England, where he attended public (that is, private) schools.

After being graduated from Dulwich Public School, of which P. G. Wodehouse also was an alumnus, he studied in Europe for the British civil service exam, did very well on the exam and began work as a civil service clerk.

Finding that he disliked the civil service, Chandler worked for a time as a reporter for the *London Daily Express.* He also wrote and placed a few juvenile poems. In 1912, he returned to the U.S., briefly living in San Francisco before moving to Los Angeles, where he took a job as a bookkeeper in Los Angeles and brought his mother to live with him.

In 1917, Chandler enlisted in the Canadian Army Expedition Forces and was sent to France, where he suffered a concussion from artillery fire. He then transferred to the Canadian Royal Air Force, but the war ended while he was still in training. Chandler returned to Los Angeles and went into the oil business with a company called the Dabney Oil Syndicate. In 1924, after the death of his mother who opposed the marriage, he married Cissy Hurlburt, a woman 18 years his senior. Despite the difference in ages, initially the marriage was a happy one, and Chandler prospered in the oil business, rising to the position of vice president of Dabney.

The onset of the Great Depression and problems at work with female employees and drinking, however, put an end to Chandler's success in the oil business. He reportedly was dismissed by the company in 1931. It was then that he seriously began to thinking about writing professionally. Chandler discovered Dashiell Hammett and other mystery writers in the pulps, especially *Black Mask.*

In 1933 and 1934, his first short stories appeared in *Black Mask.* After experimenting with a number of different protagonists, he settled on Philip Marlowe as the central character in his short stories. Over the course of the 1930s he published about 20 stories in *Black Mask.*

Unlike his literary mentor Hammett, Chandler did not have personal experience with detective work. He learned about police work and the PI business from reading about it.

Chandler's first two novels, *The Big Sleep* (1939) and *Farewell My Lovely* (1940) were expansions and combinations of his previously written short stories. After publishing four Philip Marlowe novels, Chandler began working as a screenwriter for Hollywood, mostly at Paramount but also at Warner Brothers, MGM and Universal. He was well paid – one year he earned $100,000 working on a script, well over a million in today's dollars.

Two of his efforts, for James M. Cain's *Double Indemnity* and *The Blue Dahlia,* for which Chandler wrote the original screenplay, were nominated for Academy Awards. Humphrey Bogart played Philip Marlowe in *The Big Sleep* (1946).

However, like many other novelists before him, Chandler was unhappy working for Hollywood. He was especially dissatisfied with the MGM movie version of his novel, *The Lady in the Lake.*

The last time he worked as a screenwriter was in 1950 when he collaborated with Alfred Hitchcock on *Strangers on a Train.* That effort was a disaster. Years after his death, two more of his novels were the basis for films *The Little Sister* in 1969 and *The Long Goodbye* in 1973.

Problems with his work and with his marriage likely contributed to Chandler's heavy drinking, which had become more and more of an issue. He stopped appearing in public, and his friends no longer invited him to dinners and parties.

What most critics consider his greatest work, *The Long Goodbye,* appeared in 1953, one year before the death of his wife, Cissy.

By this time, years of hard drinking began to take its toll, and in the 1950s Chandler spent time in at least two sanatoriums for treatment of his alcoholism.

The last and weakest of Chandler's Marlowe novels, *Playback,* appeared in 1958. Soon after, Chandler was elected president of the Mystery Writers of America. In the late winter of 1959, he flew to New York to give his inaugural address.

The weather in New York was bad, and Chandler came down with a cold. Due to his weakened condition from constant drinking, the cold turned into pneumonia, and he died on March 26, 1959, at a hospital in La Jolla. He was 71.

At the time of his death, Chandler was working on a story in which Marlowe gets married and lives in Palm Springs, the tony Southern California town Chandler called "Poodle Springs." Years later, Robert B. Parker completed Chandler's unfinished novel. It was published as *Poodle Springs* in 1989 with Chandler and Parker listed as co-authors. In 1990, Parker also wrote *Perchance to Dream,* which he termed a sequel to *The Big Sleep.*

Philip Marlowe Novels by Raymond Chandler

The Big Sleep (1939)
Farewell, My Lovely (1940)
The High Window (1942)
The Lady in the Lake (1943)
The Little Sister (1949)
The Long Goodbye (1953)
Playback (1958)
Poodle Springs (left unfinished at Chandler's death in 1959; completed by Robert B. Parker, 1989)

Philip Marlowe Short Story Collection

The Simple Art of Murder (1950)

Notable Works on Raymond Chandler

Hiney, Tom, *Raymond Chandler: A Biography* (1997). A controversial biography faulted for a number of factual errors.

Lester, Herb and Cooper, Kim, *The Raymond Chandler Map of Los Angeles* (2017). A map covering the important places in Los Angeles related to Marlowe and Chandler.

MacShane, Frank, *The Life of Raymond Chandler* (1976). One of the earlier biographies of Chandler.

Travis McGee

From the Travis McGee series by John D. MacDonald (1916-1986)

Plaque mounted at Bahia Mar Marina, Slip F-18, in Fort Lauderdale
Photo by Jonathan Schilling

Boat bum, self-described "salvage consultant" and occasional existential philosopher who takes his retirement in chunks as life goes along, Travis McGee is the first-person narrator of 21 novels by John D. MacDonald. The McGee novels, starting with *The Deep Blue Good-by* in 1964 and ending with *The Lonely Silver Rain* in 1984, are among the best detective-adventure stories written in the 20th century.

All the McGee series books have a color in the title – amber, cinnamon, gold, indigo, copper, turquoise – and are at least partially set in Fort Lauderdale, at the Bahia Mar marina. There his hulking 52-foot houseboat, *The Busted Flush,* won in a poker game, is moored.

As a salvage consultant, the last resort for those who have lost something valuable, McGee is paid a standard recovery fee of 50 percent of anything he recovers. However, he often accepts less than the full fee. Among the items he's been hired to recover are: a $400,000 stamp collection, blue sapphires worth $40,000, Mexican gold figurines worth $300,000 to $400,000 and cash or other valuables worth from about $29,000 to $900,000.

In the series, McGee is in his late 30s to mid-40s, stands 6 feet 4 inches tall and at his prime weight is around 205 pounds. He wears a size 46 suit and shirt with 17½-inch neck and 36-inch sleeves. Most people seem to think he is larger than he is, frequently remarking on his size.

McGee is a Korean War vet, discharged as a sergeant with a Purple Heart, played semi-pro football for two years, is deeply tanned, quick on his feet and a talented brawler. However, McGee frequently loses his physical battles. He has been knifed, shot and badly beaten up a number of times. He has lost three teeth, has had several serious concussions and has been shot in the right side of his waist, his left shoulder and his right *gluteus maximus.* He ages some over the series, perhaps to his early 40s, and by the end is worried that he is not as quick as he used to be.

The salvage consult plays chess, bridge, poker and backgammon. He likes classical music and jazz and seems knowledgeable about modern art. McGee often wears old blue jeans and tee-shirts, khakis and boat shoes. He enjoys traditional food, especially rare or medium rare steaks with baked potato, beef stew, chili, Irish stew, hamburgers, broiled flounder and scrambled eggs with country ham. McGee likes black coffee, preferring fine-ground Colombian and espresso.

Women seem to like McGee, and he usually ends up in bed with one or two in each book. A guestimate is that he has had sex in the novels with at least 50 women. McGee frequently compares himself to a knight-errant avenging wrongs and rescuing fair maidens. Sometimes, friends and he himself view him as Don Quixote with an existential side.

Trav McGee's best friend and sometimes sidekick on his adventures to Mexico and elsewhere is the multilingual PhD economist, semi-retired, a hairy bear of a man known only as Meyer, who (until the boat is destroyed by a bomb) also lives at Bahia Mar in his cabin cruiser, the *John Maynard Keynes.*

Meyer then buys another boat, which he names the *Thorstein Veblen.* Meyer speaks at least seven languages, including German, Swedish and Hawaiian. He attracts young women like honey attracts flies.

McGee's Digs: McGee famously lives in his 52-foot houseboat, *The Busted Flush,* at Slip F-18 in Bahia Mar marina in Ft. Lauderdale. He named his boat after he won it in a 30-hour high-stakes poker game. In a round of five-card stud, he was dealt the deuce of clubs face down, the deuce of hearts face up. His next three cards were all hearts. McGee bet heavily, and when everyone else dropped out, he collected the pot, "accidentally" showing his hole card to be a club, so he took the pot with a busted flush. This had the result of making the other players think he bluffed frequently. By the end of evening, the big loser in the game was down $30,000, and McGee lent that player the 30 grand against the guy's big houseboat. McGee left the game as the owner of the boat.

The houseboat is a custom-built barge with a 21-foot beam and a displacement of 38 tons. Its draft is only 4 feet. Powered by twin 58-horsepower diesels, *The Busted Flush* has a range of up to 600 miles at about 6 knots. It carries 500 gallons of fresh water and has a 10 kilowatt gas generator to provide air-conditioning and kitchen power when not in port. However, the big houseboat rolls badly in seas and can be taken out in the ocean only in good weather with low seas.

The Busted Flush has a master bedroom with king-size bed, a master head with 7-foot-long bath tub, a guest stateroom, a large lounge with curved couch, big and small chairs, bookshelf, hi-fi record systems and a small TV. The well-equipped, stainless steel galley has two refrigerators, a freezer locker and a canned food locker and propane stove. In the bilge area is a well-hidden safe, and there are other hiding places around the ship. Topside there are good-sized aft, bow and sun decks, along with an enclosed wheelhouse with dual controls.

McGee's Rides: Parked at the marina where *The Busted Flush* is moored, and rather incongruously so given McGee's preference for a low profile, sits *Miss Agnes,* his vintage 1936 Rolls-Royce. This possibly was based on the large Phantom III with V-12 engine, one-shot lubrication system and road damping adjustable by the driver. Only 710 of these motorcars, now highly collectible, were manufactured in 1935 and 1936.

However, it possibly could be a Wraith or a 20/25 or 25/30, as the chassis of all these also were made by Rolls-Royce in 1936, with custom bodies and interiors by coachbuilders.

The exact model is never clearly specified. At any rate, it has been bastardized by a previous owner, converted into a pick-up and painted an ugly neon blue.

After an accident dumps the Rolls-Royce into a Florida drainage canal, McGee further defiles the original hand-built motorcar, putting in a modern V-8 engine from a 1972 Lincoln Mark IV Continental, along with a new transmission and power train, a Dodge truck suspension, power steering, disc brakes, 12-volt electrical system and air-conditioning. The converted Rolls will do more than 140 mph on the highway.

McGee's Drinks: McGee is a gin man, preferring to drink Plymouth gin by the "flagon" straight on ice. For a time, when Plymouth was no longer distilled in England, he switched to Boodles. Occasionally, McGee drinks the McGee Special Martini, swirling an old-fashioned glass filled two-thirds full of shaved ice with dry sherry, pouring out the sherry and adding Plymouth gin to the top of the ice, with a lemon peel rubbed on the rim. McGee also likes cold beers on a hot day, preferring Mexican lagers such as Carta Blanca and Dos Equis. McGee also has been known to drink bourbon and water and when in Mexico sips aged tequila straight.

The liquor locker on *The Busted Flush* is well-stocked, with Wild Turkey bourbon, Jack Daniels, Plymouth, Boodles and Booth's gin, Metaxa tequila, Irish whisky, red wine and Rose's sweetened lime juice and bitters.

Plymouth Gin on Ice

Plymouth Gin

Ice cubes

Take a "flagon" of Plymouth brand gin (if not available, use Boodles) and pour it straight over a glass full of ice. Sip, preferably when sitting on the deck of a houseboat in Florida.

McGee Special Martini

Plymouth gin

Old-fashioned glasses, two-thirds full of cracked ice

Slosh of dry sherry

Lemon peel

Pour an unmeasured "big slosh" of any dry sherry into an old-fashioned glass two-thirds full of cracked ice. Quickly swirl the sherry around the glass, then pour it out. Fill the glass to the top of the cracked ice with Plymouth gin. Rub the lemon peel around the top of the glass and pinch a drop or two of citrus beads on top of the drink. Sip and repeat.

McGee South-of-the Border Beer

Carta Blanca or Dos Equis beer

Put good Mexican lager beer on ice or refrigerate until frosty cold. Pop cap and take deep swigs straight from the bottle.

About Author John D. MacDonald:

Born in Sharon, Penn., in 1916, John Dann MacDonald grew up in a middle-class family in Utica, N.Y. He attended Wharton School of Finance at the University of Pennsylvania, but dropped out. He later obtained a bachelor's degree in business administration at Syracuse University, where he met and married Dorothy Prentiss, and then earned an MBA from Harvard. MacDonald worked in collections, insurance sales and for Burroughs Adding Machines before being commissioned as a lieutenant in the U.S. Army in 1940. He served in the China-Burma-India Theater in World War II, including a stint under Joseph "Vinegar Joe" Stillwell, rising to the rank of lieutenant colonel.

MacDonald's first published short story was in *Story Magazine* in 1946, for which he received $25, and shortly thereafter sold a story for $40 to *Detective Tales.* By working 14 hours a day, he became a prolific contributor to pulp magazines, earning enough to support his wife and young son.

After the pulp market disappeared, he switched to paperback thrillers, some of which sold millions of copies for Fawcett and Dell. MacDonald's first novel that drew national attention from critics was *The Executioners,* published in 1957. The dark novel is the story of an attorney who testifies against a rapist. After being paroled from prison 14 years later, in a murderous vendetta the rapist stalks the attorney and his family.

MacDonald began working on the Travis McGee series in 1962, finishing the first three novels in the series – to be sure he could live with a long-term series – before allowing the first to be published in 1964. McGee originally was to be called Dallas McGee, but after President John F. Kennedy was killed in Dallas, MacDonald decided to change the first name, choosing Travis from the Air Force base in California.

By his death at age 70 of heart disease in 1986, he had written more than 600 short stories and 70 novels, along with a number of non-fiction books, collections of short stories and articles. Many were set in his adopted home of Florida, where he and his wife lived on Siesta Key near Sarasota.

His novel about shady real estate development in Florida, *Condominium,* was on *The New York Times* best-seller list for six months. In 1972, MacDonald won the Grand Master award from the Mystery Writers of America, and in 1980 he won the National Book Award for *The Green Ripper*, the only mystery novel ever to win the award.

John D. MacDonald was often confused with his contemporary Ross Macdonald, main pseudonym of Kenneth Millar (1915-1983), creator of a the hard-boiled detective series featuring Lew Archer. *(See the chapter on Lew Archer.)*

Several of MacDonald's works have been made into movies, including 1962's *Cape Fear,* starring Gregory Peck and Robert Mitchum, based on *The Executioners.* The movie is set on the Cape Fear River near Wilmington on the coast of North Carolina, although the film was shot on location in Savannah. *Cape Fear* was re-filmed in 1991 by Martin Scorsese. In 1970, his Travis McGee novel, *Darker Than Amber,* was made into a movie starring Rod Taylor as McGee and Theodore Bikel as Meyer. *The Empty Copper Sea* was made as a TV movie in 1983, starring Sam Elliott as McGee and with the Florida setting changed to California.

Stephen King called MacDonald "the great entertainer of our age, and a mesmerizing storyteller." Kurt Vonnegut said MacDonald's works would be compared by future archeologists to the "treasures of the tomb of Tutankhamen."

Travis McGee Novels by John D. MacDonald

The Deep Blue Good-by (1964)
Nightmare in Pink (1964)
A Purple Place for Dying (1964)
The Quick Red Fox (1964)
A Deadly Shade of Gold (1965)
Bright Orange for the Shroud (1965)
Darker than Amber (1966)
One Fearful Yellow Eye (1966)
Pale Gray for Guilt (1968)
The Girl in the Plain Brown Wrapper (1968)
Dress Her in Indigo (1969)
The Long Lavender Look (1970)
A Tan and Sandy Silence (1971)
The Scarlet Ruse (1972)
The Turquoise Lament (1973)
The Dreadful Lemon Sky (1974)
The Empty Copper Sea (1978)
The Green Ripper (1979)

Free Fall in Crimson (1981)
Cinnamon Skin (1982)
The Lonely Silver Rain (1984)

Notable Books about John D. MacDonald

Merrill, Hugh, *The Red Hot Typewriter: The Life and Times of John D. MacDonald* (2000). The best biography of MacDonald.

Shine, Jean and Walter, *JDMBibliophile* (1979). Fascinating self-published newsletter on John D. McDonald, with a "Special Confidential Report" on Travis McGee.

Jim Rockford

From the The Rockford Files TV series (1974-1980) starring James Garner

"Jim, I have finally finished 12 long years of psychotherapy, and I'm now able to tell you just what I think of you. Would you please call me?"

Message on Jim Rockford's answering machine

James Garner receives the Purple Heart with Oak Leaf Clusters – he was wounded on two occasions in the Korean War

Jim Rockford, played by James Garner (1928-2014), is a free-spirited, wisecracking Los Angeles private detective in *The Rockford Files* television series that debuted in the fall 1974 season on NBC. The popular series has been rated as one of the best shows of all time by *TV Guide* and other publications.

As portrayed by Garner, who was 46 when "The Rockford Files" debuted, Jim Rockford is an ex-con who served time in San Quentin but who was later pardoned. Rockford has a Los Angeles private investigator's license, but legally he frequently gets close to the line. While not a con artist, Rockford has a big collection of business cards with various names and business titles.

Rockford relies on his wits and his gift of gab to gather information and get the job done for his clients. He rarely resorts to the use of his Colt revolver and only uses his fists when absolutely necessary. More often than not, Jim is sluggee rather than the slugger.

Rockford claims to only handle "cold cases," no active cases that might draw too much attention from the police, although over the series that rule is violated a number of times. He does a lot of insurance investigations and missing person cases. Rockford's only good friend on the LA police force is he long-suffering Sergeant Dennis Becker (played by Joe Santos), who is promoted to Lieutenant late in the series. Rockford charges $200 a day plus expenses, although many times he ends up working for nothing.

In the first four seasons, the lovely, bright Beth Davenport (Gretchen Corbett) is Jim's attorney and off-and-on girlfriend. Among his other love interests during the series are Dr. Megan Dougherty (Kathryn Harrold), a blind psychiatrist, and Rita Capkovic (Rita Moreno), a former prostitute.

Rockford's father, Joseph "Rocky" Rockford (played by Noah Beery Jr.), a former tractor-trailer truck driver, appears in most episodes. Jim and Rocky love to go fishing together.

Angel Martin (Stuart Margolin), Rockford's former prison mate at San Quentin, shows up frequently, usually as a result of trying to pull some small-time scam. Soft-hearted Jim remains Angel's friend, despite all the problems he causes Rockford. Jim's nemesis is Lance White (Tom Selleck, in his pre-Magnum days), a suave, highly successful, impossibly perfect PI who always gets the bad guy while collecting large fees and winning awards for his brilliant detecting, leaving Rockford with mud on his face.

Rockford's Digs: Jim Rockford lives in a dilapidated singlewide trailer on the beach in Malibu. In early episodes, Rockford's trailer is located in a parking lot at 2354 Pacific Coast Highway. For the rest of the series, the trailer is at 29 Paradise Cove adjacent to an ocean pier and a restaurant, the Sand Castle, sometimes called the Sand Pebble, later known as the Paradise Cove Beach Café.

Rockford uses his trailer as his office. Every episode of the series starts with a call on Rockford's home answering machine. Usually the messages are humorous, to viewers if not to Rockford, and rarely have anything to do with the episode coming up. Many of the messages are from bill collectors, old girlfriends or deadbeat friends and clients.

Typical messages:

"It's Norma at the market. It bounced. You want me to tear it up, send it back or put it with the others?"

"Jim? It's Shirley at the cleaners. You know that brown jacket, the one that I said looked so great on you? Your favorite. We lost it."

"It's Jack. The check is in the mail. Sorry it's two years late. Sorry I misfigured my checking account, and I'm overdrawn. Sorry I stopped payment on it. So, when it comes, tear it up. Sorry."

"Jim, this is Cal of the Leave the Whales Alone Club. Our protest cruise leaves from the pier Saturday at 3 a.m. The whales need you, Jim."

"This is The Baron. Angel Martin tells me you buy information. Okay, meet me at 1 a.m. behind the bus depot, bring $500 and come alone. I'm serious."

"Here's the tally, Jimbo. You had Atlanta at even money, tough break. And you got bombed in the Duke-Wake Forest fiasco, and you split the quinella at Hollypark. So you owe the book for $450. Anytime before Friday, huh, buddy?"

Rockford's Drives: One of the stars of *The Rockford Files* is Jim's Pontiac Firebird. It's the Esprit model (at least the 1974 was the Esprit model, with later models being the performance-oriented Formula 400 model, with beefed-up suspensions), in a gold/copper color with tan interior. In most episodes, the car's California license tag is 853 OKG. According to Oklahoma-born James Garner, he OKG stood for "Oklahoma Gamer," but the origin of 853 is unknown.

The show had new, essentially identical, Firebirds each season, from 1974 through 1978 model years. Most years, the show had three different vehicles to use in simultaneous filming or in case the script called for the car to be wrecked or blown up. Firebird *aficionados* may be able to spot the slight design and detail differences of each year's vehicle, and in a few episodes footage from a previous year was reused. (The biggest difference in the model years is in the headlights.) Reportedly, James Garner didn't like the front grill-less design of the 1979 Firebird, so the 1978 model was used in the last season (1979-80) of the show.

Rockford, with James Garner doing the driving himself (Garner was a motorsports enthusiast and for a time owned an auto racing team), made the "J-Turn" or "Rockford Turn" famous. It was a high-speed turn-around used by Jim to evade a tail or when cornered by another car. It works this way: Rockford suddenly brakes to a stop, shifts into reverse, speeds up backwards in a straight line, then sharply turns the steering wheel. This causes the front end to swing around 180 degrees, allowing Rockford to shift out of reverse and speed off in the opposite direction. Don't try this at home.

Rockford's Drinks: Jim Rockford was mostly a beer drinker. He kept beer in his fridge in his trailer, popping one to enjoy with some Oreo cookies, or while watching a ballgame with Rocky, or drinking one with a spicy taco with extra hot sauce at Casa Taco.

The beer was in "generic" cans without an obvious brand name. Beers popular during the 1970s included classic domestic brands such as Bud, Miller, Schlitz and Pabst Blue Ribbon.

In a restaurant with a date, Rockford might order wine or, occasionally, a bourbon and water.

Malibu Trailer

Cold can of domestic beer (any American brand – Bud, Miller, PBR)

Open the fridge, grab a can of cold beer and pop the top. Drink it straight from the can.

About The Rockford Files:

The Rockford Files was created and produced by Roy Huggins (1914-2002) and Stephen J. Cannell (1941-2010).

Huggins in the 1950s had created the pioneering television series *Maverick,* a Western comedy-drama also starring James Garner. He also created *The Fugitive,* a highly successful program in the mid-1960s. During his long career, Huggins wrote more than 350 screen and television scripts.

In most credits, Huggins is listed as John Thomas James, a pseudonym taken from the name of Huggins' three sons.

Cannell wrote or co-wrote 35 of the *Rockford* shows, including the pilot. He directed several episodes. Cannell is credited with creating or co-creating more than 40 television shows, including, in addition to *Rockford, Baretta, The A-Team, Black Sheep Squadron, Jump Street* and *The Comish.* By his own count, over his career he wrote more than 450 TV scripts and produced more than 1,500 episodes. Cannell also wrote 18 novels.

The Rockford Files ran for a total of 123 episodes, plus a pilot. After the final episode aired on NBC in January 1980, eight made-for-TV *Rockford* movies, also starring James Garner, by then in his 60s, aired on CBS from 1994 to 1999.

Stuart M. Kaminsky (1934-2009), a prolific mystery writer who did some two dozen books featuring his Toby Peters detective character, penned two novels based on the characters in the television series, *The Green Bottle* (1996) and *Devil on My Doorstep* (2001). Both novels are set at a later time in Rockford's life, after the death of his dad, Rocky. Another writer, Mike Jahn, also did a couple of novels based on the *Rockford* series that appeared while the program was on the air.

Star James Garner was born James Bumgarner in Norman, Okla., in 1928. He left high school to become a merchant seaman before moving to Los Angeles where he attended Hollywood High. Returning to Norman, he joined the Oklahoma National Guard. Garner was called up for duty in the Korean War, during which he saw combat and was awarded the Purple Heart before his discharge in 1952. He briefly attended the University of Oklahoma before returning to Hollywood.

Garner's first notable role was as Marlon Brando's friend in the film *Sayonara,* and he went on to star in about 50 movies. His big break, though, came in television, in the role of Bret Maverick in the 1950s series, for which he shared a Golden Globe award and was nominated for his first Emmy. In some ways, Jim Rockford was a reprise of the Maverick character.

Among his best movies roles were with Julie Andrews in *The Americanization of Emily* (1964) and *Victor/Victoria* (1982); in *Grand Prix* (1966), considered one of the best racing movies ever made and in which Garner did much of his own driving; as Philip Marlowe in *Marlowe* (1969), based on Raymond Chandler's "The Little Sister," following in the acting footsteps of Humphrey Bogart, Dick Powell and Alan Ladd.

Garner also starred with Sally Fields in *Murphy's Romance* (1985), for which he received an Academy Award nomination; and as an ex-president opposite Jack Lemmon in *My Fellow Americans* (1996), which was filmed around Asheville, N.C.

Garner won an Emmy for his performance in the highly rated *The Rockford Files,* one of two he won in his career and one of 15 nominations. In *Rockford,* Garner took pride in performing most of his own stunts.

Still popular with television audiences, *The Rockford Files* remains in syndication. It also is available on Netflix, Hulu and other online services.

Sam Spade

From the novel The Maltese Falcon by Dashiell Hammett (1894-1961), and the 1941 movie directed by John Huston starring Humphrey Bogart

'She put her mouth to his, slowly, her arms around him, and came into his arms. She was in his arms when the door-bell rang."

Dashiell Hammett, *The Maltese Falcon*

U.S. postage stamp honoring director and screenwriter John Houston – Humphrey Bogart and the Maltese Falcon are in the background Photo credit Shutterstock.com

The Maltese Falcon is a jewel-encrusted gold sculpture, and Dashiell Hammett's novel is the crown jewel of his body of work. In the view of many, it is the nearly perfect detective story, and the 1941 movie made from it, which follows the novel closely, is arguably the best private eye film ever made.

The novel is set in downtown San Francisco over a five-day period, between Wednesday and Sunday, in the first half of December 1928, contemporaneously with the time it was being written.

The plot is so well known it is only necessary to briefly summarize it here. A beautiful young woman, Brigid O'Shaughnessy (played in the film by Mary Astor), comes to the offices of Spade & Archer, where she meets with Samuel Spade (played by Humphrey Bogart.)

Brigid initially gives a false name, Ruth Wonderly, and tells a tale about wanting to find her sister, who supposedly has come to San Francisco with a boyfriend, Floyd Thursby. She wants either Sam or his partner, Miles Archer (Jerome Cowan), to shadow Thursby and find her sister. Sam doesn't believe her story, but he accepts a $200 retainer (about $2,500 today) anyway.

Archer decides to do the shadowing. During the course of the evening, he is shot to death, as is Thursby. Sam Spade, who is having an affair with Archer's wife, Iva (played by Gladys George) is immediately suspected of the killings. Police detectives Dundy (Barton Maclane) and Polhaus (Ward Bond) pay a visit to Sam at his apartment. Spade, both out of a kind of duty to his partner, even though he didn't particularly like him and has been bedding his wife, and also to avoid being charged with the murders, sets out to solve the case.

It is soon obvious that the beautiful Brigid is up to her neck in something. She is after the 16th century golden, bejeweled falcon, worth a huge fortune. The bird was given as tribute to the King of Spain by a group of crusaders, the Hospitallers of Saint John of Jerusalem, who had made their homes on the island of Malta and several nearby islands. Brigid has been hired by the aptly named Kasper Gutman, a fat man (played wonderfully in the film by Sydney Greenstreet), to help find the falcon. She also hooks up with the homosexual Joel Cairo (played in the film without much gay undertone by Peter Lorre) but betrays them both.

Gutman, who claims to have been searching for the precious bird for 17 years, offers Sam, whom he believes to know the whereabouts of the falcon, sizeable amounts of money for it. Spade finally does get the bird, delivered by the dying captain of a freighter that has arrived from Hong Kong carrying the falcon hidden in the hold. The captain has been shot multiple times and expires in Spade's office. Spade leaves his trusty assistant, Effie Perine (played by Lee Patrick) to explain it all to the police. Sam delivers the bird, and Gutman is ready to pay him $10,000 (about $125,000 today), much less than he was originally promised. But it's all to naught, as Gutman discovers this is just a worthless replica made of lead.

By this time, Spade has slept with and is close to falling in love with O'Shaughnessy, but he realizes it was she who killed Miles Archer and Floyd Thursby. Brigid makes a final play for Sam, and he admits he probably is in love with her, but he decides to turn her over to the police. His famous line "I won't play the sap for you" sums it up.

The Maltese Falcon, unlike the *Continental Op* novels that preceded it, which were written in the first person, uses a third person narrator, a technique that works especially well with this book.

Sam Spade's Digs: During most of the time he was working on *The Maltese Falcon* Dashiell Hammett was living in a fourth-story corner apartment, likely number 401, in Charring Cross Apartments at 891 Post Street in San Francisco. This is also the apartment that Sam Spade occupies in *The Maltese Falcon.*

Except for a brief excursion out of the city by rented car and driver, all of the action in both the novel and the movie takes place in a relatively small area of downtown San Francisco. As noted, Spade's apartment is at 891 Post Street. A plaque was placed on the building in 2005, citing it as a "Literary Landmark" and the home of both Sam Spade and Dashiell Hammett. The Spade & Archer offices are in the Hunter-Dulin Building at 111 Sutter Street, about a 15-minute walk from Spade's apartment. The Hunter-Dulin Building was no run-down dump. The 25-story building had been completed in 1927, just the year before the time of the novel and about the time when Spade said he had moved to San Francisco from Seattle. Its design combines Late Gothic Revival and French Renaissance Revival styles. Supposedly Spade's office was on the fifth floor. In the real world, the building served as the West Coast headquarters of the National Broadcasting Company (NBC) from 1927 to 1942. In 1997, it was listed on the National Registry of Historic Places.

In the book, Archer shadows Floyd Thursby from the lobby of the St. Mark Hotel to Burritt Alley, where they are both killed. There is a plaque on what is now Burritt Street noting that this is where Miles Archer died. The St. Mark likely is modeled on the St. Francis Hotel on Union Square, which had opened in 1904 and rebuilt after the 1906 earthquake. The St. Francis was then an institution in San Francisco, and Hammett claimed to have worked his most famous Pinkerton Detective Agency case here. In 1921, the movie star Roscoe "Fatty" Arbuckle was accused, many said falsely, of raping the young actress Virginia Rappe, who died as a result. He was tried three times for the alleged rape, with two hung juries and a final acquittal. However, the scandal ruined his career.

Other landmarks in *The Maltese Falcon* include John's Grill on Ellis Street, where Spade had a dinner of two pork chops, a baked potato and tomatoes for 50 cents. The chophouse and seafood restaurant is still open today, at 63 Ellis, near the original site.

Kasper Gutman is said to have stayed at the Alexandria Hotel. There was no hotel named that in San Francisco at the time, but Hammett in 1928 had stayed at the Alexandria Hotel in Los Angeles. The fictional Alexandria may have been the Sir Francis Drake at Sutter and Powell streets or possibly the Clift Hotel on Geary Street.

Sam Spade's Drives: Like Hammett himself, Spade does not have a car or even a driver's license. Spade uses taxis, a hired car and driver and the San Francisco streetcars to get around.

Sam Spade's Drinks: At one point in *The Maltese Falcon* novel Spade drinks several wine glasses of straight Bacardi rum and then falls asleep in his apartment on Post Street. He keeps a bottle of pre-mixed Manhattans in his desk drawer at his office in the Hunter-Dulin Building. The following Sam Spade Manhattan is made from scratch.

Spade Manhattan

2 oz. rye
1 oz. sweet vermouth
Several dashes of Angostura bitters
Luxardo cherry for garnish

Put ice in a shaker and add rye and sweet vermouth. Shake well and drain into a cocktail glass. Garnish with cherry.

About Dashiell Hammett:

(For additional biographical information on Dashiell Hammett, see the section on The Thin Man.*)*

Samuel Dashiell Hammett wrote *The Maltese Falcon*, his third novel, in 1928, completing a draft in December of that year. He revised it in the first half of 1929 and sent the manuscript to his publisher, Knopf, in June 1929. Hammett thought the book was the best thing he had done to the time, and he asked both the publisher, Blanche Knopf, and his editor at Knopf, Harry Block, not to edit the story too much.

Block liked the novel and in fact edited it lightly. The main changes were to downplay the sexual attraction of Spade to Brigid O'Shaughnessy and to eliminate some references to the homosexuality of Joel Cairo. In the film, Peter Lorre plays Cairo as a louche loner.

The book was serialized in five parts in *Black Mask,* beginning with the September 1929 issue. It was published by Knopf in 1930. Later, Hammett used Sam Spade as a character in three short stories.

A motif that runs throughout the novel is how people deal with unexpected, random events.

At one point, Sam Spade tells an odd story – in the novel, but not in the movie about a man named Flitcraft, who was living a well-ordered life with a successful real estate business, a wife and children in Tacoma, Wash. One day, on his way to lunch, he is almost killed by a falling construction beam. The man then deserts his business and family (but leaving his wife and children well off) and moves to Spokane. There, under a new name, Charles Pierce, he starts over in a new business, a car dealership, builds it into a success, and marries a woman much like his former wife. He has a child and in time his life becomes as well ordered as it was before.

About this odd event Spade explains: "He adjusts himself to beams falling, and then no more of them fell, and he adjusted himself to them not falling." Spade doesn't bother to explain that Charles Peirce, spelled only slightly differently from the man in Hammett's story, was a 19th century philosopher who wrote about chance, randomness and how people live with their illusions.

The Maltese Falcon received high praise from the top critics of the time. Alexander Woollcott called it "the best detective story America has yet produced." Other critics compared Hammett to Hemingway.

The novel was also a commercial success. It went through seven printings in its first year of publication. The movie rights were sold to Warner Brothers.

About the 1941 Film:

The famous 1941 movie was actually a remake. The original *The Maltese Falcon* was produced in 1931 with Ricardo Cortez as Sam Spade and Bebe Daniels as Ruth Wonderly/Brigid O'Shaughnessy. It was a box office success. In a second version, this one a 1936 comedy titled *Satan Met a Lady,* the Sam Spade character was renamed Ted Shane and played by Warren William. The 1936 version bombed at the box office.

Today, it is impossible to separate Sam Spade from Humphrey Bogart, so completely did he take over the role. The Spade described in Hammett's novel – 33 years old, 6 feet tall, 185 pounds, with a V-shaped face and blond hair – was physically very different from Bogart, who was then in his early 40s, with dark hair, craggy features, standing only 5 feet 8 inches tall with a slight build.

Spade rolls his own cigarettes, using Bull Durham tobacco and brown cigarette papers. Unlike most PIs, he doesn't carry a gun.

John Huston's script for the movie is faithful to Hammett's novel. Only a few, mostly minor, scenes from the novel are left out of the film.

One has to do with Kasper Gutman's daughter, who is in the novel but not in the film. This change is an improvement, helping the movie move forward more effectively. Another scene, when Spade forces Brigid to strip naked so she can prove she didn't steal a $1,000 bill (Gutman had in fact palmed it), doesn't make it to the movie, likely because it wouldn't have passed Code.

Huston uses Hammett's terse, often sarcastic dialogue almost verbatim, making cuts mainly for the sake of time.

It is nearly impossible to think how the casting for the movie could have been any better. Bogart simply *is* Samuel Spade. He would receive an Academy Award nomination as Best Actor for the role. Sydney Greenstreet and Peter Lorre are perfect in their roles, respectively, as the fat man with a heart of cold steel and the mincing, cowardly but sinister and vicious Joel Cairo. The more minor roles – Iva, Effie, the detectives and others – also are well cast. If there is a weak link, it's Mary Astor as Bridget. She provides a very credible performance, but a little something is missing in the chemistry between Bogie and her. She's a liar and a manipulator, and it doesn't quite make sense that the tough, no-nonsense, practical Spade would fall for her, despite her beauty. *The Maltese Falcon* would prove to be Astor's last starring role in a major picture, as three divorces, drinking, a tangled personal life and an attempted suicide took their toll.

As for director John Huston, this was his first big shot as a director in Hollywood, and he made the most of it. Huston, the son of famous actor Walter Huston, had considerable experience as a screenwriter and had also appeared as an actor in films and on stage, but in the early 1930s he had tried his hand at becoming a painter in London and Paris, failed and had ended up briefly a homeless beggar. Returning to America in 1933, he had better luck, starring as Abraham Lincoln in a movie about the Civil War president. Warner Brothers also made regular use of his writing talents. The studio was so impressed with him that it hired him as both the screenwriter and director for *The Maltese Falcon.* Huston went on to direct a number of the greatest films in Hollywood history, including *The Treasure of the Sierra Nevada, Key Largo, The African Queen* (all with Bogart, with Huston winning Oscars for directing and screenwriting for *Sierra Nevada*), *The Asphalt Jungle* and *The Red Badge of Courage.*

Other Versions: There have been a number of radio versions of *The Maltese Falcon.* Edward G. Robinson played Spade in a 1943 *Lux Radio Theatre* production. Bogart rehashed his film role in both a 1943 *Screen Guild Theater* production and a 1946 *Academy Award Theater* production.

A series, *The Adventures of Sam Spade*, which appeared consecutively on all three networks, ABC, CBS and NBC during the period 1946-1951, starred Howard Duff (and later Steve Dunne) as Sam Spade.

One of the worst detective films ever made, *The Black Bird,* released in 1975 to terrible reviews and poor box office, had George Segal as Sam Spade Jr.

The estate of Dashiell Hammett in 2009 permitted mystery writer Joe Gores to use the original Hammett characters in *Spade & Archer: The Prequel to Dashiell Hammett's The Maltese Falcon.*

Dashiell Hammett's Sam Spade

The Maltese Falcon (1930)

"A Man Called Spade" (1932, *The American Magazine*; also in *A Man Named Spade and Other Stories,* 1944)

"Too Many Have Lived" (1932, *The American Magazine*; also in *A Man Named Spade and Other Stories,* 1944)

"They Can Only Hang You Once" (1932, *The American Magazine*; also in *A Man Named Spade and Other Stories,* 1944)

Notable Works on The Maltese Falcon and Dashiell Hammett:

Cline, Sally, *Dashiell Hammett Man of Mystery* (2014). A biography of Hammett.

Herron, Don, *The Dashiell Hammett Tour* (1979, latest edition 2009). Herron is well known for his Dashiell Hammett tours of San Francisco.

Layman, Richard, *Shadow Man, The Life of Dashiell Hammett* (1981). Arguably the best biography of Hammett.

Spenser

From the Spenser series by Robert B. Parker (1937-2010)

Robert Brown Parker's Spenser is a tough guy with a tender side, the protagonist of 39 novels by Parker, as well as several posthumous novels by contract writers, notably Ace Atkins.

Spenser is introduced in *The Godwulf Manuscript* in 1973 as a 37-year-old ex-boxer, Korean War veteran, former Holy Cross football player and former Massachusetts State Trooper who has left the force due to insubordination. Born in Laramie, Wyo., like Raymond Chandler, on whom Robert Parker wrote part of his PhD dissertation, Spenser works as a private investigator with a small office in Back Bay Boston. In the early drafts of the first Spenser novel, Parker gives Spenser the first name of David, after Parker's elder son, but after this he is known only as Spenser ("like the poet"). Over the course of the books, Spenser ages only a little, perhaps reaching his mid-40s.

The ex-pro fighter, who stands about six feet tall and weighs 195 pounds, still works out with heavy weights, jumps rope, hits heavy and speed bags and runs. Spenser uses his boxing skills to great advantage, rarely losing a fight even against several opponents at a time. Over the course of the series, Spenser is responsible for the deaths of several dozen people, frequently using a .38 Smith & Wesson snub nose revolver or a 9 mm Browning. He also has a .357 Magnum as a backup and at various times uses other weapons including rifles and shotguns and a variety of handguns. In the 1985-88 TV series *Spenser: For Hire,* Robert Urich playing Spenser carries a Beretta 92.

Spenser is a hard-boiled tough-guy PI with a heart. After the first couple of books, he maintains a monogamous if sometimes rocky relationship with Susan Silverman, who at first is a high school guidance counselor and later a successful psychologist in private practice with a PhD from Harvard. Her office is in her home on Linnaean Street in Cambridge. Spenser's relationship with Dr. Silverman, described as a "Jewish princess," is romantic, even sentimental.

Another major and continuing character in the Spenser novels is Hawk, originally introduced in *Promised Land,* the fourth Spenser novel. Hawk, an African-American in his 30s, is if anything even tougher than Spenser. If Spenser is a detective for hire, Hawk is a thug for hire, and he is often involved in violent events on the shady side of legality. Spenser and Hawk frequently box and work out together at a Boston gym, the Harbor Health Club, owned by Henry Cimoli. The gym does well and over the years becomes increasingly upscale.

Rita Fiore is a sexy, redheaded lawyer who appears in many of the Spenser novels. Initially she is an assistant DA in Norfolk County. Later she works as a senior litigator for the law firm of Cone, Oakes & Baldwin.

Paul Giacomin appears first as the teenaged son of a divorced couple and reappears in later Spenser novels. Spenser takes an interest in Paul in *Early Autumn* and becomes a surrogate father to him. Paul studies dance at Sarah Lawrence College and later becomes a professional dancer.

Patricia Utley runs a high-class prostitution business on the East Side of Midtown Manhattan. She figures in several of the Spenser novels including *Ceremony, Taming a Sea-Horse, Mortal Stakes* and Small *Vices,* often helping Spenser.

Spenser and Susan's companion is Pearl, the Wonder Dog. The original Pearl is a chocolate German shorthair pointer. In *Back Story,* the original Pearl has died, and Spenser goes to Toronto to pick up another chocolate German shorthair pointer, this one 15 months old. Spenser and Susan call her Pearl as well.

Spenser often checks in with Martin Quirk (in early novels a lieutenant, later a captain) of the Boston Police Department. Among Spenser's other regular police contacts are Sergeant Frank Belson, later a lieutenant, and Detective Lee Farrell, who is openly gay, both homicide investigators under Quirk's command, and Captain Healy, a captain of the Massachusetts State Police. An equal opportunity private eye, Spenser also maintains relations with mobsters and criminals such as Joe Broz, whose right-hand man is Vinnie Morris, and with Tony Marcus and his shooter Ty-Bop Tatum.

Like many cops and PIs, Spenser likes donuts. He frequents Dunkin' Donuts. If Spenser and Susan are going out for a good meal, they go to a place like the Bristol Lounge at the Four Seasons Hotel. Spenser also favors Grill 23, a steakhouse at 161 Berkeley Street and, until they closed, Casablanca and Rialto, both in Cambridge. He also likes the bars at the Four Seasons and the Taj Hotel Boston, formerly the Ritz-Carlton.

Diversity is part and parcel of the Spenser novels, with a number of gay and lesbian (both of Robert B. Parker's sons are gay), African-American, Mexican-American, Native American and other characters. Spenser is a good cook and frequently prepares dinner. Susan, attractive and slim, has a near-anorexic attitude toward food, often eating only a few bites of her meal.

Spenser is not the kind of traditional detective who seeks out clues. Instead, he stirs things up by poking at hornets' nests to see what may fly out.

The novels are written in the first person, and the later books are almost entirely dialogue, with only brief bits of narrative.

This is an example of the dialogue in the last Spenser novel by Parker, *Sixkill,* published in 2011:

"We were having breakfast in the café at the Taj Hotel, which use to be the Ritz. Our table was in the small bay that looks out on Newbury Street, and the spring morning was almost perfect.

'He's asleep on my couch,' I said. [Spenser is referring to Zebulon Sixkill, a Native American.]

'You've taken him in,' she said.

'For the moment,' I said.

'Good God,' Susan said.

I smiled becomingly.

'Sometimes,' Susan said, "I think you are far too kind for your own good.'

I ate a bite of hash.

'And some other times?' I said.

'I think you are the hardest man I've ever seen,' she said.

'So to speak,' I said.

'No sexual allusion intended,' Susan said.

She broke off the end of a croissant, put very little strawberry jam on it, and popper it in her mouth."

Most of the Spenser books are set in the Boston area, and in many hardcover editions the inside covers have a map of Boston, with places of interest to Spenser, such as his apartment and office and Susan's residence and office, noted. In various books the detective travels to Los Angeles, London, Amsterdam, Washington, D.C. and elsewhere.

Spenser's Digs: Spenser lives in Boston's Back Bay neighborhood, in a four-story brownstone on Marlborough Street near Boston Public Garden. In most of the novels, his small office is nearby, at the corner of Boylston and Berkeley streets. There's an entrance on Boylston and also one from an alley off Berkeley. Spenser's office is on the second floor.

Spenser's Drives: Spenser doesn't care much about cars, driving a series of nondescript vehicles including in later novels a Ford Explorer SUV. Sidekick Hawk has more appreciation for a nice ride and in later times drives an expensive Jaguar.

Spenser's Drinks: Spenser is an equal opportunity drinker. In the earlier novels, such as *God Save the Child* and *Mortal Stakes,* he drinks a lot of beer, with Amstel being one of his favorites. But he also swigs Miller, Labatt and even Schlitz. He also drinks bourbon, notably Wild Turkey.

Spenser enjoys a few fingers of Bushmills   Photo by Van Helsing

In later novels, in beers he tends toward Heineken, Sam Adams and Rolling Rock, and then settles on Coors Blue Moon. However, over the course of all the books he tries at least three dozen different beers, along with a variety of wines and champagnes.

As the years go by, Spenser hits the hard stuff a little harder. He often keeps a bottle of Bushmills Irish whiskey at his office. Bushmills is believed to be the world's oldest operating distillery, founded in 1608.

In the last books by Robert B. Parker, Spenser typically drinks scotch, especially Glenfiddich, Johnny Walker Blue and Laphroaig. His sidekick, Hawk, prefers expensive French champagne, especially Taittinger, Krug, Cristal and Dom Pérignon. Spenser's great love, Susan, usually drinks white wine.

Spenser's Old Irish

Bushmills Irish whiskey

Mug or glass

Pour a couple of fingers of Bushmills Irish whiskey in an old coffee mug or any handy glass. Drink straight.

About Author Robert B. Parker:

Robert B. Parker was born September 17, 1937 in Springfield, Mass., from 1921 to 1931 the site of the only Rolls-Royce factory outside of Britain and for several decades the home of Indian motorcycles. He went to Colby College in Maine, graduating in 1954, and then received master's and PhD degrees in English from Boston University. His doctoral dissertation was on the work of Dashiell Hammett, Raymond Chandler and Ross Macdonald. He married Joan Hall, whom he had gotten to know at Colby, in 1956.

In the late 1950s and early 1960s, Parker worked as a technical writer for Raytheon and then as a copywriter and editor for Prudential Life Insurance. For a short time he owned a small ad agency and was a food writer for a Boston magazine. He also taught at Massachusetts State College in Lowell, Suffolk University in Boston and at Massachusetts State College in Bridgewater. From 1968 until 1979, he taught at Northeastern University. He became a full professor in 1977. After finishing five Spenser novels, he left academe for the life of a full-time writer.

Besides the Spenser series, Parker wrote Westerns, finished a Raymond Chandler Philip Marlowe novel, *Poodle Springs,* and wrote a sequel to Chandler's *The Long Sleep* called *Perchance to Dream.* He created two other mystery series, one featuring female detective Sunny Randall and the other Jesse Stone, a police chief in a small Massachusetts coastal town, an ex-pro baseball player and former Los Angeles cop who wrestles with a drinking problem. There is some crossover among characters in the Spenser, Stone and Randall books.

Parker shared a large Victorian house in an affluent area of Cambridge near the Charles River with his wife, Joan Hall Parker. It was an unusual marriage as they lived on separate floors of the house until his death from a heart attack at age 77 in 2010. Most of Parker's books are dedicated to Joan.

A prolific writer, Parker published nearly 70 books. Besides the 39 Spenser novels, he authored nine Jesse Stone novels, six Sunny Randall novels, five Westerns, four non-fiction volumes, two Philip Marlowe novels and other works. His Spenser novels, especially the earlier ones, won high praise from critics. He received the Edgar Grand Master Award. In 1985, his Spenser books became a TV series, *Spenser: For Hire,* starring Robert Urich. In the TV series, which ran for 66 episodes, Spenser drives Ford Mustangs, including a beautifully restored '66 Mustang GT. There also were four made-for-TV Spenser movies. Several of Parker's Jesse Stone novels were made into TV movies starring Tom Selleck.

In an interview, Robert B. Parker said of the television programs: "I was theoretically a consultant on *Spenser: For Hire* but in fact contributed little. I had a large role in three movies we did for A&E starring Joe Mantegna. In neither case did I think the movies got it right (including the ones in which I had a large role)."

Since Parker's death, his estate has continued three of his most popular series, using contract writers: Ace Atkins for the Spenser series, Michael Brandman and Reed Farrel Coleman for the Jesse Stone series and Robert Knott for the Cole/Hitch Westerns.

Spenser Novels by Robert B. Parker
The Godwulf Manuscript (1973)
God Save the Child (1974)
Mortal Stakes (1975)
Promised Land (1976)
The Judas Goat (1978)
Looking for Rachel Wallace (1980)
Early Autumn (1981)
A Savage Place (1981)
Ceremony (1982)
The Widening Gyre (1983)
Valediction (1984)
A Catskill Eagle (1985)
Taming a Sea Horse (1986)
Pale Kings and Princes (1987)
Crimson Joy (1988)
Playmates (1989)
Stardust (1990)
Pastime (1991)
Double Deuce (1992)
Paper Doll (1993)
Walking Shadow (1994)
Thin Air (1995)
Chance (1996)
Small Vices (1997)
Sudden Mischief (1998)
Hush Money (1999)
Hugger Mugger (2000)
Potshot (2001)
Widow's Walk (2002)
Back Story (2003)
Bad Business (2004)
Cold Service (2005)

School Days (2005)
Hundred-Dollar Baby (2006)
Now and Then (2007)
Rough Weather (2008)
Chasing the Bear: A Young Spenser Novel (2009)
The Professional (2009)
Painted Ladies (2010)
Sixkill (2011)

Posthumous Spenser Novels by Ace Atkins
Lullaby (2012)
Wonderland (2013)
Cheap Shot (2014)
Kickback (2015)
Slow Burn (2016)
Little White Lies (2017)

Posthumous Spenser Novel with Helen Brann
Silent Night (2013)

Notable Works on Robert B. Parker and Spenser
Dean, James and Foxwell, Elizabeth, *The Robert B. Parker Companion* (2005). A useful little book on Parker and his work. It contains an interview with Parker, along with a bibliography, summaries of the Spenser novel plots up to 2005 and short bios of characters in the novels.

NEW WOMEN

Illustration: Shutterstock.com

Women have writing detective fiction for well over a century, and female detectives made appearances early. Agatha Christie's Miss Jane Marple, of course, was the grande dame of amateur detectives *(see the chapter on her in this book),* and Harriett Vain, in the Lord Peter Wimsey series by Dorothy L. Sayers, was an Oxford-educated crime novelist who virtually took over the last four Wimsey books.

However, it was in the early 1970s, with the rise of feminism, that a new kind of detective began to appear – the resourceful, smart, independent woman. We have included one of the first, P. D. James' **Cordelia Gray**. Gray is not as well known as James' male detective, Chief Inspector Adam Dalgliesh, but especially in *An Unsuitable Job for a Woman,* she carves a lasting place in the genre for herself.

Sharon McCone, the creation of Marcia Muller, is often considered the first liberated female private detective. She is also a professional, with her own detective agency.

Her agency is later merged with her lover-husband's international security business, making it quite a successful operation.

Kinsey Milhone, featured in to date 25 novels by Sue Crafton, is perhaps the most popular female detective of the late 20th and early 21st centuries. **Stephanie Plum** is plucky New Jersey lady of Italian and Hungarian descent, created by Janet Evanovich in a series of more than two dozen novels. **Judge Deborah Knott** is more low-key than some of the other feminist detectives, and much of the interest in the novels by Margaret Maron derives from Knott's family and deep roots in the central North Carolina county of Colleton, just southeast of Raleigh. Knott is a lawyer and district court judge.

As to why we didn't include Victoria Iphigenia"Vic" or "V. I." Warshawski, the outgoing, fiercely independent and sexually liberated ex-lawyer and now Chicago private detective created by Sara Peretsky, we have no excuse, except that we haven't read enough of these highly touted detective stories. Yet.

Cordelia Gray
From the Cordelia Gray Novels by P. D. James (1920-2014)

"A private eye is hardly a comfortable dining companion."
– Cordelia Gray in P. D. James' *The Skull Beneath the Skin*

P. D. James at age 93, in Cologne, Germany

P. D. James, labeled "the queen of crime" by *Newsweek,* is best known for her Inspector Adam Dalgliesh series – in 14 novels and five short-story and novella collections – but her Cordelia Gray private detective was one of the first of the "new women" in modern detective fiction. Gray, proprietor of the Pryde's Detective Agency in London, appeared in only two novels, *An Unsuitable Job for a Woman* (1972) and *The Skull Beneath the Skin* (1982).

Gray is young, just 22 at the time of *An Suitable Job,* and only slightly older in *The Skull.* Like P. D. James herself, she has been denied a university education. She had been educated for a while in a convent school, to which she had been admitted by mistake due to a mix up in names. Her father had been a well-known revolutionary idealist. Gray did not get to know him well, but she spent six months with him in Germany and Italy, doing things for his comrades, just before his early death. This nomadic existence came at a bad time, because it made it impossible for her to take her place at Cambridge, so she went to work instead including as a junior assistant at Pryde's agency.

Cordelia inherited the second-rate detective agency from its owner, Bernie Pryde, who committed suicide after learning he has cancer. While lacking much detective experience, Gray is smart, observant and mature for her years.

Rather than try to sell the agency, Gray decides to try to run it. Her first major client is Elizabeth Learning, assistant to Sir Ronald Callendar, a distinguished scientist. The case is an apparent suicide by hanging of a former Cambridge student, Mark Callendar, the 19-year-old son of Sir Ronald. Gray go to see Sir Ronald, who is taken aback by her age and gender, but through her professionalism Gray convinces him to let her handle the case. She goes to Cambridge and moves into the gardener's cottage where the young man was living after he dropped out of Cambridge, working as a gardener and handyman, and where he found hanging. She begins to talk with Mark's oh-so-clever friends at Cambridge, who try to put her off the scent. Nonetheless, Cordelia enjoys being at Cambridge and the student life there that she had not been able to experience herself. She soon learns, based on the way he was hanged and other evidence, that Mark's death was not a suicide but murder.

In the process, Cordelia is thrown down a well near the cottage and left to die. She escapes and waits, with the unlicensed pistol, a .38 semi-automatic, that Bernie Pryde has left her, for the would-be killer to return. The assailant turns out to be Sir Rodney's lab assistant. The assistant escapes in his van but then dies in a collision with a truck.

Cordelia is convinced that it is Sir Rodney himself who killed Mark. She goes to Sir Rodney's house, meets again with Elizabeth Learning, who takes Cordelia's gun and leads her to Sir Rodney. Cordelia confronts him. Sir Rodney confesses to killing Mark, sure that it cannot be proved.

But then Elizabeth comes in and shoots and kills Sir Rodney. She tells Cordelia that she was Cordelia's true mother. Cordelia has sympathy for Leaming, and the two rearrange the scene to look like another suicide. The case is referred to Chief Inspector Dalgliesh of New Scotland Yard, the protagonist of James' more widely known series, who suspects what really happened. Dalgliesh, who used to supervise Bernie Pryde but later fired him, gains new respect for Pryde, as Pryde's training of Cordelia allows the young detective to stand up under tough police questioning. Cordelia, we learn later, is secretly in love with Dalgliesh.

In the second Cordelia Gray novel, *The Skull Beneath the Skin,* Gray is engaged by Sir George Ralston, a baronet, former career soldier, World War II hero and, it turns out, now head of a fascist-style organization, the Union of British Patriots, to accompany his wife, the actress Clarissa Lisle, posing as a secretary-companion but actually as a kind of bodyguard, for a weekend at Courcy Castle, a Victorian castle on the fictional island of Courcy on the Dorset coast. Clarissa is starring in a play, *The Duchess of Malfi*, being presented by an amateur company, the Cottringham Players, privately to among others her husband George, her stepson Simon Lessing, her cousin Roma Lisle, a noted theater critic who had been Clarissa's lover but now was dying, in the castle, which is owned by a best-selling novelist, Ambrose Gorringe.

The title of James' novel is a reference to the T. S. Eliot poem, "Whispers of Immortality," about great Jacobean dramatists including John Webster, who wrote *The Dutchess of Malfi.* It includes the line "And saw the skull beneath the skin." Lisle has been receiving apparent death threats in form of quotations from plays where she had the main role. Her husband does not take the threats too seriously.

On arrival at the island by boat, Cordelia meets the castle owner and some of the guests. They take a tour of the castle, with its collections of Victoriana, including a newly purchased marble arm of a child. Cordelia gets settled in her room, adjoining Clarissa Lyle's. They have dinner, with Simon then playing Chopin and accompanying Roma and Cordelia singing Victorian ballads. Cordelia sings in a sweet convent-trained soprano voice.

The next morning, another message comes, slipped under Clarissa's door during the night. This one is short, two lines from Webster's play, on a piece of paper with a skull drawn at the top:

Thus it lightens into action,
I am come to kill thee.

After breakfast on the second day, Ambrose leads Clarissa, Cordelia and others to a Norman-period crypt on the island. It is filled with skulls on rough oak boards. Ambrose tells the story of a de Courey in the 17th century who brought local maidens to the island, and raped, tortured and killed them. In a trial marked by bribery and corruption, de Courey was acquitted. The father of one of the dead girls stood and cursed the de Courey and all his clan.

The curse may have taken hold, for in 1635 the bubonic plague came to the coast of Dorset. Many caught it, including the father of the dead girl who had stood in the court and cursed de Courey. Knowing that he had little time, the man got a boat, went to the island, flung his arms around de Courey and kissed him full on the mouth. Soon, de Courey and all his family caught the plague and died. The line went extinct.

Then Ambrose takes the party to another part of the crypt, where he shows them a trap door that opens to the sea. In the early part of World War II, in 1940, a group of about 50 Nazi sympathizers had been interned on the island. One of the group, George Blythe, a boy of about 22, was accused by the others of being a British agent who had infiltrated the group and told its secrets to the British authorities. The Nazi sympathizers tried the boy, sentenced him to death and took him to the trap door, where he was tied up and thrown into the sea and drowned. As it happened Sir George Ralston knew the boy, as they had been at the same school together, and George was stationed here at the time.

On the way back to the castle, Cordelia finds another threatening note. Cordelia does not show this or the previous note to Clarissa, as it might make her upset and nervous before the play.

With the play set to begin at 3:30, Clarissa takes a nap. She locks herself in her room.

When Cordelia goes to awaken Clarissa, she finds her dead in her bed, her face and head beaten to a bloody pulp with the Victorian marble child's limb, now covered in blood. The murderer appears to have escaped through Cordelia's adjoining room and out the bathroom window.

Sir George and Ambrose organize a search party, using members of the audience and some players, to scour the island for the murderer. They ring for the police. Cordelia admits that she is a private detective, not a secretary. She blames herself for not staying with Clarissa.

The local police soon arrive, led by Chief Inspector Grogan.

One of the other police officers is Sergeant Robert Buckley, a good-looking and shrewd young man. Buckley, who had done well in sixth form, had chosen to join the police rather than go to university, as he figured success would come quicker in a job for which he was overqualified.

Chief Inspector Grogan and Sergeant Buckley grill Cordelia, and Grogan tells her straight out that he, not she, is here to solve the crime.

During the investigation, Ambrose's manservant, Munter is found dead in a pool, apparently drowned. It is then learned that Munter was in fact the illegitimate son of George Blythe, the young man who had been killed by the Nazi sympathizers in 1940. *Munter* is German for Blythe. It is also learned that Sir George was on duty the night and considers himself responsible for not preventing the death.

The novel has many echoes. The island off Dorset brings to mind the isolated island and its guests in Agatha Christie's *Ten Little Indians*. The castle owner, Ambrose Gorringer, a collector of Victorian pieces, has a butler and manservant, Munter, who is named about as closely as possible to Lord Peter Wimsey's valet, Butner. P. D. James was often compared to Christie and Dorothy L. Sayers.

Many critics loved the first Cordelia Gray book, but they were less enthusiastic about the second, and final, one, with its convoluted plot and retrograde echoes of earlier Gothic detective mysteries. Gray, while observant and competent, plays a relatively small role in this novel, and she is more driven by events than the driver. The exception comes near the end of the book, when she decides that the motive of the murders derive from a newspaper clipping from 1977, in which the castle owner accidentally appeared. He had unexpectedly made a large amount of money from his novel, *Autopsy,* and to save the 80% income tax then in effect became a tax exile from Britain for the next year. However, he had to return for a day or two at the behest of his uncle and by chance was photographed by a newspaper reporter. Clarissa had discovered the photograph and had been blackmailing Ambrose.

Cordelia learns that Ambrose did take the marble arm and beat Clarissa's face to a pulp, but that, in fact, she was already dead. She had been killed by ... but, wait, we'll save that final complication for you to learn for yourself. The murderer soon commits suicide, so it all works out in the end. There is even a new case waiting for her back in London, a lost Siamese cat.

Cordelia's Digs, Drives and Drinks: Cordelia Gray has a shabby third-floor office, up narrow, linoleum covered stairs, on Kingly Street in the SoHo area of London. She occasionally shares the two-room office with Bevis and Miss Maudsley, typists she gets on an as-needed basis from a temp agency, and with Tomkins, a small black-and-white kitten. Cordelia lives in a sixth floor flat off Thames Street in the City of London, the historic part of London that contains its central business district.

Gray was able to buy the flat after the Sir Ronald Callendar case with funds from the sale of a house in Paris that came to her from her father's estate. The flat had a large, sparsely furnished sitting room and a small (only five by eight feet) but luxuriously finished bedroom.

Gray takes wines, at dinner or a party. She prefers claret. In *The Skull Beneath the Skin,* she drinks Chateaux Margaux with the suspected murderer. In *An Unsuitable Job,* she drives the iconic British car, a Mini, made by British Motor Corporation.

About P. D. James:

Phyllis Dorothy James was born in 1920 in Oxford, England. She had to leave school at age 16, before graduating even from secondary school. The reasons were lack of money and also because her father, an Inland Revenue tax inspector, didn't believe in higher education for girls. Her schooling did give her a good grounding in Shakespeare and the King James version of the Bible, which James said were crucial for a writer.

In 1941, she married Ernest White, an army doctor. Returning from World War II, Dr. White experienced severe mental illness, probably schizophrenia, and had to be put in an institution, where he remained off and on until his death in 1964. This left P. D. to provide for the family, including their two daughters. She worked for a hospital board in London and for the National Health Service from 1949 to 1968 and later spent a total of 11 years in the Home Office in police- and criminal-related departments. Her civil service career in Britain spanned three decades.

James also began trying to earn money by writing, starting in the 1950s. She mostly wrote in the early mornings, before going to work. In her book *Talking About Detective Fiction,* James said: "When I settled down in the mid-1950s to begin my first novel, it never occurred to me to make a start with anything other than a detective story. Mysteries were my favorite relaxation reading, and I felt that if I could write a good one successfully it would stand a good chance of acceptance by a publisher."

Her first published novel, *Cover Her Face,* a Dalgliesh, came out in 1962, when she was 42. Much later, she revealed that she had first written another Dalgliesh novel, *The Private Patient,* which was not published until 2008.

For years, James wrote and published but made only modest sums from the royalties from Faber and Faber. Her fourth Dalgliesh book, *A Shroud for a Nightingale,* published in 1971, became a huge international bestseller, and the royalties started to pour in.

Then, in 1980 she really turned the financial corner: *Innocent Blood,* one of her few novels not to feature Dalgliesh, earned 380,000 pounds for the paperback rights and 145,000 pounds for the film rights (about 2½ million in U.S. dollars today), more than she had earned in a decade at the Home Office. She happily retired from her civil service job.

James was named an Officer of the Order of the British Empire (OBE) in 1983 and was given the title of life Peer as Baroness James of Holland Park) in 1991. In 1999, she was honored as a Grand Master by the Mystery Writers of America. She was inducted into the International Crime Writing Hall of Fame at the inaugural Crime Thriller Awards in Britain in 2008.

James died at her home in Oxford on 27 November 2014, aged 94.

Besides the two James novels, Cordelia Gray also appeared in one film. *An Unsuitable Job for a Woman* was produced in Britain by Boyd's/Castle Hill in 1982 with Pippa Guard as Cordelia. ITV/PBS, a British-American partnership, did a four-part series featuring Gray from 1997 to 2001.

With a total running time of 600 minutes, the series was originally broadcast in six one-hour episodes and two two-hour episodes. Only the first 180-minute program, "An Unsuitable Job for a Woman: Sacrifice," is straight from P. D. James' work.

The other three are based on James' characters, with some additions, but are written by others. Helen Baxendale played Cordelia in all four episodes. In the television series, after a short fling in Italy, Cordelia becomes pregnant, one of the few fictional pregnant private detectives in the history of the genre.

P. D. James was unhappy with the way her work was translated to film and television.

Cordelia Gray Novels by P. D. James

An Unsuitable Job for a Woman (1972)
The Skull Beneath the Skin (1982)

Notable Works on P.D. James

James, P. D. *Time to Be in Earnest: A Fragment of* Autobiography (2001). Over the course of a single year, James set down the events of her the year in dairy form. It also includes her recollections of past events.

James, P.D. *Talking About Detective Fiction* (2009). Elegant little book by James on her views on detective writers and their works.

Sharon McCone

From the Sharon McCone series by Marcia Muller

"Secrets, I thought. Most said money was the root of all evil, but in my experience it was secrets, many of them not involving cold, hard cash."

Sharon McCone in *City of Whispers* by Marcia Muller

Marcia Muller's detective, Sharon McCone, has been called by many as "the first liberated female detective of modern times" – a statement that some would dispute – but certainly she was one of the first who broke out in a big way from the "cozy" category of women sleuths. At the very least, she was the first of the popular hard-boiled female detectives, and it can be argued that she is the first feminist PI.

Sharon McCone is tough enough and always ready to get out and try new things. She carries a .38 Special (in the past she used a .45 but keeps coming back to the .38), has been known to gulp down a glass of straight bourbon, flies a plane and drives a sports car, first an old MG and later a Mercedes. In the line of work, she has killed. McCone got her start moonlighting as a security guard during college at Berkeley and was briefly trained by a private detective before being fired. Her first real job as an investigator is at a low-income legal co-op, All Souls Legal Cooperative.

The initial Sharon McCone novel, *Edwin of the Iron Shoes,* came out in 1977. Her first investigation involves vandalism in a run-down San Francisco neighborhood of junk and antique shops, which eventually ends in the murder of an antique dealer, a client of the legal co-op.

In the second McCone book, *Ask the Cards a Question* (1982), Sharon investigates the strangling of a neighbor in her apartment building. The All Souls Legal Cooperative cases continue for years.

After some changes at the co-op – it finally closes – McCone starts her own private investigation agency, McCone Investigations, along with two co-workers from the poverty law center. The change is announced in the 15th book in the series, *Till the Butchers Cut Him Down* (1994).

Then, later, she and her then lover, Hy (Heino) Ripinsky, first introduced in *Where Echoes Live* (1991), a shadowy environmental activist who is a co-owner of a successful international security firm, Renshaw and Kessell International (RKI), merge their agencies.

After 24 McCone books, McCone and Ripinsky get married. Together they run M&R, a sizeable, profitable security and private investigation company. Among her associates at M&R, besides Hy, are her nephew Mick Savage, office manager Ted Smalley and her old All Souls associate Rae Kelleher.

The later McCone novels have migrated more toward the thriller genre.

Although McCone is listed in this chapter about New Women detectives, she just as well could be listed under The Professionals chapter, as now she is far from being a lone wolf private eye like Kinsey Milhone. While she started as a novice investigator for a legal co-op, and then opened her own small private detective agency, she now operates from a large and fancy office building, has a staff of investigators, an office manager, computer experts and other specialists, some shared with her husband's security business.

McCone is of Shoshone Indian heritage, but the extent of this heritage changes during the series. Initially, she admits to being only one-eighth Native American, through a grandmother, although in every book she comments in one way or another on her appearance reflecting her ethnicity. McCone was raised as the middle child of five, with two older brothers and two younger sisters, in San Diego. The McCones eventually separate and both her mother and father remarry. It is only when, going through the papers of her father after his death, that Sharon learns she has been adopted.

Her actual birth father, Elwood Farmer, a nationally known painter, lives on the Flathead Indian Reservation in Montana. Her birth mother, Saskia, also is a Shoshone Native American who has become an attorney.

Shar, as many call her, has had relationships with a number of men, including a male chauvinist police lieutenant, Greg Marcus, head of the homicide division of the SFPD, who nicknamed her "papoose"; a free-spirited disc jockey, Don Del Boccio, and a college professor. None of the relationships clicked until she met Hy, whose background was in intelligence, possibly with an organization similar to the CIA.

McCone, like Sue Grafton's Kinsey Millhone, ages through the long series, but as with Millhone, she ages more slowly than the rest of us. When we first meet McCone, she is in her late 20s. Thirty years and more than two dozen books later, she is only in her mid-40s; today she is edging into true middle age.

Sharon McCone's Digs: McCone's first workplace, All Souls Legal Cooperative, is located in a classic Victorian house in the Bernal Heights section of San Francisco. McCone Investigations, the detective she sets up with other former staff of the legal co-op, is in the fictional Pier 24½, which sounds a lot like the real-life Pier 24 in the South of Market (SoMa) area below the Bay Bridge. M&R, the company resulting from the merger of McCone Investigations and Hy's firms, owns a four-story headquarters in a circa 1932 restored Vermont granite building in the financial district, with all the latest security bells and whistles. The first floor is leased out to upscale clothing shops and Angie's Deli. The second floor has the administrative offices for clerical, billing and other support services for M&R. The third floor has residential suites, a kind of high end safe house for clients, M&R operatives from offices in other cities and for hospitality functions and parties. The top floor, which has a roof garden, houses the offices of Sharon, Hy and senior and key staff.

The first four novels in the McCone series are set entirely in San Francisco. Beginning with the fifth novel, *Leave a Message for Willie* (1994), McCone ventures outside the city to other locales. A number of the later novels in the series take place partly in areas other than San Francisco; however, the City by the Bay is the main setting of most the McCone books.

When we first meet McCone in San Francisco she is living in a cheap apartment in the Mission District. Later, she lives in a house on Bernal Street near the legal co-op and then buys a house, a so-called "earthquake cottage" on Church Street that was built to house survivors after the 1906 earthquake. (Marcia Muller built a highly detailed miniature model of the Bernal Street and Church Street houses.) When the Church Street house is burned down, she and Hy build a new house on Avila Street in the tony Marina District. Hy and Sharon also own a getaway beach cottage, Touchstone, and Hy has a sheep ranch on a lake in Mono County, a lightly populated area of east central California.

McCone's Drives: Sharon drives a beat-up vintage red MG two-seater sports car for many years. Later, after she becomes more financially established, she graduates to a Mercedes. As a pilot, McCone flies the single-engine, two-seater Citabria Decathelon that Hy Ripinsky owns.

McCone's Drinks: Sharon likes wine. When dining out she might order a chardonnay or, with Italian food, a zinfandel. At home, she and Hy relax with a bottle or two of Dry Creek zinfandel or Deer Hill chardonnay. However, she also drinks the harder stuff, usually either bourbon or tequila.

About Marcia Muller:

Marcia Muller was born September 18, 1944, in Detroit and grew up in Birmingham, Mich. She attended the University of Michigan at Ann Arbor and graduated with a major in English. Among her jobs was a stint at *Sunset* magazine.

Marcia Muller married the prolific mystery writer, Bill Pronzini, in 1982. This was Pronzini's third marriage. Pronzini is best known for his *Nameless Detective* series, which to date total 46 books, but he has authored more than 130 novels and some 300 short stories. In addition, he has edited more than 100 anthologies of detective, Western and science fiction writing. The two writers have collaborated on eight novels and anthologies. In 1986, the couple also published *1001 Midnights: The Aficionado's Guide to Mystery and Detective Fiction,* an 879-page reference work that includes 1,001 plot summaries, author biographies and critical evaluations of important crime and espionage novels and short stories.

To date, Muller has written more than 35 novels, seven short-story collections and a number of non-fiction articles. Besides 33 Sharon McCone novels and two short-story collections, she has written three novels each in her Elena Oliverez, Joanna Stark and Soledad County/Cape Perdido mystery series. In addition, she has written, co-written or edited 16 short story collections and anthologies, a stand-alone novel, plus five Carpenter and Quincannon mysteries co-written with her husband.

So far, none of her books has been made into a movie, although several were optioned. In 2005, Muller received the Grand Master award from the Mystery Writers of America. Her novels have been nominated for five Shamus awards, and her 2006 Sharon McCone novel *Vanishing Point* won the Shamus for Best P.I. Novel. Her novel *Wolf in the Shadows* won the Anthony Boucher Award, and she received a Lifetime Achievement Award from the Private Eye Writers of America.

Muller's advice for would be authors: "Plant butt on chair in front of whatever device you use. Face blank page. Stare at it until a word comes to you. Input it. The rest will follow."

Muller and Pronzini live in a very expensive house in Sonoma County, Calif.

Sharon McCone Mysteries:

Edwin of the Iron Shoes (1977)
Ask the Cards A Question (1982)
The Cheshire Cat's Eye (1983)

Games to Keep the Dark Away (1984)
Leave A Message for Willie (1984)
Double (1984) (co-written with **Bill Pronzini**)
There's Nothing to Be Afraid of (1985)
Eye of the Storm (1988)
There's Something in A Sunday (1989)
The Shape of Dread (1989)
Trophies and Dead Things (1990)
Where Echoes Live (1991)
Pennies on A Dead Woman's Eyes (1992)
Wolf in the Shadows (1993)
Till the Butchers Cut Him Down (1994)
A Wild and Lonely Place (1995)
The Broken Promise Land (1996)
Both Ends of the Night (1997)
While Other People Sleep (1998)
A Walk Through the Fire (1999)
Listen to the Silence (2000)
Dead Midnight (2002)
The Dangerous Hour (2004)
Vanishing Point (2006)
The Ever-Running Man (2007)
Burn Out (2008)
Locked In (2009)
Coming Back (2010)
City of Whispers (2011)
Looking For Yesterday (2012)
The Night Searchers (2014)
Someone Always Knows (2016)
The Color of Fear (2017)
The McCone Files (1994) (short story collection)
McCone and Friends (1999) (short story collection)

Notable Works on Marcia Muller:

Howe, Alexander N and Jackson, Christine A. (eds.) *Marcia Muller and the Female Private Eye* (2008). Academic essays on the works of Marcia Muller, with emphasis on the feminist side of Sharon McCone.

Judge Deborah Knott

From the Deborah Knott mystery novels by Margaret Maron (1939?-)

"Every time we start thinking we're the center of the universe, the universe turns around and says with a slightly distracted air, 'I'm sorry. What'd you say your name was again?'"

Deborah Knott in *Bootlegger's Daughter* by Margaret Maron

Margaret Maron, creator of the Judge Deborah Knott series, in North Carolina

In Margaret Maron's novels, Deborah Knott is a lawyer and a district court judge in fictional Colleton County, a rural county southeast of Raleigh, with the county seat being the town of Dobbs. Colleton Countrry resembles Johnston County with its county seat, Smithfield.

The series began with the *Bootlegger's Daughter* in 1992, a publishing sensation that swept all four major mystery awards as best mystery of the year: the Edgar, Agatha, Anthony and Macavity awards. That was the first and so far only time a book won all four awards. The series ended with the 20th book, *Long Upon the Land*, published in 2015.

We meet Deborah Knott when she is practicing law among the good 'ol boys of Colleton County. In *Bootlegger's Daughter* she runs for district court judge but loses the election; however, in the next book in the series, *Southern Discomfort,* following the death of a judge the governor appoints her district judge.

The Knott novels are written in the first person, and Deborah Knott comes across as a folksy, down-to-earth woman with plenty of common sense, but one who is not afraid to express her opinions. At the beginning of the series, she has just turned 35; by the last novel, she hits 40, so she ages only about five years in more than two decades.

Here's a short sample of Judge Deborah's style:

"This was our second day of *voir dire,* a tedious, time-consuming process. Some people are eager to serve, usually for the wrong reasons, but most would rather not spend the time listening to legal jousting, when they had planned to spend the week doing other, more interesting things.

"'Your Honor, I have a hair appointment for this afternoons,' a blonde woman said.

"'Color?' I asked, noticing a thin line of dark roots at the hairline of her forehead.

"'Just shampoo and cut,' she said brightly.

"I denied her request. Color appointments aren't all that easy to get, but there was no reason she couldn't reschedule a simple cut.'"

Deborah Knott comes from a large family, and she has kinfolk all across the county and the state. She was the youngest and only girl of 12 children. Her father, Kezzie Knott, is a grade-school dropout, the son of a bootlegger and a bootlegger himself during the Depression who spent time in federal prison for income tax evasion. Despite his lack of formal education, he is smart as a whip and has not done badly for himself.

Kezzie's first wife, Annie, mothered eight sons, the first when she was just 15. After Annie's death, Kezzie meets and marries Sue Stephenson, the daughter of a prominent local family, a union that was not much appreciated by the Stephenson family.

By the time the series ends, the Knott family together have bought this parcel and that and accumulated enough property so that instead of original 100 acres of tobacco farm they end up owning 2,500 acres, likely enough to make them millionaires several times over.

Various family members show up regularly in the Judge Knott novels, especially Deborah's half-brothers Robert, Franklin, Andrew, Herman, Haywood (Herman and Haywood are twins), Seth and Jackson, along with their wives and children, and also full brothers Will, Adam and Zack (the latter two are another set of twins) and their families. With her parents' and brothers' extended families of cousins, nephews and nieces, sisters-in-law and aunts and uncles, it sometimes seems Deborah is related to, or at least knows, nearly everyone in Colleton County. The connections are so complicated that the author provides a family tree at the beginning of the books.

About midway through the series, Deborah begins to fall in love with a childhood friend of some of her brothers, Dwight Bryant, a deputy sheriff in the Colleton County sheriff's department. They eventually tie the, ahem, knot. After Dwight's former wife is killed, their son Cal comes to live with Dwight and Deborah.

These are murder mystery novels to be sure, but many of the murders are connected to Deborah's large family or to her courtroom. Knott is not a private detective. She's a judge and family member first, detective second.

The solutions to the mysteries almost always can be found buried in clues in the books, but often Knott seems to stumble upon them. Especially in the later novels, she depends on her husband Dwight's investigative skills.

Maron doesn't shy away from controversy in her Judge Knott novels. In different volumes she tackles racism, immigration and the way North Carolina is transitioning from a rural state to an urbanized one.

North Carolina plays an important role in the Knott series. As a district court judge her home courtroom is in Dobbs in Colleton County, but district court judges sometimes fill in for vacationing or ill judges in other districts in the state, and they attend judicial conferences in different cities, so this gives Maron the opportunity to set some of her books in different parts of the state.

High Country Fall is set in the mountains of Western North Carolina; *Shooting of Loons* takes place on Harkers Island and in Beaufort on the Crystal Coast; *Uncommon Clay* is set in Seagrove, known for its pottery; *Killer Market* takes place in High Point during the huge furniture trade show held there; and *Sand Sharks* is set during a judges conference in Wilmington, on the Cape Fear Coast.

Maron, who herself grew up on a farm in a rural area of Johnston County, knows best the local people of Colleton County, a rural area described as located at the point where the North Carolina Piedmont meets the Sandhills.

Her neighbors are rural and small-town folks. Many hold blue-collar jobs. As a review in the *Raleigh News & Observer* by Mary Cornatzer notes, "Maron knows the people she's writing about – and more than that, cares about them. She captures the rhythms of speech and life here, the fierceness of a sudden summer storm, the changes around us, and she even throws in a few whacks at the legislature (over budget cuts to the judicial system and education) for good measure."

A lot of the family gatherings in the Knott novels revolve around food, mostly Southern and North Carolina staples. Margaret Maron includes a recipe that is mentioned in several of her Knott novels: Granny Knott's Baked Toast, a local take on French toast.

Granny Knott's Baked Toast
Serves 6

Ingredients
1 loaf good bread cut into 1" slices
3 eggs
2 cups whole milk
1 cup light brown sugar, plus additional 3 tablespoons
1 stick (8 oz.) unsalted butter
¼ cup honey, molasses or maple syrup
1 teaspoon vanilla
Directions
Cover the bottom of a 9"x12" casserole dish with brown sugar
Melt butter and stir in honey, molasses or maple syrup, then drizzle that over sugar
Lay slices of bread on top of the sugar
Beat eggs, milk and vanilla and pour over the bread slices
Sprinkle additional brown sugar on bread and pour egg, milk and vanilla mixture over it
Cover with plastic wrap and refrigerate over night
Bake in 350 degree oven for about ½ hour or until brown sugar caramelizes on bottom and top and is well browned
Serve immediately

In interviews, Maron has said some of he readers have told her they moved to North Carolina after reading her novels, but that scares her, she says. Maron says she likes it better when readers tell her that they have come to understand the state better due to her books.

Deborah Knott's Digs: Deborah and her husband, Dwight Byrant, and Dwight's son Cal (adopted by Deborah) live in a white frame house Deborah built on the Knott family farmland. When Dwight and Deborah married, they expand the house, adding a master bedroom to the original two bedrooms. There's a pond near the house for swimming. By the time the series ends, the family farm has grown to 2,500 acres.

Deborah's Drives: Deborah doesn't much care about cars. She drives a nondescript and unnamed sedan. Her daddy Kezzie drives a new white Chevrolet pickup. Husband Dwight also drives a pick-up, as do most of the Knott brothers.

Deborah's Drinks: Although her father and grandfather were bootleggers, Deborah Knott isn't a heavy drinker. She occasionally has a glass of wine at lunch, but not when she's holding court in the afternoon. She doesn't care much for beer. At parties, out for dinner and when on vacation, she usually drinks tequila or bourbon. Usually trying to watch her weight, she takes her bourbon with a Diet Pepsi.

Judge Knott's Bourbon and Diet Pepsi

2 oz. Jim Beam or other bourbon

Diet Pepsi

Put ice in an old-fashioned glass. Add the bourbon and fill the rest of the glass with Diet Pepsi.

About Margaret Maron:

Margaret Maron was born Margaret Brown just before World War II near Greensboro, N.C., the daughter of C. O. Brown and Claudia Stephenson Brown. The family soon moved to a rural part of Johnston County just southeast of Raleigh, to a tobacco farm owned by her grandparents. This is where Margaret grew up. The county then had a population of about 64,000, with most people involved in agriculture of some kind, especially raising poultry and hogs or growing tobacco, then the top farm crop in the state.

Today it is to a great extent a commuter suburb of the greater Raleigh-Durham-Chapel Hill metro area. Johnston County has a population now of about 180,000, while the Triangle's population is more than a million, with its economy anchored by three nationally known research universities, Duke, UNC-Chapel Hill and NC State, and by the Research Triangle Park, one of the largest technology and pharmaceutical centers in the country.

Maron attended UNC-Greensboro, then the women's college of the University of North Carolina system, for two years. In 1959, while working as a secretary at the Pentagon in Washington, D.C., she met and married Joseph (Joe) Maron, a Navy officer. Joe stayed in the Navy for another tour of duty, this time in Italy, and he and Maron lived for three years in Naples. The couple then moved to Joe's hometown of Brooklyn, where they lived for about 10 years. Joe earned an MFA in art and taught painting in Brooklyn and later at Meredith College in Raleigh.

Returning to a farm in Johnston County that had been in the family for more than 100 years, Margaret Maron began trying to establish herself as a working writer. Initially she was interested in poetry and short stories. Her first sale, according to husband Joe, was to *Alfred Hitchcock Mystery Magazine,* for $65.

After selling stories to a number of mystery and women's magazines for about a dozen years, she was encouraged to try her hand at longer form novels, as the short story market was drying up. The result was her first mystery novel, *One Coffee With*, featuring New York Police Department Lieutenant Sigrid Harald, published in 1981. Harald is in many ways the opposite of Deborah Knott – a loner without much family or many friends, a professional cop and a big city girl. (Harald does, however, have a North Carolina connection, as a grandmother is from Colleton County, and she makes an appearance in two Judge Knott books, in New York in *Three-Day Town* and in North Carolina in *The Buzzard Table.*) She followed this up with seven more Sigrid Harald novels, ending the series in 1995. However, in 2017, she did another Harald book, *Take Out,* which Maron says will be her last novel.

Besides having won all the major mystery writer awards, some multiple times, Maron has served as president of Sisters in Crime, an organization for women mystery writers that she helped found, the American Crime Writers League and Mystery Writers of America.

Altogether, Maron has published 33 books: 20 Deborah Knott books, nine Sigrid Harald mysteries, two stand-alone novels and two collections of short stories. As of 2017, Maron says she is finished with deadlines and novels but plans to concentrate on her first love, short stories.

Judge Deborah Knott Novels by Margaret Maron

Bootlegger's Daughter (1992)
Southern Discomfort (1993)
Shooting at Loons (1994)
Up Jumps the Devil (1996)

Killer Market (1997)
Home Fires (1998)
Storm Track (2000)
Uncommon Clay (2001)
Slow Dollar (2002)
High Country Fall (2004)
Rituals of the Season (2005)
Winter's Child (2006)
Hard Row (2007)
Death's Half-Acre (2008)
Sand Sharks (2009)
Christmas Mourning (2010)
Three-Day Town (2011)
The Buzzard Table (2012)
Designated Daughters (2014)
Long Upon the Land (2015)

Kinsey Millhone

From the Kinsey Millhone "A to Z" series by Sue Grafton (1940-)

"I didn't take the death-and-dismemberment talk very seriously. Where could you rent a chainsaw at this time of night?"

Kinsey Millhone in *F is for Fugitive* by Sue Grafton

Sue Grafton in 2009 *Photo by Mark Coggins*

Kinsey Millhone is the protagonist of Sue Grafton's best-selling "alphabet mystery series" that started with *A is for Alibi* in 1983 and is currently at *Y is for Yesterday* (the 25th book in the series), published in the late summer of 2017. The series is expected to end in 2019 with *Z is for Zero.*

Born in 1950, Millhone is a former high school pot smoker and mediocre student, community college dropout and ex-cop (for two years) who now is a licensed private investigator in the fictitious oceanside small city of Santa Teresa, Calif., about two hours north of Los Angeles. Santa Teresa bears a close resemblance to Santa Barbara, and her creator Sue Grafton has a home in Montecito, an affluent unincorporated area of Santa Barbara County.

The Kinsey Millhone books are told mostly in the first person. Millhone finds the killer or otherwise solves the mysteries through a slow, diligent process of finding and interviewing all of the possible suspects and turning up clues. She is very well organized, writing reports and keeping key details of the case on a stack of hand-written notecards. Spunky, with her own strongly held opinions, a good liar, brave (but usually not reckless) and bright though not highly educated, Kinsey is one of the first modern female detectives and still the best-known of contemporary female PIs.

Most of the Kinsey Millhone books begin slowly, with a chance happening or prospective client meeting creating a chain of events that lead to Kinsey digging more deeply into the case. Kinsey is not above a little harmless breaking and entering if it seems to offer a promising result. A number of the novels have Millhone reconstructing long-passed events to solve an old murder. Most of the series novels are set in and near Santa Teresa, although occasionally Kinsey must drive to another part of California, or fly go another state to find a key witness or uncover evidence. Among cities she visits are Las Vegas, Dallas, Louisville and Boca Raton, Fla. Frequently, the novels end in a violent episode.

In the early novels, Millhone is about 30, and she ages slowly, very slowly, through the series and through the decade of the 1980s in which the series is set. By *V is for Vengeance,* Kinsey is 38 and is 39 in *Z is for Zero.* Kinsey has had two brief marriages, one ending in divorce after Kinsey leaves her husband, and the other in desertion by her husband. Kinsey dates periodically and over the years has several fairly serious relationships, often with cops or PIs.

All of the series is set in the 1980s before cell phones and the widespread use of the internet. Although the novels reference computers, including personal computers, Millhone isn't an early adaptor.

Named after her mother, Rita Cynthia Kinsey, Millhone was orphaned at age 5 when her mother and father were killed in an auto accident. She was raised by her Aunt Gin, who dies when Kinsey is in her 20s. She does not realize until *J is for Judgment* that she has any living family.

Millhone, who is 5 feet, 5 inches tall and around 118 pounds, keeps fit by jogging three miles most days, but she is a little careless about her diet. Her favorite foods are peanut butter and pickle sandwiches and Quarter Pounders from McDonald's. At home, Millhone also likes to sup on a gooey grilled cheese sandwich with a bowl of canned tomato soup. She often eats bad Eastern European food at Rosie's, a nearby neighborhood joint owned by the Hungarian Rosie, who is married to her landlord's brother, William Pitts, a hypochondriac in his 90s who is the bartender at Rosie's. By the *X* installment, Rosie's has become something of a cop hangout.

Kinsey only occasionally carries a gun. In the penultimate novel in the series, to defend herself against the psychopathic killer, Ned Lowe, who nearly choked her to death in the previous book, she has purchased a 9-shot Heckler & Koch VP9, a German-made 9 mm semi-automatic handgun, although she usually keeps it locked up. She also is taking martial arts/self defense classes.

Kinsey's Peanut Butter & Pickle Sandwich

Whole grain bread

Jif Extra Crunchy peanut butter

Vlasic or Mrs. Fanning's Bread 'n Butter pickles (you can substitute dill but not sweet pickles)

Spread peanut butter on the bread. Add pickles. Cut bread diagonally.

Millhone's Digs: In the first Kinsey Millhone novels the PI trades for office space from California Fidelity Insurance in exchange for working on two or three insurance cases a month. Later, she rents an office in a three-story building owned by the small law firm of Kingman and Ives. Toward the end of the series she takes another rented space, a three-room office in the center bungalow of three cottages in downtown Santa Teresa, within walking distance of the main police station, the courthouse and public library. Her rent is $350 a month.

At age 32, Kinsey moves into a small studio apartment in converted from a garage. Situated not far from the ocean, the apartment is fitted out like a boat, with plenty of storage and a place for everything. It is owned by Henry Pitts, a former commercial baker in his late 80s who lives next door with his cat, Ed. Kinsey and Henry are close friends. On occasion, Millhone will meet a client at her apartment, and clients and contacts often leave messages on her home answering machine, but as much as possible the detective tries to keep her home life separate from her professional work.

Millhone's Drive's: In the earlier novels, Kinsey drives a beat-up 1968 beige Volkswagen Beetle. It was featured on the cover of the hardback edition of *G is for Gumshoe.* After that Bug was wrecked, she buys a blue 1974 VW Beetle, which was buried in a hole on an isolated rural road after a car chase. Then, in a big switch, she buys a 1970 Mustang, a "Boss 429" model in an eye-popping blue color. Today, these rare high-performance Mustangs – the 429 cubic-inch engine with four-barrel carburetor generates over 500 horsepower. (Well-preserved examples now can go for more than $400,000 at muscle car auctions.) In *X,* to be less obvious when trailing a suspect or on a stakeout, she has replaced the Mustang with a nondescript 1980s Honda.

Millhone's Drinks: Kinsey usually drinks white wine, typically Chablis or chardonnay. Her favorite watering hole is Rosie's, a Hungarian restaurant and tavern within walking distance of her apartment in Santa Teresa. She rarely drinks more than a glass or two of wine. At times, she keeps a bottle of white wine chilling in a small fridge in her office.

Kinsey's White
Chardonnay or Chablis white wine
Pour any inexpensive Chablis or chardonnay in a wine glass and sip.

About Author Sue Grafton: Sue Taylor Grafton was born April 24, 1940, and raised in Louisville. Her father, C. W. Grafton, was a bond attorney but also authored three mystery novels. Both her father and mother, Vivian Harnsberger Grafton, a teacher, were alcoholics, according to the author. Grafton received a bachelor's degree in English literature from the University of Louisville.

Before turning to the Millhone series, Grafton wrote screenplays for film and television, along with seven other novels, only two of which were published. Because of her experience writing screenplays, Grafton has refused to sell the rights to any of her Kinsey Millhone books to television or movies.

Grafton has said that in some ways Kinsey Millhone is the author's alter ego. The writer herself owned 1968 and 1974 VW Beetles, as did Millhone. Grafton and her husband have a home in Montecito, a suburb of Santa Barbara, the small city on which Kinsey's hometown of Santa Teresa is based. Grafton and her husband, Steven F. Humphrey, a university professor, also have a home in Louisville.

According to Grafton, the biggest influence on her work was Ross Macdonald. Kenneth Millar (1915-1983), writing as Ross Macdonald, lived for 30 years in Santa Barbara, and some of his classic hardboiled-detective Lew Archer novels are set there. Macdonald, too, called it Santa Teresa. The recipient of the Mystery Writers of America Grand Master Award, Grafton has won numerous other honors, including two Edgars, three Anthony awards and three Shamus awards.

Kinsey Milhone Novels by Sue Grafton

Listed in order of publications.

A Is for Alibi (1982)
B Is for Burglar (1985)
C Is for Corpse (1986)
D Is for Deadbeat (1987)
E Is for Evidence (1988)
F Is for Fugitive (1989)
G Is for Gumshoe (1990)
H Is for Homicide (1991)
I Is for Innocent (1992)
J Is for Judgment (1993)
K Is for Killer (1994)
L Is for Lawless (1995)
M Is for Malice (1996)
N Is for Noose (1998)
O Is for Outlaw (1999)
P Is for Peril (2001)
Q Is for Quarry (2002)
R Is for Ricochet (2004)
S Is for Silence (2005)
T Is for Trespass (2007)
U Is for Undertow (2009)
V Is for Vengeance (2011)
W Is for Wasted (2013)
X (2015)
Y is for Yesterday (2017)
Z is for Zero (scheduled for 2019)

Notable Works on Kinsey Millhone and Sue Grafton

Kaufman, Natalie Hevener and Kay, Carol McGinnis, *G is for Grafton:*
The World of Kinsey Millhone (1997). Details of Kinsey Millhone's life up to the time of the book.

Stephanie Plum

From the Stephanie Plum "number" series by Janet Evanovich (1943-)

"I took the barstool next to one of the Russians and crossed my legs, letting my skirt ride up to a couple of inches below my doo-dah, and asked the bartender for a champagne cocktail."

Stephanie Plum, in *Top Secret Twenty-One*

Stephanie Plum is about as subtle as a Saturday night in New Jersey. That's to be expected, because Plum was born and raised in "the Burg," the Chambersburg section of beautiful Trenton. After briefly working as a lingerie buyer, she gets a job as a bounty hunter, working for her cousin Vinnie of Vinnie Plum Bail Bonds, along with the self-admitted former "ho" Lula and the tough Connie, who doesn't admit her alleged Mob connections.

Most of Plum's family still lives in the Burg, including her mother Ellen, father Frank and her mother's mother, Grandma Mazur, whose main entertainment is going to funerals and visitations, whether or not she knew the deceased.

A 30-ish, five foot seven, 130-pound high-energy package of Italian-Hungarian heritage, with curly shoulder-length brown hair, Plum can get into more trouble in a day than most people do in a lifetime. When she's not out collaring FTAs (Failure to Appear bond jumpers) she's hooking up with her boyfriend, Joe Morelli, a vice cop with the Trenton police (his name, perhaps not so coincidentally, comes from a minor character in the original *The Thin Man* movie). At other times, she's hanging with Ricardo Carlos Mañoso. aka Ranger, a latte-skinned Cuban-American who runs Rangeman, a high-tech security company, drives various black SUVs and a Porsche 911 and usually dresses all in black.

Plum narrates her stories in the first-person, using short sentences and snappy language. A lot happens in these stories. For example, in *Top Secret Twenty-One*, about a dozen people are killed (you quickly lose count), five apartments including Plum's are wrecked with rocket fire, two men are poisoned by radioactive polonium, several cars are blown to smithereens, a gang of wild Chihuahuas terrorizes Trenton and a one-eyed, tattooed Russian leaves a human heart on Plum's kitchen counter as a warning (the heart is then eaten by her boyfriend's dog).

Plum's Rides: Plum goes through cars like mud through a goose. Her cars get wrecked, blown up, repo'd, stripped for parts and stolen. The only car that seems to last is her grandmother's 1953 powder blue and white Buick Roadmaster. It's called "Big Blue."

Plum's Digs: Plum lives in a decent but not fancy one-bedroom, one-bath apartment on the northern edge of Trenton. Most of the residents of the building are senior citizens. Plum shares her apartment with Rex, the world's longest-lived hamster.

Plum's Drinks: Most commonly Plum chugs beer, usually a Bud or some other domestic brand, usually with a pizza or grilled cheese sandwich. In a bar, she's likely to order a champagne cocktail or a black sambuca, the deep blue-colored, liquorice version of the colorless anise-flavored Italian liqueur.

Plum Black Sambuca
2 oz. Black Sambuca
Pour the black sambuca in a liqueur glass. Sip.

About Author Janet Evanovich: Like her best-known creation, Stephanie Plum, Janet Evanovich was born and grew up in New Jersey. In her 30s, Evanovich started writing romance novels. She published a dozen of them before switching to mysteries, writing what she calls romantic adventure novels. Her first effort, *One for the Money,* featuring the "barely competent" bounty hunter Stephanie Plum, got good reviews and by the sixth installment of the "numbered" series, she was hitting the top of the national best-seller lists. Through 2017, she has published 22 novels in the series, the last being *Tricky Twenty-Two,* plus four holiday novellas and a short story.

Although much older than her hero Plum, Evanovich claims that the two share many characteristics, from their New Jersey background, hamster ownership and love for junk food.

Evanovich also has authored several other adventure/mystery series. She lives with her husband, Pete, in New Hampshire and Florida.

Stephanie Plum Novels by Janet Evanovich
One For the Money (1995)
Two For the Dough (1996)
Three to Get Deadly (1997)
Four to Score (1998)
High Five (1999)
Hot Six (2000)
Seven Up (2001)

Hard Eight (2002)
Visions of Sugar Plums (2003)
To the Nines (2003)
Ten Big Ones (2004)
Eleven on Top (2005)
Twelve Sharp (2006)
Plum Lovin' (2007)
Lean Mean Thirteen (2007)
Plum Lucky (2008)
Fearless Fourteen (2008)
Plum Spooky (2009)
Finger Lickin' Fifteen (2009)
Sizzling Sixteen (2010)
Smokin' Seventeen (2011)
Explosive Eighteen (2011)
Notorious Nineteen (2012)
Takedown Twenty (2013)
Tricky Twenty-two (2015)
Turbo Twenty-three (2016)

About Lan Sluder

A former newspaper editor in New Orleans, Lan Sluder is the author of more than 20 books. Most of them are on the subjects of travel, retirement and relocation, especially in Belize and Central America and in the Southeastern United States, including the Carolinas and Georgia and the city of Asheville, N.C. Among his books are *Fodor's Belize, Easy Belize, Amazing Asheville, Asheville Relocation, Retirement and Visitor's Guide, Frommer's Best Beach Vacations, Living Abroad in Belize* and *Buying a Classic Rolls-Royce or Bentley.* His articles also have appeared in many publications around the world, including *The New York Times, Caribbean Travel & Life, Chicago Tribune, Miami Herald, Belize First, New Orleans Business, Bangkok Post, The Tico Times, The Globe & Mail* and *Where to Retire.* Sluder and his wife live on a mountain farm near Asheville.

www.ingramcontent.com/pod-product-compliance
Lightning Source LLC
Chambersburg PA
CBHW031157270326
41931CB00006B/312

* 9 7 8 0 9 9 9 4 3 4 8 0 2 *